PN3355.R6

0 0068 000

Rockwell, F. A/Modern

Whitworth College Librar

D0687494

355
R6

60,806

College Library
Washington

MODERN FICTION TECHNIQUES

MODERN FICTION TECHNIQUES

F. A. Rockwell

BOSTON

THE WRITER, INC.

PUBLISHERS

COPYRIGHT © 1962, by F. A. ROCKWELL

Library of Congress Catalog Card Number: 62-14074

Printed in the United States of America

60,806

Acknowledgments

MY THANKS to the professional writers, whose material I have quoted as beacons of skilled techniques to guide unestablished writers through the wilderness of learning; to my students, who have requested me to put into this book my classroom advice which they have followed with brilliant success; to the friends who have helped in the book's final preparation so that it could be made available to writers everywhere who cannot attend my classes; and to *The Writer, Writer's Digest,* and *Author & Journalist,* where some of the material first appeared in article form.

—F. A. Rockwell

CONTENTS

MODERN FICTION TECHNIQUES

I | GIVING UP AMATEUR STATUS

WRITING AFFORDS a wonderful opportunity of sharing ideas with others, if, of course, your writing is professional enough to be published and to be accepted by a wide audience. The purpose of this book is to help you make your stories professional by clarifying the necessary techniques plus giving you some extra-special tips and tricks to help you sprint ahead of the competition.

Before we plunge into the ingredients that make up today's successful stories, let's see where you stand now. Are you a pro? An amateur? Or what Charles F. Kettering called a "professional amateur" because, as he put it: "We are amateurs because we are doing things for the first time. We are professionals because we know we are going to have a lot of trouble . . . a certain amount of intelligent ignorance is essential to progress; for if you know too much you won't try the thing." Which are you at this stage of your writing career? Test yourself according to the following:

THE DIFFERENCE BETWEEN THE AMATEUR
AND THE PROFESSIONAL

1) The obvious difference is that the amateur *dreams* of selling whereas the pro *sells* regularly enough to support himself and his family (partially or completely) and be recognized as a success in his field.

2) The amateur splashes words on paper and then asks "Where will this story sell?" rather than mastering the techniques that will make it the kind of story editors want to buy. The pro never confuses writing that is therapeutic with writing that is salable.

3) The amateur is victimized by inspiration which he relies upon too heavily. Sometimes he'll write incessantly like an erupting volcano, and then be inactive for long periods of time. The pro writer, like the pro in any field, can be depended upon to give as good a performance when he's *not* in the mood as when he *is*. As Nathan Bond tells his son in Sloan Wilson's *A Sense of Values:* "One difference between an amateur and a professional is that the professional is trying his best. He doesn't have the excuse that he could do better if he only had the time. Professionals don't horse around."

4) The amateur writes *when he* feels like it and *what he* feels like writing. He thinks in terms of himself, not his reader. He is subjective, not objective; he thinks of writing as *self-expression,* whereas the pro considers it *communication.*

5) The amateur is hypersensitive, and has a subjective and extreme attitude toward his work—it's either "great" or "terrible." The pro develops a healthy balance between

his creative and his critical faculties. He realizes that the domination of one destroys the other.

6) The amateur reveres and trusts every idea that comes to him *as it is*. The pro researches, thinks, ponders, plans, plots and reworks each idea until it has dramatic and universal meaning. He adds love of labor to his labor of love.

7) The amateur says "I want to write." The pro says "I want to think!" and he prepares for a career of thinking as well as a career of writing. G. B. Shaw was aware of the fact that most people do very little thinking, and he claimed he gained a tremendous reputation for himself by thinking just two or three times a week.

8) The amateur puts a story down "as it really happened" or "as it came to his mind," whereas the pro consciously uses every means to make others see, smell, hear, taste and experience life more keenly than they could without his writing. The professional writer is wholly dedicated to the re-experiencing of reality, for, as Robert Frost put it: "The best thing that we're put here for's to see," and to make others *see*. The pro does this thoroughly, without the amateur's frantic haste to mail the story immediately, for the pro realizes that a manuscript that is submitted in haste will be returned at leisure.

9) The amateur bristles at criticism and defends his brain children, whereas a pro welcomes constructive suggestions to improve his techniques and omits clichés, taboos, coincidences and other weaknesses. He welcomes criticism, agreeing with the Chinese proverb: "One can see one's faults only with other people's eyes."

10) The amateur works haphazardly and where and when he wants to. The pro establishes regular writing hours at a usual writing place.

The professional has one trouble that the amateur does not have: deciding what to do with the checks he receives. But if you still want to be a pro, it'll help to have: a) a good typewriter, b) an undisturbed place to write, c) plenty of paper, reference books, a good thesaurus and dictionary, d) a knowledge of people, life, philosophy and psychology, f) a large coffee pot. It'll help even more if you do *not* have: a) a phone, b) lots of visiting friends, c) a large appetite, d) a huge, noisy family. On the other hand, a family will probably make you buckle down, work hard, and stop wasting time.

If you do not fit all the above descriptions of a professional, then you will want to know how to become one. The personal traits that make a writer are Imagination, Logic, Vitality, Integrity and Persistence. But these characteristics will help you only if you have intriguing, worthwhile ideas to write about and know how to present them. Where do you get ideas? From everywhere and everyone. The ubiquity of ideas is what makes writing a popular profession; the application of professional techniques is what makes writing difficult. Ideas are all around you all the time. You cannot escape them, and you do not have to work to get them. In fact, as James Norman Hall once said, "Loafing is the most productive part of a writer's life. Your most valuable time is that spent in idleness. That's when you get your ideas. The writing is merely the fulfillment of the inspiration dream from the loafing."

Good ideas may be likened to uranium, and you must develop your cranial Geiger counter to detect the valuable from the worthless ore. Then, use technique to convert the raw material into the nuclear energy of salable stories.

Ideas are funny things; they won't work unless you do, and the harder you work, the better the results. A Ripley cartoon once pictured a plain bar of iron worth $5 as it was. But when it was made into horseshoes, its value increased to $10.50. Made into needles, it became worth $3,285, and if turned into balance-wheels for watches, $250,000. The same thing can happen to a good idea, which a writer could use for a $10- to $100-anecdote or develop into a best-selling novel and movie script. The basic idea isn't as important as what you do with it; in fact the idea-nucleus doesn't even have to be original. There aren't any really original ideas, merely fresh idea-combinations, the best of which result from stocking your mental storehouse with a multitude of thoughts. Since ideas are everywhere, the obvious dangers are confusion or trying to use those that are trite, or taboo. In choosing ideas for fiction development, a) be selective and discriminating, choosing ideas that affect the reader; b) concentrate on ideas with which you have an emotional involvement. If you do not *care* deeply about your subject, how can you give your reader an *emotional experience* which is the *must* of fiction? c) know the sources of any idea or quotation you use; don't trust the "someone told me" or hearsay ideas, which may lead you to unintentional plagiarism or inaccuracies.

WHERE CAN YOU GET IDEAS?

1) *Reading.* The best writers have always been omnivorous readers. Every author realizes that unless he reads, his writing is sterile and superficial. From the ancient Chinese sage who wrote "After three days without reading, talk becomes flavorless"; to Somerset Maugham who said

"To acquire the habit of reading is to construct for yourself a refuge from almost all the miseries of life," all thinkers have enriched their mental endowment by reading the works of others. Always carry with you paperbacks, pocket-sized tomes or something to read wherever you go. Read books, magazines, newspapers, fiction, non-fiction, poetry, *everything,* for you never know what will ignite your greatest ideas.

2) *Listening* has provided a kernel for thousands of magnificent stories, for most authors learn to be sharp-eared eavesdroppers on life's dramas.

Becoming a good listener will make you a better writer and thinker, a finer person and a more efficient worker.

A final word to the wise: there is so much to read and listen to nowadays that it's vastly important to be discriminating and not be like a) the funnel (everything goes in one ear and out the other; b) the strainer (lets out the wine and retains the dregs); or c) the sponge (absorbs everything, whether worthless or worthwhile.) (Quoted from *Chapters of the Fathers.*)

3) *Experiences:* Jobs, travel, people, and living. Reading and listening are *vicarious. Living* is direct. What inspires one person may not move another at all. James Michener was thrilled to articulation by the Pacific islands, but Sloan Wilson (who was in the South Pacific at the same time) received no charge out of that atmosphere whatsoever. Life in dramatic Australia has sparked many fine stories like *The Sundowners,* but Morris L. West, a patriotic Aussie, finds his greatest inspirations in Italy.

To enrich your writing and stock your mental storehouse, read, listen and live to the hilt. Collect thoughts and experiences as avidly as a philatelist collects valuable stamps, and learn to give your ideas universal meaning by carrying them to a philosophical conclusion. Balance inspiration with what Thorstein Veblen named "The Human Instinct for Workmanship." Thomas Wolfe once wrote, "If a man has a talent and cannot use it, he has failed. If he has a talent and uses only half of it, he has failed. If he has a talent and learns somehow to use the whole of it, he has obviously succeeded and won a satisfaction and a triumph few men ever know."

II | TRANSLATING REALITY INTO THE ILLUSION OF REALITY

THE MAIN TOOL of a fiction writer is Imagination, and if you are to succeed at all in fiction writing, you must keep this tool sharpened, polished, and in constant use. In short, you must learn to be an "imagineer." This requires you to use your imagination to engineer facts into fiction, and reality into the illusion of reality.

But-it-really-happened writers who feel that a true-life story is necessarily a good fiction story must learn that the reverse is true and that if you copy stories and characters from life, the result may not be authentic or believable.

You must face this vital fact of writing life squarely, and if you have a George-Washington-and-the-cherry-tree complex that won't let you tell a lie, and you pride yourself on telling the truth, the whole truth, and nothing but the truth, so help you, you belong in a court as somebody's witness, or perhaps in the technical article-writing field, but *not* in fiction. A story must give the reader truth with meaning, or "truth on a trestle," with the human values pointed out much more clearly and with more sense than life seems to do.

Commercial fiction gives us life as it ought to be instead of the frustrating thing that life often is, and people have a basic need for this affirmation that virtue is rewarded. You should be glad it is this way. If the reader wanted a story to be a copy of life as it is, he'd be satisfied to read newspapers or listen to people talk about themselves. There wouldn't be any need for fiction.

Don't think that "imagineering" annihilates truth or glorifies falsehood. It doesn't. In fact, it rearranges small, insignificant actual happenings into greater, significant whole truths. The actual incidents in books like *Uncle Tom's Cabin* or *Ramona,* for example, never really happened, but they add up to moral truths about human relationships. Liza crossing the ice in a Southern river that's warm all year round is almost as gross an untruth as other fictional fabrications like the Dutch boy, Peter, sticking his finger in the dike to save the town, or the Pied Piper luring all the children out of Hamelin, or Pinocchio's nose growing longer with each fib he told. But each tells a more important truth: the courage of an oppressed mother in trying to save her child, the unselfish courage of a boy, the punishment that may follow a broken promise and deception.

How do writers go about transcribing life into fiction? Most of them follow the advice Mark Twain once gave Kipling: "Young man, first get your facts, then distort them as you please." To which Lion Feuchtwanger added the idea that the writer must "take over from the past the fire, not the ashes." Extract the meaning, the emotional conflicts, the human values that have meaning to contemporary readers. These are the major truths. Aristotle compared the truth to a barn door which no man can avoid hitting, but which no man can hit all of at once. He insisted that "the artistic representation of history is a more serious pursuit than the exact writing of history, for the art of letters goes to the heart of things." That's why some historical novels are considered the most authentic pictures of their times: Paul Wellman's *The Female* is studied in college history courses as the top authority on the Byzantine period.

Leonard Wibberley (*The Mouse That Roared* and *Take Me to Your President*) calls the novel "the human voice of the time in which it is written . . . an expression of the conscience of a people . . . a statement of attitudes . . . customs, hopes, fears, loves, hates, deaths and births. Sometimes it is even a deeply moving statement of abiding faith." Surely these are more meaningful truths than cold facts and dates. We highlight truth by embellishing it.

Jan de Hartog keeps this reminder above his typewriter:

> Never let the truth come between me and a good story, but never let me tell a lie that does not reveal the truth.

As his criterion of whether a story is good, he asks, not "how true is it?" but "how interesting is it?" He learned this trick when he was a boy on a schooner and he told a story that was a total flop. The bosun told him, "Next time you dream up a story, tell it to the cook first. Then wait outside the galley and listen. If the cook tells your story to the next man in, go ahead with it. If he doesn't, forget it." A good measuring stick for all writers!

Instead of testing a story idea by asking, "Did it really happen?" measure it up to the following questions:

1) Is it so interesting and suspenseful that it will capture and hold reader attention?

2) Is it a mere undeveloped incident or is it a real story all the way from the presentation of a knotty problem to a satisfactory solution?

3) Does it move dynamically or do the characters and action stay more or less the same?

4) Does it prove a philosophical point or illustrate a universal truth?

5) Is this premise in line with what I sincerely believe? In other words, if I am true to my beliefs I will be telling a truth that will be more true and more salable than incidents or stories that I take from life. After all, life plagiarism is certainly not as honest as using your God-given, self-developed imagination to "imagineer" a really meaningful well-constructed story.

Why can't you sell pure, undiluted true facts to fiction publications? Because the truth is:

1) Too humdrum, dull and boring

2) If at all dramatic, it's probably libelous

3) Too fantastic and coincidental

4) Too chaotic, pointless or incongruous

5) Without motivation or a moral lesson that will give the reader insight into his own problems.

There's an old Arabian saying that Allah delights in many kinds of truth and truth in many degrees, but that even Allah doesn't want the entire truth. Neither does the fiction editor or the reader. The latter paradoxically turns to fiction to escape from life, and yet he wants a reasonable facsimile, an illusion of reality: people who are identifiable, events that are recognizable.

Truth is a good starting point, and many successful novels and short stories emanate from true facts. But true facts need as much tossing and seasoning as a successful salad.

Never is the purpose of a short story to imitate life to the letter. The average real-life happening is illogical, plotless, without motivation, rhyme or reason. The average fiction plot, on the contrary, starts with an intriguing situation (often taken from life), but follows through with a logical probable sequence of events. The emphasis is on the tight relationship between cause and effect; and the ideal set-up is for the characters themselves to be the active agents (especially when it comes to the protagonist extricating himself from the plot's stranglehold). Uniqueness is less important than verisimilitude (the convincing lifelike quality needed in fiction).

Any newspaper you pick up is studded with unusual happenings which the "but it really happened" boys seize but cannot sell as short stories. Here are a few (guaranteed true!):

> A Harrisburg, Pennsylvania, woman, examined for a bronchial infection, was found to have her chest covered with Christmas seals. When the amazed doctor questioned her, she explained:
> "I've been doing it for 30 years, Doc. It says on each seal that it's one way to fight T.B."

> A Burlington, Vermont, chap put his shoes on the wrong feet and when he turned a corner, his shoes crossed and he broke both legs.

> An injured soldier, sent home to recuperate, was watching a power lawnmower at work in his front yard. It picked up an old spoon left on the grass and hurled it with such force and accuracy that it penetrated the calf of his leg, and it had to be removed by surgery.

A twelve-year-old girl died from drinking too much water. While playing "saloon" with other children, she drank three quarts in twenty minutes, which proved fatal within twelve hours. So much water was absorbed by her bloodstream that it filled her lungs and produced all the symptoms of actual drowning.

They really happened. Honestly! But their obvious unsalability proves Aristotle's wisdom when he insisted that in drama the *probable impossible* is always preferred to the *improbable possible*.

The very quality that makes these 100%-true incidents fascinating—their freakishness—makes them implausible and unsalable as they occurred. There's too much coincidence here for fiction, and even though chance is acceptable, pure coincidence is not. Both words, "chance" and "coincidence," are derived from the Latin word, *cadere*—"to fall." "Chance" means "falling out," whereas "coincidence" means falling out on top of each other. One "falling out" or chance, the reader enjoys, but several piled up on each other make him feel that the cards are marked, the dice loaded. He imagines himself tricked and deceived, his intelligence insulted by the manipulations that only a genius like Hitchcock can get away with.

No matter how authentic, coincidence should be avoided because it strains the reader's credulity. It's unacceptable in fiction because it doesn't represent the way things *usually* happen. They happen that way once or twice, but the fiction-reader will say "So what?"

You can use a true incident or character as a springboard for fiction *only* if you develop the objective ability to translate the reality into the improved illusion of reality. This means adding, subtracting, or in some way altering

Whitworth College Library
Spokane, Washington

it to create credibility and significance for the reader. You must be able to tell what's good and what's bad about a life story, what's salable and what's not salable. For instance, the example of the little girl dying from drinking too much water is so gruesome that it outrages our sense of justice. It might also frighten mothers into not letting a child out of sight. However, there is an interesting gimmick involved which could be used as a murder-method devised by a villain who has strong motivation for wanting to get rid of a victim (not necessarily a child). Or you could work out a fraternity hazing story in which the villain tries to expose the hero as a coward or keep him out of the fraternity by daring him to drink so much water or apple cider or other liquid, knowing the probable results; a twist reversal could make the scheme boomerang for a happy ending, or it could work unhappily for a mystery story.

Keep a file of news happenings that can serve as *the starting point* for fabricated fiction. An item about a horse that was snowbound on a mountain ledge might have inspired the delightful children's story about the boy whose pet horse ran away and was later spotted from the air snowbound in an inaccessible spot. Through ingenuity, the boy persuades the pilot who located the horse to fly a haylift to save the horse, as Elisha, in the Bible, was fed from the skies. This develops into a great news story that attracts community help, teaches both boy and horse a lesson in caution and provides a name for the horse.

Conflict, contrasting characterization and premise are three "musts" you add to real-life happenings. It is also necessary to set abstract values in conflict as Gerald Green does in developing the life story of his dedicated doctor-father into the unforgettable Dr. Sam Abelman of *The Last*

Angry Man. Idealism is set up in conflict with commercial-
ism and sincere love of humanity versus exploitation for
profit.

These are some of the additions you must make to satisfy
reader-expectancy when you translate reality into the illusion of reality. Whatever alterations you make, always
remember to be the creative artist, not the photographer or
imitator, for, as Nancy Hale puts it: "Fiction is an artistic-
ally-controlled personal myth, which in its coming-together
into a form releases overtones of the universal. In both
these aspects it has a value that can be said to exist in the
world of reality—its value to the world as a work of art,
and its value, realized or not, to the artist. If, seen nega-
tively, all phantasy is self-regarding, so, affirmatively
speaking, phantasy, fiction, bears upon the conscious personality of its creator to compensate it.

"The territory of fiction is thus the other half of the
world of reality: the dark side of the moon, the mantel-
piece mirror that reflects the room, the dream between the
wakings, the shadow within the sunlight. If there is an
Open Sesame of talent to let the artist into the world of
imagination, there is a password of understanding to let
him out again into a reality which he has, perhaps, come to
value also."

Abrupt coincidence interferes with the plan of Char-
acter-makes-Destiny. It destroys verisimilitude—the illusion of reality—that is more convincing than any cold re-
production of true facts. A vivid, colorful oil-painting
hangs better on a wall than a blurred photograph; and scintillating costume jewelry shines better from the stage than
a tiny genuine diamond.

III   PREMISE

THERE'S A SAYING that a woman will wear a swim suit when she can't swim or jodhpurs when she doesn't know how to ride, but when she puts on a wedding dress, she means business. Editors are on the constant lookout for stories that are like the girl in the wedding gown—stories that mean business, that have something to say. This is true of all fiction, from vignettes to novels.

What your story says is its most important feature. You can have the best plot in the world, convincing characters, scintillating dialogue, strong emotion and suspense, but if your story lacks premise, theme, or basic moral, the editor will reject it as "much ado about nothing."

That's why it is best to formulate your premise before plotting your story. Select a proverb, quotation, or aphorism in which you sincerely believe and one that is in harmony with the policy of the magazine at which you're aiming the story. Write it down: in typewriter type, indelible pencil, or lipstick letters large enough to remind you to follow the premise throughout. Then plan your characters and plot action to best dramatize this theme for your readers. The premise is usually proved at the *end* of the story. Therefore, you start out with the negation or doubting of the real premise. As each complication tests it more and more, you build up to the emotionally satisfying climax which proves the validity of the premise.

You can start with a minus and develop it into a plus at the end.

Let's take Lincoln's favorite maxim: "If you make a bad bargain, hug it all the tighter." Comparing women to horses, he insisted that trading a horse whose faults you know for one with unfamiliar faults is a mistake in judgment. It's the same with wives. They all have faults, and changing a wife requires adjusting to a whole series of new faults. It's senseless to experiment with futility. This premise, of course, can easily be developed into a story that's timely in these divorce-ridden times. A husband is irritated by the fact that his wife isn't the glamour girl of their dating days. In fact, with the coming of the babies, her well-groomed immaculateness has vanished, and he plans to divorce her and marry his impeccable secretary or a gorgeous model. A dramatic incident proves that the gorgeous gal is so vain and selfish she wouldn't make him a good wife, wouldn't let him smoke cigars or bring fish home from fishing trips, and certainly wouldn't jeopardize her figure and her smoothly-scheduled life by having babies. He decides to keep wifey—faults and all. Perhaps she has been scared enough by the prospect of losing him to tidy up a bit.

Another variation of Lincoln's favorite aphorism occurs in Truman Capote's *Esquire* yarn, "Among the Paths to Eden," in which widower Ivor Belli feels so happy in his single blessedness, released from his late wife's constant yakking, clucking over him and nagging, that he's in no hurry to visit her grave. When he finally does go, however, he is set upon by a solicitous, friendly but definitely predatory spinster who lurks in the cemetery. (In her desperate desire to land a husband, she makes a specialty of giving peanuts and soft words to recently widowed men who come to their wives' graves.) Her faults make those of his late wife, Sarah, seem like virtues, and he readjusts his own emotional response to Sarah and her death. We feel at the end that Mr. Ivor Belli has a better understanding of himself, that his lack of a feeling of normal grief was a symptom and that he will now have a better rapport with his children who have been resenting his cold-blooded attitude toward their mother's death.

How can you promise a premise and keep your promise? First of all, in or near the beginning state or imply a moral question that intrigues the reader. The subsequent story action exploits and develops various aspects of this problem and the climax takes a stand, answering the moral question according to the author's beliefs. There are many possible answers to any given moral question, and a modern reader expects you to prove one specific answer convincingly and dramatically. The question "Should you always tell the truth, and nothing but the truth to a child?" has many possible solutions. In Thornton Delehanty's *Cosmo* story, "At First Sight," daughter Doris asks mother Susan how she met Daddy, and the mother doesn't want to fib, but she knows the true story of the "pickup" meeting would be damaging to the girl's moral standards, so the author's answer comes in this premise: "Telling the truth is like eating an artichoke. You move inward toward the heart from the outer edge, pulling the leaves in even rows around and around, and you can, just before you get to the heart, skip a row. What could it matter? It was the truth . . . with just one silly little row left out. Doris wouldn't understand anyhow."

Of course the opposite stand is often taken, and "Honesty is the best policy" about telling a child that he is adopted, or exploding the Santa Claus or Good Fairy or Stork-Brings-the-Baby myths, or relaying a painful truth to a child before he learns it more painfully from others.

In some stories a premise is boldly stated in the beginning, but usually this will be drastically changed by the end of the plot action. In Margaret Cousins' *McCall's* story, "Romantic Names, Exotic Places," the husband-hunting heroine has a definite philosophy of life. The story opens with:

> When I was young and single, I entertained a good many convictions about the way things should be . . . I was a dreamer with my eyes wide open on the twin subjects of love and life, and I had the whole thing pretty carefully arranged. I had plans. Plan your work and work your plan —that was my motto. With organization and singleminded purpose, practically anybody can make progress. . . . I never saw it fail.

Planning to marry a rich, distinguished man, she goes to work in the Sweetwater National Bank. Her only "catch" is Archie Snodgrass who also worked at the bank for $10 more a week than she earns. An expensive trip to Europe nets her dates with a Marchese Francesco Tornabuona and a handsome dreamboat named Winthrop Hastings—both of whom deceive and swindle her. Her strong beliefs are totally reversed by the end of the story when she unromantically meets and marries Harold Hoeppell-finger, a junior geologist for the Humble Oil Company, and lives in a hick town remote from the "exotic places" she had in her plans. The story ends with: "Of course I still have dreams, but there's one thing I've learned. When it comes to love, you don't have to plan. It's just a waste of time."

In the above story, Margaret Cousins' answer to the moral question "Can you manipulate love and chart romance?" is "No!" But the same question is answered affirmatively in Jean Scott's *Teen* story, "The Stars and Stephanie," in which the fifteen-year-old heroine consults her horoscope every day and uses it as a sort of a battle-map in her campaign to land a boy friend. On days when the horoscope advises her to be aggressive, she is. When it says, "Don't force things today; above all, keep your temper under control," she is shy and retiring . . . and it works.

Watch for the moral question in published stories and analyze the way the author works out the answer according to his own beliefs. Develop the habit of stating the moral question, the answer, and the plot action the author uses to prove his solution.

Make a careful study of proverbs and premises and develop the ability to translate premise into plot and vice versa. When you think of a moral, try to remember a story that serves as a parable to it. For instance, "A guilty conscience needs no accuser" or "conscience doth make cowards of us all." In Jeanne Barry's "Eyewitness," a man murders his wife in their apartment. The only possible witness is a baby in his playpen on the terrace beyond their window. Each time the murderer passes the baby, the child cries and the man cringes until conscience forces him to confess. The twist is that the baby *always* cries when it sees anyone but its mother.

The Bible says, "Love thine enemy," a difficult task for most of us. The heroine of Mary D. Lane's *Redbook* story, "Her Big Moment," learns enough from her enemy, Ceil Morton, to insure her own future happiness. Ceil is the golden, glamour-charm-girl to Henny's quiet, freckled prettiness. When good-looking Rex Saunders, the new personnel manager, takes Henny out, the always-popular Ceil warns Henny that he can't possibly be serious about a plain-Jane like Henny, that he probably doesn't like to compete for attention and it builds up his ego to be with a girl like Henny—a girl who listens. In a crisis scene with Rex, Henny blows up and instead of being the sweet, quiet girl who listens, she erupts and is as explosively outspoken as Ceil has always been. This awakens Rex to the tune of a proposal, and when Henny is showing her engagement ring to the girls in the office, she is especially kind to the miserably jealous Ceil. She concludes the story with: "After all, if it hadn't been for Ceil, I wouldn't have known enough to stop listening and start talking."

After you choose a premise with which you heartily agree, plan your story to illustrate it. There are three types of premise:

1. Positive
2. Negative
3. Middle-of-the-road

Positive premises are the best for the slicks—surely for all light fiction. There will always be a demand for Cinderella, Horatio Alger, Boy-Gets-Girl, and adventure stories which prove that virtue, honesty and perseverance will triumph over villainy. Several authors have used positive premises to illuminate whole books. For example, Lloyd Douglas' books illustrate his belief that life moves according to God's plan and that Man has within him a spiritual power which enables him to conquer all obstacles and move on to heroic success. Again, Robert Louis Stevenson's work illustrates the premise that might makes right; that simplicity, childlike hope, faith, and a pure heart make a full man. Both authors had a positive philosophy and passed it on to their readers through their fiction.

Negative premises, which appear in Broadway plays, serious novels, and quality magazines like *The Atlantic Monthly, Harper's* and *The New Yorker,* deny this positive attitude. Most of them echo the Man-Is-Doomed theme of Dostoyevsky and Strindberg who shout: "All's wrong with the world!" They are what Nietzsche calls the "Nay-Sayers to Life." You won't find these negative premise stories in the *Post.*

The *middle-of-the-road premises* have a bitter-sweet realism to be found in off-trail fiction that is printed in the pages of *Harper's Bazaar,* the *Ladies' Home Journal,* and *McCall's.* Some writers, like Chekhov, believe that "nothing ever turns out as well as we expect, but the hope that it might more than makes up for our disappointments." James Thurber was another optimistic cynic whose premises from *Fables for Our Time* include:

"He who hesitates is sometimes saved."

"Stay where you are—you're sitting pretty."

"Youth will be served, frequently stuffed with chestnuts."

"The paths of glory at least lead to the grave, but the paths of duty may not get you anywhere."

" 'Tis better to have loafed and lost than never to have loafed at all."

"It is better to ask some of the questions than to know all the answers."

"A new broom may sweep clean, but never trust an old saw."

Most middle-of-the-road premises coincide with the idea that if you can't have what you want, the secret is to want what you have.

The important thing is to fit your premise to the proper market. You can't sell a premise to the wrong magazine any more than you could sell a size 5 shoe to a size 13 foot! In fact, so antipodal are slick and quality premises that you can write down the theme of a *Post* yarn, reverse it, and find its negative in a tragic play, novel, or quality story.

Try it and see!

Here are a few quotations taken at random, which suggest splendid characters, perhaps for your next story:

"The secret of being a bore is to tell everything."

"Curiosity is one of the forms of feminine bravery."

"How sharper than a serpent's tooth it is to have a thankless child."

"Never marry a widow unless her first husband has been hanged."

"The wife that loves the looking-glass hates the saucepan."

"A woman is charitable toward the man who would ruin her and so exacting toward the man who worships her."

"No man finds himself until he loves a woman."

The premise can be the seed that contains the whole plot. For example, the proverb, "Yielding is sometimes the best way of succeeding," suggests a person giving ground to gain a bigger victory. It could be a war story, a sports yarn, or a psychological piece like the *This Week* story of the bride whose mother advised her: "Be sure to win the first battle and you'll always have your way. Your marriage will be a success, then."

When the first battle came up, Mrs. Bride was tempted to obey Mama's warning, but an objective analysis of her parents' marriage convinced her that Papa was henpecked, submissive, and unhappy. Climax: Bride decided to let hubby win their first crucial battle!

Start a premise-to-plot file of published stories, like the following:

PREMISE: "Vanity can be a man's undoing."
PLOT: "The Spectacles," by Edgar Allan Poe. The hero is too vain to wear glasses, and, as a result he finds himself in an embarrassing, ridiculous situation. Painfully, he learns the danger of his vanity—and all's well that ends well.

PREMISE: "Once burned, keep away from the fire."
PLOT: "More About Eve," by Mary Orr. Even though Eve Harrigan had broken up their happiness in the past, Lloyd and Karen let her enter their lives again . . . with resulting tragedy once more.

PREMISE: "People who live in glass houses shouldn't throw stones." Or: "No man can set himself up on a pedestal and criticize other people for acting lower than the angels. They are only human and so is he."
PLOT: "Panic," by Larry Marcus. A newspaper columnist berates the selfish behavior of men in a fire because the men

trampled women and children in their efforts to save their own lives. When he receives a letter that threatens his life and contains a promise to kill him within the next twenty-four hours, he reacts as primitively and selfishly as the men he has criticized.

PREMISE: "If you don't like what you see in the mirror, don't blame the person who gave you the mirror for the wart on your nose."

PLOT: "The Spellbound Village," by Julia Truit Yenni. A woman writer who lives in a small town is ostracized by the townspeople because her book exposes small-town scandals. Finally they are forced to realize that every town is like theirs and she had no special village in mind when she wrote the book.

PREMISE: "Beware of idols with feet of clay."

PLOT: *The Great Man*, Al Morgan. A honey-voiced, home-spun radio personality is killed in an auto accident. Although he is idolized by all, the flashback story reveals him to have been a lecherous, profane opportunist who had a reverse Midas touch with all his relationships.

Start other files of premises that suggest titles, characterizations and plots. Studying proverbs, folk sayings, parables and quotations from every source will spark your inspiration, enrich your writing, increase your sales and up the ante of your checks. Professionals are on to this trick, as you can see from the following titles: *Paths of Glory* (from "The paths of glory lead but to the grave"), *Of Mice and Men* ("The best laid plans of mice and men oft go astray"), *Grapes of Wrath* ("In the soul of the people the grapes of wrath are filling and growing heavy, growing heavy for the vintage"), *The Time of Your Life* ("In the time of your life, live—so that in that wondrous time you shall not add to the misery and sorrow of the world, but shall smile to the infinite delight and mystery of it"). Write down all the titles-from-premise you think of. A few more include *Room at the Top, Raisin in the Sun, You Can't Take it with You, Voice of the Turtle, For Whom the Bell Tolls, No Place Called Home, Where There's a Will, Strange Fruit, By Love Possessed, Look Homeward, Angel, The Sun Also Rises, The Time of the Cuckoo, All the King's Men, The Sound and the Fury.*

Premises can be easily created by posing contradictory proverbs against each other. You'll find that every quotation has its opposite. Just as a boy scout rubs two pieces of flint together to make a fire, you can rub opposite aphorisms together to produce clashing conflict and plot. A few:

"Sweet are the uses of adversity." "He jests at scars who never felt a wound."

"Absence makes the heart grow fonder." "Out of sight, out of mind."

"A man's reach should exceed his grasp or what's a heaven for?" "Ambition is but avarice on stilts and masked."

"Children and fools have merry lives." "The days of childhood are but days of woe."

"In trust is truth." "In trust is treason."

"A thing of beauty is a joy forever." "Beauty is only skin-deep."

There's no limit to how much the proper use of the proper premise will enhance the appeal of your stories and increase your sales. Never, *never* write a story without planning the premise first. Just as you shouldn't open your story or article until it has something worth saying. Select a basic truth that will give voltage to your script and will contain the seed of the plot. Look at this theme squarely, mull it over in your mind, and ask yourself:

1. Is this an idea I really believe in, so that I can prove it with wholehearted sincerity?

2. Is it fresh and original or is it a hackneyed platitude?

3. Will my premise develop clearly and consistently throughout the whole script?

4. Does it offer my reader insight into problems he himself may meet? In short, is it universally appealing?

5. Is it *worth while?* Or "much ado about nothing"?

6. Does it follow the philosophical line of the market to which I wish to sell the story?

7. Have I selected the characters and plot which will best illustrate and dramatize my premise?

Keep in mind what Emerson said: "The permanence of all books [and stories] is fixed by no effort, friendly or hostile, but by the intrinsic importance of their contents to the constant mind of man." It is your job to make everything you write have something to say, something to tell as well as something to sell.

IV HOW TO BRING YOUR CHARACTERS TO LIFE

WHEN YOU WRITE a story, you are actually creating a sort of fiction world. No matter how clever your plot is, how intriguing your atmosphere or subject matter or how profound your message, your story will not achieve the rank of "grand, eternal drama" or even salability unless it is peopled with living, breathing characters.

Throughout literary history, the successful authors are those who have created fictional people who are more real than they themselves and who often outlive them according to the prophetic words which Sax Rohmer heard his fiction character, Dr. Fu Manchu, whisper in his ear long ago: "It is your belief that you have made me; it is mine that I shall live when you are smoke."

You can probably think of many instances of the created characters being more real than their creators, so you should learn to delineate lifelike characters not only to make your fiction salable, but also to insure yourself a kind of immortality, along the lines of William James' words: "The great use of life is to use it for something that outlasts it."

Along with the advantages of bringing characters to life, there are some disadvantages. Once you have created real-life people, you are stuck with them: you cannot forget them, you can seldom control them, and you cannot kill them if they want to keep on living. Sometimes they'll upset the plot you have in mind for them and write their own story, and when characters are believable and likable, the author is controlled not just by them, but also by readers and publishers. But how pleasant compared to the constant rejections if they do not come to life! Once a never-selling writer sent his story to an editor stating: "The characters in this story are purely fictional and bear no resemblance to any person, living or dead."

The story bounced back with the pencilled notation: "That's what's wrong with it."

More stories are rejected on the basis of poor, inadequate characterization than for any other cause, for it stands to reason that readers cannot become interested in *what* happens if they don't care to whom it happens.

You must create characters who are so true-to-life that the reader identifies with them, shares their grief, exults in their triumphs, knows them more intimately than it's possible to know a real person since no one but an analyst can look into the innermost thoughts and feelings of a man or woman the way the reader can delve into the viewpoint of a fiction character. That's probably why Oscar Wilde said, "The only real people are those who have never lived." These are the people who never die, who wield influence over readers as well as their co-characters, and who convert a lifeless plot into "grand eternal drama."

How can you be sure your stories will be peopled with characters who come to life and bring exciting, suspenseful action into being? Not by physical description alone. This produces "looking-glass" characters, whom we can see as surely as dress models or store window mannequins, and who inspire as much sympathy. To create characters who stimulate story action and who make the reader care what happens, you must start building from the inside out. Start with the main inner trait that rules your main character's personality, the dominating trait that distinguishes each character from others even more specifically than his physical appearance does. Fiction people are really personified traits, as you can see when their names are used to describe someone else with a similar idiosyncrasy. "He's a regular Walter Mitty" (impractical dreamer); "My boss is a Simon Legree" (sadistic slave-driver); "She's a Pollyanna" (goody-goody optimist); "I wouldn't ask that Scrooge for anything" (stingy misanthrope).

Many elements go into creating fiction characters. The major or dominating trait must be expressed in eight ways. Work out each of these methods of dramatizing the trait *before* plotting your story or play.

Test people you know and characters you want your readers to know by these elements. But even if you build them up separately to work out the profile of your fiction people, be sure to integrate them smoothly with plot action and character interaction.

Study and analyze the ways in which the master fiction writer, Paul Gallico, brings to life and dramatizes the London charwoman in his book, *Mrs. 'Arris Goes to Paris:*

Background: When and where your character was born. Her educational, financial, social, physical conditions and how they affected her. Her schooling, religion, experiences that contribute to her major traits at the time we know her. Mrs. Harris, a work-worn widow nearing sixty, is what she has always been, an uneducated London char:

> The world in which she usually moved was one of per-petual mess, slop and untidiness . . . several times a day she faced dirty dishes in the sink, unmade beds, clothing scat-tered about . . . and all the litter that human pigs are capable of leaving behind when they leave their homes in the morning. She came to these rooms to find them pigsties; she left them neat, clean, sparkling and sweet-smelling.

✓*Emotions:* What and how the character feels about people, things and situations reveals inner traits. Example:

> She had awakened that morning with a feeling that some-thing wonderful was about to happen, and she had attuned herself to receive further communications.

Later that day, when she learns that the dogs are running at White City that evening:

> That was it! There was nothing to do but to find the right dog, the right price, collect her winnings and be off to Paris.

Her determination makes her dream materialize.

✓*Setting:* Clothes, hairdo, car, home, office, or the sur-roundings and environment that reveal the character's traits. Mrs. Harris maintains the same apple-cheeked, spar-kling-eyed dignity in every setting: in the rooms she is hired to clean; in her own basement flat where she grows geraniums to feed her hunger for beauty; and in Christian Dior's elegant Paris salon.

✓*Thoughts and Philosophy:* When Mrs. Harris tries to win the money at the dog races, she loses, but when she find a diamond clip and turns it in, she is rewarded. According to her thoughts:

> . . . A kindly fate had returned half her money with the plain admonition that if she were faithful, she might have her dress. But she was not to gamble. It was to be earned by work and self-denial. Well, she was prepared to give all that.

Her adventures in Paris make her realize that

> . . . French people are just like anyone else. . . . She had ventured into a foreign country among a foreign people she had been taught to suspect and despise. She had found them to be warm and human, men and women to whom human love and understanding was a mainspring of life. They had made her feel that they loved her for herself.

Notice how the evolvement of her personal philosophy establishes the premise of the book.

✓ *Speech:* What your character says, how he says it—whether about himself or others—must reveal the type of person he is: compassionate, impatient, selfish, critical, bigoted, brave, kind, or whatever you wish your reader to think him to be. Note how Mrs. Harris's speech reveals her tenacity when she admits that it would take her years to pay for one Christian Dior dress:

> "I'll 'ave it if it takes the rest of me life."

Later in Paris, when she is refused admission to the Dior sanctuary, she fumes:

> "See 'ere, Miss Snooty-at-the-Desk, if yer don't think I've got the money to pay—'ere! . . . What's the matter with that? Ain't my money as good as anybody else's? . . . Ain't you Frenchies got any 'eart? You there so smooth and cool! Didn't you ever want anything so bad you could cry? Ain't

you never stayed awake nights wanting something and shivering, because maybe you couldn't never 'ave it?"

✓ *Opinions of Others:* Subjective characterization that reveals traits from within a person through his own words, acts or feelings should be balanced by objective characterization through words of other people. This adds the "as others see us" angle for dimension. When Mrs. Harris gives up her favorite flicks (movies) to save money for the Dior dress, Mrs. Butterfield shakes her head in admiration, and says,

> "Character, that's what you've got. I could never do it meself."

Later in Paris, Mrs. Harris is loved by everyone at Dior's as the symbol of accomplishing the impossible:

> By late afternoon . . . the most remote corner of the establishment had heard the tale of the London charwoman who had saved her wages to buy herself a Dior dress, and she had become something of a celebrity. Members of the staff from the lowest to the highest, including the Patron himself, had managed to pass by the cubicle to catch a glimpse of this remarkable Englishwoman.

✓ *Actions:*

> She walked instead of taking the bus and when holes appeared in her shoes she wadded them with newspaper. She gave up her cherished evening papers and got her news and gossip a day late out of her clients' wastebaskets. She scrimped on food and clothing.

✓ *Physical Description:*

> The small, slender woman with apple-red cheeks, graying hair and shrewd, almost naughty little eyes . . . Only in the hat she wore did her ebullient nature manifest itself.

It was of green straw, and to the front of it was attached a huge and preposterous rose on a flexible stem which leaned this way and that. Any knowledgeable London housewife, or for that matter any Britisher, would have said: "The woman under that hat could only be a London char."

You must know your characters so well that each has traits that are not just general, but specific, and which make him stand out from people who are like him in many ways. Notice how, in a group of people with similar characteristics, there are always specific traits that differentiate them from each other. This is true of any group, whether it be neighbors in the same housing tract, members of a faculty, a political party, a garden club, fraternity, sorority, office firm or advertising agency.

No matter how much your characters have in common, they must have individual differences which will generate suspense and conflict. If they are too similar, either build up contrasting individual traits or telescope characters who are alike. As has been said of two partners, "If they don't disagree and are not different, one of them is unnecessary."

Normally in planning a story, it's best to select characters who have contrasting personalities because this more easily leads to conflict which of course is the basis of all plot and suspense. Most authors avoid similar characters even among the minor actors, and if they seem too much alike, the writer either changes or telescopes them. Most critics and writers will tell you, "Never give two characters in a story the same traits." But you can disregard this rule and have a successful story if you give these characters enough different traits to offset the similar ones.

O. Henry did this in his short story, "Two Thanksgiving Gentlemen," in which Stuffy Pete, a hobo, has been treated to a lavish dinner every Thanksgiving Day for nine years by a dignified, aristocratic Old Gentleman who always meets him in Union Square. *Consideration* is their mutual trait. Stuffy has already eaten and is uncomfortably full but rather than disappoint his benefactor, he says he's hungry and grateful for the Thanksgiving invitation. After Stuffy eats again while the other man watches, they part as usual. But around the next corner Stuffy "seemed to puff out his rags as an owl puffs his feathers and fell to the sidewalk like a sunstricken horse." He is rushed to the hospital and tested for strange diseases and while the doctors are still trying to diagnose, the ambulance brings in the Old Gentleman who has collapsed from starvation . . . he hasn't had a thing to eat for three days.

The major trait of these two men is the same: consideration (thinking of the other fellow before his own comfort and welfare). But in other ways, sloppy, overweight Stuffy Pete and the slim, black-clad, fastidiously-dressed Old Gentleman are antipodal.

The main objections to character-sameness are monotony and lack of suspense. If you relieve monotony with other contrasts and conflicts, and build suspense in other ways, your story will not suffer.

Your characters will be more vivid and alive if you imbue them with the *flavor* of their culture and surroundings so that they would not be precisely the same if they had been brought up in another environment. John P. Marquand's George Apley is as distinctly Bostonian as Harriet Simpson Arnow's people are Kentucky hill folk, Edith Wharton's characters are Old New York, Willa Cather's are Nebraskans, Jessamyn West's are Quakers, Ellen Glasgow's are of the Virginia aristocracy and Pearl

Buck's are Orientals. That's why wise authors write about the people they know, whose customs, philosophy, idiosyncrasies, vices and virtues are thoroughly familiar to them and can easily be made real to the reader.

Don'ts of Characterization

1) Don't forget that brilliant imagery is a valuable aid to professional characterization, so try to use similes and metaphors that are fresh and graphic.

2) Don't ever stop looking for characterization ideas all around you. Remember that "the workshop of character is everyday life. The uneventful and commonplace hour is where the battle is won or lost."

3) Don't copy and pattern fiction characters exactly after real people. Not only does this indicate lack of imagination, but it could lead to troublesome and expensive lawsuits. You think you are creating a flattering likeness, but the original subject may disagree with you and sue for libel or possibly invasion of privacy. Even writers who have gone to great pains to steer clear of using real people in their stories have been accused, so why go out and buy trouble? Sometimes you can get away with a composite character inspired by individual traits of several real persons.

4) Don't begin writing your story or novel until you have developed complete character sketches of all the principals. Ben Ames Williams would write many thousands of words about each main character before planning a novel and most other pros construct biographies of their characters before even thinking about the plot.

5) Don't forget to work out principles of character-balance. Plan each fiction person's strong point and his

weakness; keep sculpturing him until your own attitude toward him is equally balanced between subjective empathy for him and objective evaluation of him.

6) Don't use *any* name for your characters, but give their names and nicknames as much conscious thought as you would those of your real-life children. Sometimes it is effective to focus the traits in a name like Cash McCall, Scattergood Baines, Becky Sharp, or Mike Hammer.

7) Don't use names that are confusingly similar, such as a Philip, Phyllis and Filbert in the same yarn.

8) Don't create all-good or all-bad characters throughout the story or give them identical values and functions. Contrast is necessary for conflict and suspense.

9) Don't start off with unimportant characters and mislead the reader into thinking they and their problems are the main events.

10) Don't include characters unnecessary to the plot.

11) Don't clutter a short script with too many characters or use too few in a long novel.

12) Don't label the traits or ask your reader to take your word for it that the character is such-and-such kind of person. Dramatize his personality with action. Instead of *saying* he's honest, *show* him insisting on paying a higher income or property tax than he has been assessed. Instead of *saying* a woman is courageous, *show* her clawing and beating off her attacker. Instead of *saying* a teen-ager is studious, *show* him reading and working at his lessons in an iron lung. Instead of *saying* a person is hypocritical, *show* her promising one thing and doing the opposite.

13) Don't forget to use all eight methods of enlivening the characterization.

V THE MODERN FICTION VILLAIN

THERE SEEMS TO BE a trend in current fiction, as well as in television, for villains to eclipse heroes. The villains' parts are often better written, more exciting, and, on television and the stage, more sought after by actors than the heroes' roles. In fiction, the "bad guys" are getting tougher, and are breaking out of bounds from whodunits and men's magazines to the slicks, qualities, and the formerly overprotected women's slick magazines.

The only kind of villain that used to darken the door in women's slicks was the married man having an affair with our "innocent," vulnerable heroine. But even this heavy was often softened by strong motivation, perhaps a mentally or physically crippled wife, an impossible-to-dissolve marriage plus his sincere love and consideration for the heroine.

In spite of our moral objections to the foregoing antagonists, we don't hate and fear them as we do the new dyed-in-the-wool villains, like Red Dillon in the Gordons' "Operation Terror" (*Ladies' Home Journal*). Dillon is a rapist, thief, kidnapper and murderer who concocts a fiendish plan to terrorize 26-year-old bank teller Shelly Kerwood into stealing $100,000 from a Hollywood bank and giving it to him. His dastardly acts include beating her up, shattering her nerves with all-night phone calls, murdering his own sister when she opposes him, kidnapping Shelly's teen-age sister, Toby, and promising to kill both girls if Shelly doesn't play ball with him.

Red Dillon has broken the villain-barrier in the women's slicks, perhaps as a warning to the increased number of women living alone, unprotected. Whatever the reason, it's necessary for you to study the growing importance of today's villain and learn how to delineate and manipulate him. For he may very well be the most important and most difficult character to portray.

There is no story without plot; no plot without conflict; no conflict without struggle between good and evil. The villain embodies the Evil entity that fights Good, obstructing the progress of sympathetic elements, and preventing the hero from achieving his desired goal too easily. Study each villain in professional works and observe how he causes all the exciting and significant action and how there would be no story without him. What sort of a story would Robert Penn Warren's *All The King's Men* be without Willie Stark's neurotic thirst for power? *Dragonwyck* without the lustful Patroon's obsession to perpetuate his pseudo-kingdom and father a whole dynasty? Or *Rebecca* without Mrs. Danvers' sadistic persecution of the sensitive heroine?

Even in a short story, the villain's trait can set off the entire plot. In Pat Frank's "The Cool One," cold-bloodedness enables the husband to murder his wife in order to marry another woman. He flies from New York to Miami and back again, establishing an air-tight alibi by being seen in a different city. This falls through eventually because his same trait of remaining icy calm when there is trouble on the plane makes the stewardess remember him.

The modern villain must have a specific negative quality —one that is strongly motivated and explained and is offset by one or more sympathetic traits. While yesterday's villain kicked the dog downstairs, cussed children, stole egg-money from his own grandmother's cookie-jar, and, in short, was thoroughly and completely dastardly, today's villain is never nasty for sheer love of being nasty. In fact, he may be kinder to animals, kiddies, and old people than the hero is (or at least he gives that impression). He's likely to wear such a convincing mask of charm, humor or kindliness that the hero puts himself in a bad light by opposing or suspecting him. Thus the modern villain stimulates more suspense and is more of a real threat than the old-fashioned, obvious, one-dimensional Badman.

When you create an antagonist with evil traits, but add strong motivation for these bad qualities plus a few good ones, you find yourself beginning to understand him, even like him, perhaps; whereas *you must hate your villain in order to make the reader hate him, too!* This is not easy because we all admire brains, ingenuity, and initiative, and the modern villain must have plenty of these to outwit the hero for most of the story action—until the end!

Musts for Fictional Villains

1) *An immediately-recognizable, specific negative trait.* Unlike yesterday's antagonist, today's villain is never a stinker merely because you say so or because you describe

him as physically brutal or unattractive. Decide on his dominant negative trait, then bring it out through his dialogue, actions, emotion, thoughts and physical description. Obvious bad traits are variations of The Seven Deadly Sins: Pride, Envy, Intemperance, Sloth, Avarice, Ire, Lust. Or you can start with one in this Biblical phrase (Proverbs 6: 16-19): "Six things there are which the Lord hateth, and the seventh his soul detesteth: Haughty eyes, a lying tongue, hands that shed innocent blood, a heart that deviseth wicked plots, feet that are swift to run into mischief, a deceitful witness that uttereth lies, and him that soweth discord among brethren." The last fits Paul Sheparton, the money-hungry, egotistical lady-killer in Samuel Elkin's "Survival of the Fittest." Handsome, charming and confident, he woos Dora and Eva Brampton, middle-aged spinsters, turns them against each other, gives each a gun, expecting one to kill the other. Then he plans to marry the survivor and when she is convicted of her sister's murder, he will inherit their wealth. His major trait is summed up in his own words: "I am unique. I am a man without a stupid conscience. I am the survivor of the fittest."

2) *Strong motivation for the negative trait.* Usually the villain's motivation, the "why behind what," is so convincing that there are times when the reader or viewer feels that with the same provocation, he would be tempted to act as the villain does. The rustler who hates lawmen bitterly was once cruelly framed by a vote-seeking marshal up for election; the evil-doer seeks vengeance for a wrong done him or someone dear to him.

In Nancy Rutledge's *Alibi For Murder,* snobbish Bartholomew Garth kills his dominating father because his ego can no longer bear being squelched by the old man. His egotistical pride motivates his need to destroy anyone who threatens it.

Just as a sense of superiority provides Garth's motivation, an inferiority complex motivates sadistic Sergeant Keller in Robert Waldman's *End to the Glory*. Keller's cruelty drives some of his own soldiers to unnecessary death and all men and women who know him fear "the inert violence within him." He hates anyone who is smart, adjusted, friendly or popular—traits which he lacks. His motivation? Constant rejection since early childhood when he was repeatedly beaten by his drunken father. The hero, Eric Reader, sums him up thus:

> . . . the man suffered from a great inferiority complex, probably because of his awkward ugliness. Since he met Keller when they landed in Italy, he knew the Sergeant was responsible for many battle fatalities. On the surface, Keller was the ideal soldier, taking orders and executing them to perfection; but because of his personal hatred of the men serving under him, he was both despised and feared.

Sometimes the situation provides motivation, as starvation leads to murder and cannibalism in the Donner Party. In Hemingway's "The Snows of Kilimanjaro" Harry is grouchy, insulting and brutal because he is dying and is afraid of death. The woman who loves him asks:

> ". . . If you have to go away . . . is it absolutely necessary to kill off everything you leave behind? I mean do you have to take away everything? Do you have to kill your horse, and your wife and burn your saddle and your armour?"
>
> "Yes," he said. "Your damned money was my armour. My Swift and my Armour."
>
> "Don't."

". . . Harry, why do you have to turn into a devil now?"
"I don't like to leave anything," the man said. "I don't like to leave things behind."

3) *The specific negative trait must create such dramatic impact on other characters that it causes dynamic conflict which forms the bedrock of the plot action.* It also gives the villain supremacy over the sympathetic characters either temporarily or permanently. For instance, in "The Survival of the Fittest," Dora and Eva Brampton would have remained eternally devoted to each other if Paul Sheparton hadn't turned them against each other and then converted them into killers. He intended for them to kill each other, but they realized his villainy in time to turn their guns on him. The test of the antagonist's importance is: Would the story and other characters be the same without him?

4) *Don't merely label the trait but dramatize it in as many ways as possible.* For instance, in Dillon Anderson's *Atlantic Monthly* story, "The Meanest Man in Washington County," the major trait (stated in the title) is expressed by:

Background: Farmer Crusoe Dalyrumple has fought poverty, barren land and "sorry crops" all his life.

Emotion: Since the story does not go into Crusoe's viewpoint, his emotions are expressed in actions and dialogue.

Setting: Notice how his house reflects his character and sets the mood in a minor key:

In front of his red brick house . . . a pack of brindle hounds that came barking and snarling . . . slobbering and showing their yellow teeth at us.

Whitworth College Library
Spokane, Washington

Thoughts: The most he hated anybody was little children
—except, of course, Yankees and strangers. "Them damn
Yankees dreen our money off, fast as we can make it."

Speech: "What do they want here?" he barked. His voice
put me in mind of a bandsaw that has struck a knot . . .

Opinion of others: They told us how he beat his wife, his
stock, and even the hired girl. How he'd poisoned the
neighbors' dogs and kicked his own pack around something awful. He cusses before ladies . . . won't go to
church or do anything nice. He's an awful man.

Action: He bawled his wife and Nora out right there before us. He seemed to put extra heart in it for our benefit.

Physical description: Crusoe Dalyrumple was a little, fry-
ing-size guy with no meat on his bones at all. His hands
were made along the line of hawk's claws, and the leaders
in his wrists moved like baling wire. Also, he was ugly
enough to make children cry.

5) *Negative trait must be offset with at least one positive
trait.* The villain with some good characteristics is not only
more modern and realistic, but he provides a more interesting challenge to your hero and more suspense to the
story, especially if his good points fool other characters. In
Philip MacDonald's *Post* serial, "Fingers of Fear," a little
girl has been fiendishly murdered and circumstantial evidence leads Lt. Connor to arrest Frank Orbach. Later,
Connor has reason to suspect a charming, popular socialite,
Retired Naval Captain Tod Merriman. He is so charming
and clever that when Connor finally catches him and con-

fronts him with the charge, Merriman has the Chief of Police and one of Connor's fellow officers on his side ready to attack Connor. (The ensuing fight knocks open a shelf-cupboard door and out falls a broken doll that is incriminating evidence against Merriman.) Only when proved guilty beyond a doubt, does the charming, calm, confident man change:

> Merriman, composed enough, but with a gray look impinging on his tan, followed . . . a strange sound came from his throat. His mouth was twisted and he didn't look like Merriman anymore. He put his head down . . . and ran for the door.

6) *Attitude.* Villainy is not determined so much by the performance of evil deeds as by the character's attitude toward them; otherwise how could we reconcile our reverence for the Ten Commandments with our respect for the Congressional Medal of Honor?

Let us consider a bomber pilot. If his mission is to bomb an enemy target, we cannot call him a villain for following orders, especially if he suffers pangs of conscience. But if he enjoys his role as death-dealer or goes out of his way or disregards orders to slaughter more helpless people, that makes the difference. If a pilot is flying with a jammed nuclear bomb and must choose between dropping it on a heavily-populated, friendly territory or risking his own life trying to get it back to home base, the choice becomes a conflict between plus and minus moral values; between self-preservation (selfish) and self-sacrifice (unselfish). His decision between the minus or plus determines whether he's the villain or the hero.

Jonathan Swift said: "I have never been surprised to find men wicked, but I have often been surprised to find them not ashamed." Attitude makes the difference. The villain who is proud of his villainy is the dyed-in-the-wool heavy whose evil trait trips him up in commercial fiction. But the villain whose attitude is softened with conscience and contriteness, who perhaps was goaded into a crime which is basically against his real nature . . . that is the man for whom there is hope . . . the rascal who may be regenerated or do a noble deed.

Before you plot your story, it will help to create your antagonist, stressing these six basics: his specific negative trait; motivation or why he is this way; the effect of this trait on other people in the story; how you will dramatize the trait in different ways; contrasting traits to balance the bad one; and the attitude of the villain toward his villainy and your attitude toward him.

Tips on Creating the Villain

1) Make it clear that the villain is a villain because of his negative character and individual personality, *not* because of his physical appearance, his profession or job, nationality, race or religion.

2) At the beginning of the story do not give the villain *good* motives or the hero *bad* motives, even though reversal-incidents and quirks of fate may ironically give the villain's actions good results, while the hero's efforts lead to tragedy or disappointment. According to the original intentions of each, the hero's good motives are what make him the "good guy," whereas the villain's evil motives make him the "bad guy."

3) Try to make your villain consistent without being predictable, monotonous, transparent, or obvious. If he

changes character, the change must be convincing and warranted; then have the plus-traits planted.

4) Seek interesting names or nicknames for your villain. Negative characterization is colorfully implied in names like "Snakeskin," "Sneaky," etc.

5) Early or late, explain the motivation or reason for this negative trait. Exactly what in his background or experiences caused this to develop? For the sake of additional dramatic suspense, the reason for the negative trait or even the identification of the villain himself (as in a whodunit) may not be revealed until late in the story. This keeps the hero and the reader guessing and creates suspense.

6) Make certain that the specific negative trait had dramatic impact on other characters and elements in the story; that it clashes with and at times defeats the hero's sympathetic trait.

7) Avoid a villain with mental aberrations as the viewpoint character. The reader prefers to identify with a normal person whom he can understand and whose actions and thoughts will, therefore, be more convincing and credible.

8) Dramatize the character trait by contrasting the villain with a sympathetic character and making the most of character interaction. This adds dimension over the flat forms of characterization in which one person at a time is described.

9) In a commercial story, try to have the villain suffer the same negative fate he has planned for the sympathetic character. If he plans poisoning or shooting, *he* is poisoned or shot. If he pushes a victim from a high place, he is finished off this way. In Ernest Lehman's "Tell Me About

It Tomorrow" (*Cosmopolitan*), which became the movie, *Sweet Smell of Success,* overambitious press agent Sid Wallace slavishly follows Harvey Hunsecker's orders to break up Susan Hunsecker's romance with Steve Dallas. Villain Sid stops at nothing to ruin Steve's reputation by framing him with fake evidence. Susan retaliates by ruining Sid's reputation and staging a fake seduction scene that enrages her brother against Sid.

VI DRAMATIC CONTRAST IN CHARACTERIZATION

PAUL WELLMAN, the novelist, divides fiction characters into three categories: cardboard people who have just one trait; *bas relief* characters who have contrasting traits; and full-dimensioned people who have many facets to their personalities. The cardboard characters appear either in short-shorts or in minor "bit" parts; the full-dimensioned people are protagonists in full-blown novels and dramas; but the majority of characters you'll work with will have opposing traits. Unlike yesterday's actors, they are not lily-white or charcoal-bad, not vanilla or chocolate, but a marble mixture that makes them lifelike and adds suspense to their behavior and development.

The fiction characters who are remembered have contrast at their core. Scarlett O'Hara in *Gone With The Wind,* is selfish, lazy, superficial, pampered and dependent on luxuries until adversity brings out her antipodal traits and then she is self-sacrificing, hardworking, independent, and develops a tough, invincible leadership.

Evil and good co-exist within Bardone in the motion picture *General Della Rovere.* He is a clever gambler and con-man who fleeces families of captured Italian partisans during World War II by pretending he has German contacts powerful enough to free the prisoners or lighten their sentences. When the Germans force him to impersonate a dead Italian general in order to flush out a partisan leader, he reverses from unprincipled crook to true patriot and martyr. He is as marbled as John Oakhurst of Bret Harte's "The Outcasts of Poker Flat," the crooked gambler who is evicted from the camp, but later sacrifices his snowshoes and then his very life to save the others.

Sheila Sargent of Virginia Rowans' novel, *Love and Mrs. Sargent,* is a marblecake Lonely Hearts columnist who is loved by millions of readers for her charming, witty wisdom but is hated by her children, relatives and friends because of her perfection and cloying Momism. At the same time that she solves the emotional problems of strangers in her lovelorn column, she ruins the lives of her own children—Allison, whom she drives away from an art career into the Chicago debutante season, and Dicky, whom she tries to force into becoming a literary lion like his father. The war between her constructive and destructive self creates the book's major dramatic interest and is clearly defined in passages like:

> . . . an inner voice that kept questioning the Actual Sheila as to the true reason behind every word, every action, every thought. The Other Sheila was generally an outspoken, hard-boiled cynic, but she could take on a number of distressing personalities. The Actual Sheila did not always care for the companionship of the Other Sheila—but she put up with her nagging presence because she liked to feel she was completely honest with herself.

Even short story characters have antipodal qualities. Isn't this what intrigues your interest at the beginning of John Latham Toohey's *McCall's* story, "The Fabulous File":

> To twist an old saying: If you have my uncle Ferenc for a friend, you don't really need any enemies. It was Uncle Ferenc who handed me my first cigarette, at fifteen. Some three years later, in a garish roadside tavern, he presented me with my first shot of bourbon. There were other firsts along life's happy highway that need not be detailed here; Uncle Ferenc was almost invariably on hand, a wicked grin blazing on his gay Hungarian face, mockery jostling avuncular concern in his very blue, very Hungarian eyes. Please do not start thinking of my Uncle Ferenc as an ancient debaucher, tottering down the primrose path with a young innocent in tow. He is my father's much younger brother and is only about four years my senior.

Nothing stays dull with such a marblecake character around: He's naughty, he's nice, and he's a strong influence on his nephew—all of which promises fireworks. His naughtiness makes a wolf out of the boy as he investigates the girls in the file. It helps Boy meet Right Girl, but Boy loses Girl when Girl meets the Fabulous File. And then, when all seems lost, Uncle Ferenc's niceness helps him win back the girl with methods that would "melt Lucrezia Borgia into a den mother."

This paradox often creates the story itself, a timely one today. The effect of Western ways on ancient Japanese customs results in several marblecake characters in Hobart Skidmore's *Post* story, "The Eternal Blossom." Ruiko, the heroine, is sentimental and practical, torn between loyalty to her old-fashioned parents and love for wild, young Kanji. Her father, Ichiro Shiina, is proudly conventional and respectable, but also tenderly aware of his daughter's feelings. All the Japanese characters are aware of contradictions in Americans who "suspect everyone and trust everyone." But the strongest contrast is within Kenji Tanaka, the angry, young man, whose rebellion manifests itself in rejecting the age-old Japanese values of dignity, honesty and *Shuyo* (self-discipline) for uninhibited aggressiveness, which he considers the virtue of a victorious people in a modern world. Eventually, the Oriental values triumph over blue-jeaned, beatnik ideas, and Kenji returns the motorcycle which he bought with stolen money, realizing it "had never really been his. It had been an illusion, a curious migration away from the reality of himself and back. And it all had been as simple and treacherous as it had been wrong."

How do you select the opposite traits that form the marblecake? *Before* writing or even planning the overall story, work out thorough characterizations of the principals. Most professional writers write thousands of words of character-sketching that never appear in the final script, but that serve to "write the character to life." Dramatize your protagonists in every possible situation, then spotlight contrasting characteristics that are the strongest and will spark the action and drama. You should see the many phases in your fiction character, then choose the major paradoxical traits and focus on their battle for control of the character and the story.

Look for the marblecake quality in all people and your favorite fiction characters will invariably have more dimension and verisimilitude. Everyone is a Dr. Jekyll and Mr. Hyde at various times, and today's successful writer stresses this paradox, whereas yesterday's author sometimes created one-traited characters. That's why a classic that's adapted for today's audiences requires revamping of characterization to add antipodal traits. In 1912, Eleanor H. Porter delighted the world with a saccharine "glad girl," Pollyanna, who cheerfully produced good deeds and miracles. But Pollyanna Whittier would be a boring, unbelievable "square" to modern audiences if Walt Disney hadn't added the down-to-earth qualities of curiosity, terrific imagination and other normal adolescent characteristics that make both the new three-dimensional Pollyanna and the movie a heartwarming success.

A marblecake character always keeps the reader guessing. Furthermore he's more credible than an all-white or all-black cardboard personality, and the negative traits or weaknesses make him easier for the average person to identify with, whereas the super-hero gives him an inferiority complex.

Yesterday's villain would have been a consistent stinker. Not so today's Badman, who may still send the old folks to the poorhouse, but insists on paying their taxi fare! This same villain will try deviously to win the girl, but after he loses to the hero, he'll give them a wonderful wedding present or set up a trust fund for their children. If he's stuffy, self-righteous, or insufferably snobbish, he must have a balancing admirable trait.

If your stories have bounced lately, maybe it's because the characters are old-fashioned—one-dimensional and lacking the contrast of *real* people. Fictional or real, there's always "some good in the worst of us and some bad in the best of us." The most wonderful person you know may gossip, have a temper, talk too much, cheat at solitaire, or be pessimistic, sarcastic, martyrish, or vain. Conversely, the hateful heel who is selfish, vain, sadistic, merciless, aggressive, dictatorial, unethical, or rakish may have a cleverness or sense of humor that will keep any party from sagging; or perhaps he's kind to children, animals, or old ladies.

Study the rich variety of contrasts in characterization in professional works. In Kathleen Winsor's *Forever Amber*, Luke Channell, Amber's husband, is a contrast character, seeming cultured and refined, but actually coarse and bestial: "He seemed to have one great quality, his violent infatuation for her. By next morning she knew she had been cheated on that. His adoring manner had vanished altogether and now instead he was violent, crude, and over-bearing. His vulgarity shocked and disgusted her. From the first day of their marriage, he was gone most of the time, drank incessantly, and displayed almost without provocation a violent and destructive bad-temper." And then there is Mr. Martin of James Thurber's *The Catbird Seat* (which became the British movie *Battle of the Sexes*) —an unobtrusive, mild-mannered, old fuddy-duddy no-body of a clerk who suddenly acquires a devilish kind of leadership in order to outwit Angela, a woman efficiency expert who takes over. There is a final touch of contrast at the end when, after battling her desperately and viciously, he hands her a nosegay token of reconciliation.

Contrast of traits within a person creates suspenseful drama. Sometimes right conquers wrong, sometimes the reverse, but it's an exciting conflict and makes a good show. Choose and dramatize interesting, suspenseful contrasts in your fiction characters. Start keeping a file of character sketches of persons with opposite traits: the brave-in-the air jet pilot who's afraid to drive on the freeway; the drunken actress who beats up the arresting officer, then on the same day proceeds to give a heavenly performance in *Peter Pan;* the fearless stunt man who faints with terror before the camera; the Sunday School teacher who heads the juvenile crime ring; the murderer who offers his eye to a blind medical missionary while still alive; the minister who writes confessions; the ancient old lady who is more progressive, baseball-and-football-and-space-minded than any of the younger generation; the unkempt hobo who was once a college professor; the burlesque dancer who scorns social life and turns down invitations to stay home alone and read philosophy books. If people you want to write about seem one-dimensional, add characteristics that are antipodal to the ones they already have. Be sure that the paradox is convincing and well-motivated. After you have thoroughly worked out these marblecake characters, all you have to do is to introduce them to an interesting situation and the plot sparks will fly. To test your characters to see if they are suitable for modern stories, ask these questions:

1) Are there two clear-cut conflicting traits?
2) Are they dramatized through dialogue, action, emotion, reaction, and inner thoughts of the character himself?
3) Which trait is stronger?
4) Do the opposite traits represent good and evil or right and wrong?
5) Is there a suspense-filled, equal struggle between good and evil for mastery of the character?
6) Is there convincing motivation for each trait?
7) Is there a smooth, professional integration of the

major and minor traits so that there's no jerkiness?

8) Which trait triumphs to produce a sympathetic or unsympathetic character? In spite of the opposite qualities which make up each story person, his total personality must inspire a *unified emotional reaction* on the part of the reader who feels admiration, hatred, liking, pity, or other emotions toward him.

9) Is the characterization inevitable according to motivation and plot circumstances? Would real people naturally act and be the same way under similar conditions?

VII | THAT DIALOGUE DILEMMA

ONCE UPON A TIME there was a poor minister who bought a used car and didn't have the gasoline to run it. Much like the author who had a good plot (new *or* used, but good) and didn't have the dialogue to make it go. After all, that's what dialogue is:—the fuel to keep your story moving. Furthermore, professional dialogue doesn't just "come naturally." You must master the techniques and be sure it contains the necessary ingredients.

To feed your fiction high-powered dialogue that speeds it straight to publication, be sure that each line of talk does more for the story than clutter it up with yakkety-yak. Cut out talk that doesn't fulfill one or more of these dramatic functions:

1) *Does it speed up the story?*

Dialogue uses shorter sentences and fewer words than narrative, and in this way accelerates the pace of your story. Good dialogue goes right to the point and uses simple words; it should be clear and brief, understood the first time. Study dialogue openings of published stories and see how they dive-bomb into the plot, clarifying the problem, setting off conflict, and establishing suspense. Try re-writing them *without* dialogue and see how many more words and how much longer it takes to get the same story off the ground.

This example from Harriet Frank, Jr.'s "In the Good Old Summertime" (*Redbook*) opens with viewpoint character Alan Stewart tempting his wife, Janie, with a vacation-at-home alone together while their kids are away at camp:

> ". . . Tomorrow we put them on the bus, we look after them misty-eyed and we come home—alone. Alone, doll, as we used to be eight years ago. Alone, with dry martinis and a houseful of double beds.
>
> "Listen, *bon vivant*," she said with a faint smile, "tomorrow I come home, having said farewell to my children, pack a large carpetbag with a few trifles of yours and mine, and we're off on what I achingly refer to as my vacation."
>
> "I've been thinking about that," I said slowly.

2) *Does it characterize the speaker?*

One of dialogue's most vital functions is *self-description,* with the speaker's words clarifying his basic traits, aims, and desires. Each person must speak *from the inside out;* therefore you must have your characterization worked out thoroughly, with inner dialogue before you can have outer dialogue. The most effective way to accentuate characterization is, of course, by using contrasting personalities, whose opposite traits are stressed by their self-revealing words.

All the characters in Keith Wheeler's novel *Peaceable Lane* reveal their traits through their dialogue. When the crisis arises in an exclusive all-white neighborhood where a home is to be sold to a Negro, all the residents of Peaceable

Lane decide to chip in and buy this house themselves. All, that is, except the shrewd, crafty union leader, Steve Cavanidis, who is "adept in the art of enlightened self-interest." Notice how his character is revealed in his own words. When the others are angry at him for voting against their decision, therefore increasing their financial share, he says:

> I owe you no explanation, but because I've been sitting here this long I'll give you a quick one. I don't like Jigs any better than you do . . . but I'm a tall man in a big union. Some day I'll be the tallest. But it's a democratic union, which means the officers are elected." He rose to his feet. "About 35% of my members are Jigs. Good night."

Two people are characterized in this brief dialogue: "I met such a charming polite man today," she sighed dreamily. "I was carrying my umbrella carelessly, and it poked him in the eye, and I said 'Pardon me,' and he said 'Don't mention it, I have another eye left.' "

3) *Does it characterize someone through the speaker's viewpoint?*

Your characters will be lifelike and three-dimensional if, in addition to their own words of self-description (or self-revelation) you add what others say about them. Here are a few examples:

Waitress characterizes the villain in a few words:

> "He's a tough egg, always givin' us girls trouble. Likes to push people around and watch 'em squirm—as long as they're not bigger'n him. An' there ain't many that are!"

In Prentiss Combs' *Post* story "The Hostile Land," Doc Purdy and Tribus Afton are discussing the proud widow, Jessie Hilton, who needs surgery but refuses to go to the county hospital and insists on plowing the land instead:

"She's not going to the hospital," Tribus said, bracing himself for Doc's outburst. But Doc Purdy only nodded.

"Money?" he asked.

"Partly," Tribus said, and Doc nodded again.

"Too proud to go to the County. Going to stay out there and make a crop, isn't she? Going to make a crop and get Henry Hilton his triumph."

Tribus looked at him. "How come you know so much?"

"I've only come across a few like her. Not many to a dozen. Henry Hilton had himself a woman there."

"She doesn't think so," Tribus said. "Blames herself about the babies."

Doc nodded and sighed. "Keep an eye on her, Tribus."

4) *Does it state facts and give information in a livelier way than narrative would?*

Sometimes it's more interesting to learn facts from the words of a character than from the author's narrative, but not always. Readers want action, atmosphere, and sometimes a viewpoint character's inner emotions first-hand rather than through dialogue which may become tediously yakkety-yak and indirect. Many people prefer motion pictures to legitimate theatre because they can *see* battle forays, bull fights, horse races, or other action scenes that are impossible to stage and must be described for them by the actors in the theatre. So, for direct, split-second action, use narrative instead of dialogue. Another danger is artificial dialogue where a character tells another something he already knows, merely to relay it to the reader in quotation marks. Doesn't the following expositional dialogue seem synthetic in Horatio Winslow's "The Runaway"?

"I'm Mrs. Matthews, and you've told me you are Dexter Brock and that you're in the seventh grade and that your home is with Miss Weaver, who's your Cousin Grace. Well, this is the exact hour, Dex, when a seventh grader feels a need for oatmeal cookies. Lucky that I've just baked a batch. Now I'm going to lead you right to them."

Since the facts themselves can sometimes be dull fare for dialogue, it is a very clever trick to arouse curiosity and suspense before satisfying them with explanations. This rivets reader interest and makes an intriguing hook for a story beginning. You can tease the reader only so long, though, and soon after pricking his curiosity, you must satisfy him—that is, about the situation. Don't delay too long, or his mystification will annoy him or else he'll start making his own guesses and reject the situation when you do give it to him. Notice how the following openings make you wonder *what*, then promptly tell you:

Day after day they chided her. "What you did was wrong," they said. "You are still young. You have much to live for."

"Go away," she always said to them. "Go away and leave me alone!"

"You must not forget that you have a daughter; you must think of her."

Sometimes she became angry and screamed at them. "Get out of here!" she shouted. "If I want to take my own life, that's my business!"

"You cut your wrists with a razor," they said. "How could you when you have everything to live for?"

"An overdose of sleeping pills. You swallowed enough to kill the average person. You are lucky to be here at all."

"I am not lucky. You are fools . . ."

Observe how in the above opening of Gertrude Carrick's *Falling Star,* the taboo idea of attempted suicide is dramatized by dialogue that pulls out the details one at a time.

5) *Does it intensify emotion?*

Dialogue that speaks from the heart stimulates an emotional response that is greater than a narrative statement of emotion. In an emotional scene it is best to integrate dialogue with narrative to create a maximum emotional effect. They are equally important, like two hands playing one song. This is true in describing any emotion—joy or grief, hatred or love, rage or tenderness, pity or contempt. Years ago Edith Wharton described this relationship of dialogue and narrative when she called dialogue "the spray into which the great wave of narrative breaks in curving toward the watcher on the shore. This lifting and scattering of the wave, the coruscation of the spray, even the mere material sight of the page broken into short, uneven paragraphs, all help to reinforce the contrast between such climaxes and the gliding of the narrative intervals."

See how emotional narrative and dialogue blend together to fortify each other in the following passage from John D. MacDonald's "The Man Who Almost Blew His Top":

> Anger made his breathing come fast again. And he saw the black car swing out to pass. In his anger he stepped hard on the gas pedal . . . The other man stepped on it, too, and as the cars came even, Dan . . . bellowed out at the other driver, "You damn fool!"
>
> And he saw a flash of red apoplectic face, heard a similar roar of rage, torn away by the hot wind . . .

Or in Rex Stout's *Too Many Detectives:*

> Wolfe came out of his chair and took a step toward the door, then stopped, turned, and glared at me. "Dead, you say?"
>
> "Right. Strangled."

. . . He sat down, flattened his palms on the table top, and closed his eyes. After a little, he opened them. "Confound the wretch," he muttered. "Alive he gulled me, and now, dead, he gets me into Heaven knows what!"

6) *Does it add flavor, atmosphere, and local color?*

One of the best reasons for writing about the people, profession, region, or locality you know best is that you're familiar with the specific jargon or terminology, and the dialogue will ring true. One of the main reasons people read is to learn vicariously of other places, other jobs and backgrounds, and other people—with similar problems, of course, but with a different "flavor" or setting. Foreign dialects are especially unpopular in short stories where the appeal should be visual rather than auditory, and the short story reader likes flavorful talk that isn't too different from average Americanese. If you must use dialect never misspell it for emphasis ("shure now" for "sure now").

Colorful talk that the reader knows is fine: teen-age jargon; some slang, if it doesn't become stale; jive-talk; some professional expressions; horse-track or underworld terms, etc. Documentary movies and teleplays have educated the reading public to these, just as the war familiarized us with Army and Navy terms so that we don't have any trouble with a flavorful passage like:

. . . the exec's eyes moved from the 'Don't Give Up The Ship!' legend on the wall to the row of officers. "Gentlemen! We've got to fumigate our own house. I want you to drop everything else and comb your sections, fore and aft, scupper to scupper, to root this snake out. The mutineer has got to be found!"

Be sure that your characters speak in a manner appropriate to their times, age, education and personalities.

Do not use archaic dialogue for a contemporary character, although it might be perfect for a time when they really spoke in that way.

In addition to using dialogue as an aid to increasing the verisimilitude of an historical period or geographical or cultural region, you can use it to intensify seasonal atmosphere, as Florence Jane Soman does in "Interesting Stranger." In this story, two teen-age girls are discussing seasons, while, "down the wide, tree-lined street, lawn-sprinklers made glittering arcs of water in the late afternoon sun and shadows lay on the grass and the air was hot and still":

> "Summer is my season," Laurie said. "I love everything about it—sleeveless dresses and corn on the cob and outdoor barbecues and sun-tan lotion—everything."
> "Me too," Connie said, "I hate winter. Winter pinches me."
> "Galoshes," Laurie said. "All those layers you have to wear." She shook her head. "In books, the heroine's cheeks are always stung gloriously by the icy wind, but my face just gets sort of purplish, like a not-quite-ripe eggplant. In the summer I'm not nearly so revolting."

Note how dialogue makes dullish facts more palatable because they are filtered through a personality.

7) *Does it entertain?*

Lots of dialogue lightens the texture of your style. As Max Eastman said, "Repartee is a duel fought with the points of jokes." And lots of dialogue glitters, scintillates, giving the impression of humor that you should use only for light-comedy subject matter. If you see two stories, one with lots of brief dialogue, the other almost solid narrative, you expect the first to be gay and entertaining, requiring little thought and concentration; the second, serious, maybe even tragic. Use lots of dialogue for sparkling, happy stories or those which depend upon human communication for their impact; but cut down on dialogue for a tragic or serious yarn, or one in which the viewpoint character is cut off from society by a character trait (misanthropy or an inferiority complex); by an affliction (such as deafness); or geographically (as in a story about a lonely sailor shipwrecked on an island).

The lighter and funnier the story, the more dialogue and less narrative should be used. In fact, the best humor effect is created by rapid-fire, undiluted dialogue, as you often find in Max Shulman's yarns. But you cannot go on that way without describing the characters as they talk, except briefly, and only for an extremely ludicrous effect. Even in a farcical scene like the following one by Max Shulman, there are brief directions integrated with the quick-paced talking, as hero tries to win over his girl's uncle:

I extended a panicky hand. "I am proud, sir," I squeaked, "to meet the next governor of our state."

For a moment he stared at me. Then his hard red face relaxed into a soft red face. He gave my hand a cartilage-mashing shake. "Come in," he rumbled. "Come in!"

. . . "Pearl, why haven't you had Spencer over here before?"

"We just met this afternoon," said Pearl. "He is majoring in Political Science and thinks politics is the highest pursuit of man, don't you, Spencer?"

"Except maybe construction," I replied.

Pearl beamed. Her uncle beamed. I beamed. We beamed, all three.

"Sit down, Spencer," he invited. "Do you smoke cigars?"

"No, sir," I said. "But I admire a man who does."

Normally, dialogue must be stage-managed, so that we see the speaker, his actions and his gestures while he talks —the whole scene filtered through a strong narrative viewpoint. Most rejected scripts fail to do this. They have bulky passages of narrative, then undiluted dialogue in which the characters become disembodied voices, or sometimes we cannot even tell who is saying what, let alone what he is doing or thinking while he prattles on. In one story, the girl climbed a ladder to decorate a Christmas tree, and sparkling dialogue took over and the author never even got the poor girl down from the ladder.

The author must keep his eye on the character while he speaks. What is he doing? What are his emotions? What is the viewpoint character thinking, planning, or feeling while this conversation takes place? In "The Ghost Wore A Monocle," by John Davies, we know what Mrs. Whymper feels, sees, hears, does, says; it is all intermingled:

> Through a daze of terror, Mrs. Whymper heard the air hostess's polite, well-modulated voice. "Hurry, please," the hostess was saying. "We are late on take-off. Please hurry and take your seat, Mr. Whymper."
>
> Mrs. Whymper saw George come aboard and walk forward to take the seat beside her. She started up in terror and stumbled out into the aisle, putting out her hands to fend him off. But he still came on. His face swam up in front of her, and he was smiling dreadfully.
>
> Mrs. Whymper clawed at him, and her voice came out in a thin, awful scream.
>
> "No—no! You're dead . . . dead, I tell you! You're dead because I killed you! You're dead . . . dead . . . DEAD!"
>
> Then the shrieking babble strangled in her throat and she slumped unconscious to the floor . . . .

Those precious few words of dialogue fulfill three of the functions: characterization, information, and emotion —all aimed toward producing one single effect. If you use each word and phrase of dialogue for a specific purpose, you won't be guilty of pointless dialogue. Test your dialogue by using a different color for each of the seven functions, and underlining in the proper color the dialogue that fulfills them. All colorless talk should be eliminated!

Perfect your dialogue technique by listening, reading, studying professional conversational scenes *before* writing your own, and then, *afterward* by acting and talking out your dialogue scenes. As Zachary Gold said, "Good dialogue speaks; bad dialogue reads."

VIII   EMOTION

EMOTION IS THE HEARTBEAT, the pulse and soul of all fiction. It creates tension and suspense and provides the reader with a luxurious therapeutic outlet which life usually denies him.

There are many emotions you must deal with, control and exploit if you are to become a professional: The emotion you feel for your subject, your reader, for each of your characters; the emotions each of them feels for other characters; the emotions you plan for your reader to feel for the story and people in it; and surely your emotion toward writing itself. Perhaps it's frustration, fascination, enthusiasm, excitement . . . anything but indifference. Ray Bradbury calls it zest, gusto, verve. He says: "If you are writing without zest, without gusto, without love, without fun, you are only half a writer . . . you are not being yourself."

Once you have this emotional attitude toward writing itself, a strong passion for or against a subject or a person may be the starting point of a specific script. But you must use logic and careful planning to direct these emotions into successful form . . . the way you must bridle and rein a high-spirited horse or harness tumultuous waterpower into useful electricity. Illogical emotional eruption is like hot erupting lava that turns people away from the volcano. When you are emotionally aroused about a subject or person, gear your story or novel, premise and structure to arouse a pre-planned emotional reaction on the part of your reader. All social reform literature begins with emotional indignation: Harriet Beecher Stowe, incensed by the injustices of slavery, wrote so strongly about it in *Uncle Tom's Cabin* that later when President Lincoln met her, he said, "You are such a little woman to have started such a big war."

In all successful creative endeavor, emotion is tempered by logic and planned by a sure-footed knowledge of technique. Be like the heroine of William J. Walters' *Post* story "Welcome Back, Soldier," who says: "I'm a woman in love. My emotions have a frantic sort of wisdom." Plan an emotion that also has a frantic sort of wisdom, and learn all you can about the physiological and psychological nature of emotions, especially the ones you are most likely to describe in your writing . . . the primary and the secondary emotions.

What are the *primary* or major emotions? The strongest action-stimulants so common to most people that they are almost instincts?

Fear	Hope
Hate	Love
Anger	Joy
Grief	Pity

What are the *secondary* emotions? Those not so strong or fateful as the major ones, but in certain instances, they can be exaggerated out of normal proportion to cause dramatic behavior, influence characterization, cause tragedy etc. Secondary emotions include: jealousy, self-pity, loneliness, ambition, greed, vanity, courage, humility, despair, loyalty, stubbornness, timidity, boredom, gratitude, disappointment, inferiority, intolerance, amusement, envy, pride, suspicion, possessiveness, revenge, ungratefulness, shame, guilt.

You can add many more. Plan the overall emotion of your story, and the specific emotion each character feels for the others. Don't be satisfied to label or name these emotions; you must dramatize and bring them to life in the following seven ways:

1) *Through narrative viewpoint*

> The sight was heartbreaking. The boy's crutches were sinking inches deep with every twisted step. The shotgun was banging him across the back and shoulders. The wind was having its own cruel sport with him. Sometimes, it seemed, he made no progress at all; it was all he could do to hold his ground. The duck was only a speck on the water now. Jack would never make it. It was impossible. Fielding pulled his fleece-lined cap down across his face and left the blind.
>
> (Roderick Lull, "A Fighting Chance")

2) *Through dialogue*

Here emotion is dramatized in two ways: 1) The way the voice sounds: she said huskily; her words choked; she sobbed, screamed, giggled, gasped, yelled, shrieked, purred, cooed, whispered, soothed, chortled, hollered, stuttered, squawked; "his angry roar rattled the china on the shelves." 2) The words themselves: "I hate you, you vile

varmint. Get out!" "Dear God, I'd give my soul for another chance!" "You must be crazy! You can't leave me
alone now. You can't let anything happen to you! You're
all I've got!" "There's a limit," her voice rose hysterically.
"How much are you supposed to take without smashing
up?"

She laughed foolishly, shouting, "Art is all!" repeating
again the toast of the artists full of cheap wine when they
gathered in a cafe evenings to talk shop and curse the
official Salon.

(Stephen and Ethel Longstreet, "Man of Montmartre")

"Ha, ha, ha, did you see the expression on his face?" yelled
Vinny Bergerac with shuddering eagerness jumping up
around the road and grabbing G. J. to haul and push him
in a wild laughing hysterical stagger of joy.

(Jack Kerouac, "Maggie Cassidy")

3) *Through action*

Dmitri threw up both hands and clutched the old man by
two tufts of hair that remained on his temples. He tugged
at them, and then flung him to the floor. He kicked him in
the face two or three times with his heel.

(Dostoevsky, *The Brothers Karamazov*)

As in a trance, Mike walked toward the girl, carrying the
pen. Her back was to him as he came up to her.

"Excuse me. Did you lose this?" he said, holding up the
old, frazzled ballpoint pen.

Startled, she turned too quickly. The hose turned, too. A
gush of water swept across Mike's light cord suit. The girl
dropped the hose, and her hands went to her cheeks in
utter horror. "Oh, I'm so sorry! I didn't hear you," she
wailed.

(John Reese, "The Cool Kind")

4) *Through description of inner emotion
   in physiological terms*

This involves *empathy*—imaginative identification of one's emotions with those of the fictional character's. The writer gets inside the character and describes the emotions felt by the character from the inside out—his feelings, reactions, tastes. Florence Jane Soman, successful writer of slick fiction, is especially good at this. She uses many phrases like "there was a pressure in her chest," "something hurt inside him," "she gulped as if for air," "she turned her head away, feeling the longing swell inside her, deep and full," "sudden choking feeling."

Another example:

> Maurice went icy cold. The cognac pinched his nerves into a cold fury. Then rage ran like acid in his veins. "You fat, pigheaded fool! Some day you'll beg me to allow you to show my work in your museum of dead bones!"
>
> His fury grew. He loaded the paintings under his arm and crossed the golden rug, almost stepping on the neat pointed shoes of an Englishman entering the gallery. Outside in the sunlight Maurice's fury did not relax itself. His rage choked his throat, opened his mouth.
>
> (Stephen and Ethel Longstreet, "Man of Montmartre")

5) *Through physical description*

Emotion experienced by anyone except the viewpoint character must be described objectively instead of from the inside out:

> Our breaths were literally snatched from us by what we saw; so literally that Thornton actually fainted in the arms of the dazed man who stood behind him. Norrys, his plump face utterly white and flabby, simply cried out inartic-

ulately; whilst I think that what I did was to gasp or hiss and
cover my eyes.

(H. P. Lovecraft, "Rats in the Wall")

The car spurted past Paul and he had a glimpse of Harriet
sitting stiffly upright, the tears bitter and unheeded in her
eyes.
(Irwin Shaw, "Search Through the Streets of the City")

She stiffened in my arms.

(John Braine, *Room at the Top*)

6) *Through imagery*

Because emotions are abstract, they can be made more
graphic and understandable to the reader if you compare
them to concrete objects. Use similes, metaphors and symbolism—the imagery which Webster defines as "language
which gives a vivid mental picture." Hope, for instance,
may be compared to a beacon of light in a storm-blackened
night; a capsule that keeps melting and melting until nothing remains; a crocus poking its head through the snow; a
rainbow glimmering after a rainstorm; a baby's laughter;
the budding of a long-dormant, seemingly-dead tree. You
can think of many other concrete representations of the
abstract emotion, hope.

Study how professionals use imagery to describe emotions vividly and colorfully. In his short story, "Among the
Paths to Eden," Truman Capote describes impatience
metaphorically: "The fuse attached to Mr. Belli's patience
shortened," and, "For a man who believed himself a human compass, Mr. Belli had the anxious experience of
feeling he had lost his way . . ."

Always use imagery that is appropriate to the character's
background, personality and profession. A housewife's

temper can mount like coffee in a percolator or steam in a pressure cooker, but in describing the emotions of a male mechanic, you would use more pertinent terms. Williams Forrest's *Post* story, "Lesson in Courage," deals with an inarticulate mechanic, Stacy Trimble, who has an inferiority complex and a paralyzing inability to fight for his rights, even against the villain, his partner, Gus Borchard, who steals his ideas and borrows his tools without returning them. Stacy's anger at being taken advantage of and his inability to release this anger are portrayed in metaphorical terms natural to a mechanic's thinking:

> It was there in Stacy, the first whirring of motion, a switch turning and a machine beginning. The wheels moving, the cutting or punching tools beginning to move, to find their spots, to operate, to drive on to power, smoothly, surely working. But then the power was turned off, and in him there was the stillness of dead machines. The frantic clicking of a switch, trying to make it operate again—but the deadness, complete, prevailing, and then the knowing that you could not make this machine start again and do its work.

Later, after he solves his emotional problem, calls the villain's bluff and proves his foreman abilities to the boss: "Stacy sat straight on the wooden chair, a thrill of challenge and ambition going through him, scouring him, gritty and clean."

Take advantage of every opportunity to utilize the preceding six ways of dramatizing emotion in your story writing. In this way you will give your reader what he turns to fiction for: an emotional experience.

Be on the constant lookout for emotional situations that will be grist for your fiction mill. Then list all the various emotions you can extract from each and plan to dramatize them in all the six ways. They exist in almost every human relationship and abound in newspaper stories. Start clipping them and analyze the many different emotions inherent in each. Here are a few from my daily paper:

A convict breaks out of jail to attend five-year-old stepson's funeral and to comfort his wife. Possible emotions: grief, shock, worry about wife, frustration at inability to help her, determination to be with her, decision to jailbreak and take the consequences, fury at being caught again, humility in asking to go to funeral, relief and gratitude when authorities agree.

A rookie cameraman, assigned to photograph visiting leader of "enemy" nation, is suspected of assassination plot because of his elaborate Swedish camera. By the time his camera is dismantled and put together again, the Big Shot is gone. Emotions: Excitement about the assignment and pride in his extra-special camera, Anticipation as he prepares to shoot, surprise when he is arrested, indignation when his camera is seized for inspection, relief when cleared, fury and frustration when the subject is out of range.

Seventy-year-old woman regains sight after forty years. Emotions: delight, gratitude, happiness at being able to see relatives and friends, disappointment in her aging appearance, fear of recurrent blindness.

Fiction is successful when it deals with emotional decisions and problems that are faced by most people at some time, and when the emotional experiences are made vital and understandable by the combined tricks of physiological description, dialogue, action, objective delineation and imagery as well as narrative description.

IX | ACTION: THE LIFE OF
A STORY

RECENT SCIENTIFIC EXPERIMENTS prove that doing
absolutely nothing for twenty-four hours is not restful and
relaxing, but can unbalance a happy, healthy mind. The
subject rests on a comfortable bed, shut off from all work
and worry. His only activities are eating and going to the
bathroom. He wears frosted glasses, ear plugs, and gloves
to reduce his sense of touch. But this escape from noise,
work, and life's complexities is not heaven, but rather an
unbearable hell which soon makes him unable to think,
dream, hope, laugh, or have normal reactions. He has
hallucinations, fears, childish emotional responses, and
visual and psychological disturbances for many hours after
the experiment is over.

Other experiments prove that many highway, airplane,
and railroad accidents are caused by the mental disturbance
to drivers exposed to "the monotonously repeated stimula-
tion of an unchanging environment"; that "a changing
sensory environment is essential for human beings."

Science is merely admitting what editors and psychologically aware writers have always known: people want and

need action. Just as do-nothingness is humanly unbearable, story inactivity will make your script unendurable to the reader, and therefore unsalable.

This does not mean that all your characters must bounce and dash around in Keystone-comedy action from the first paragraph to the last. Story action is not always visible motion and bustle like the physical movement you find in the men's Western, adventure and sports pulps. Psychological action dominates many women's slick and quality stories in which there is no physical movement at all, and yet suspense is maintained and interest held because *something happens* to change the characterization or the protagonist's viewpoint, mood, or philosophy. And who will deny that changing the thinking and emotions of a human being is less exciting than dodging a sheriff's posse or rocketing through the sky?

Your reader will stay with your story only as long as it is dynamically alive with planned action that may be psychological, physical, or a combination of both:

1) PSYCHOLOGICAL ACTION STORIES hinge upon internal, invisible but impressionable change. This includes *character regeneration, come-to-realize* and *thought association* plots.

a. *Character regeneration.* Through a convincing series of dramatic events or emotional factors, a coward develops courage enough to perform an heroic act; a sinner changes into a saint; a tough revenge-seeker abandons his vicious purpose and shows mercy or tenderness; a stingy protagonist becomes generous; a misanthropic Scrooge develops a capacity for love and understanding; a person overcomes jealousy, intolerance, greed, hate, lust, lying, or any other negative trait. The average confession yarn is usually a study in psychological action as the narrator confesses, self-analyzes and regenerates.

✓ b. In *come-to-realize* plots, psychological action travels from minus to plus—not a character trait, however, but a mood or mental attitude toward a situation. Circumstances remain the same, but the protagonist's emotions have changed, so that even though the story may lack *physical* action, there has been effective *psychological* action that changes an attitude or philosophy.

In Anne Homer Warner's "Jet Pilot's Wife," Mary worries about Chris's flights and hates his assignments that leave her alone and frightened. It's particularly bad when he fails to return for the baby's christening. But, during the ceremony as she stares at the flaming candles and the chaplain's words drone on and the baby stirs, suddenly the "nothingness cracked"; and as the tapering light lifts away the blackness, she feels joy, as if Chris *is* with her, holding her hand and assuring her "even when I am away, I am with you, Mary. . . ." She realizes that love creates a magical togetherness that transcends physical separateness —and you're never alone when you're in love. This premise is doubly proved when she later learns that Chris survived a rough forced landing because she and the baby were with him in the same magic way.

✓ c. *Thought association* plots are currently popular, although there is nothing really new about the associative process which has given us our most valuable inventions since long before Robert Fulton watched the tea kettle boil and dreamed up his steamboat. You'll have some great never-fail plot gimmicks if your hero remembers a scientific principle, a trick of nature, or a parallel experience that suggests a similar solution to his own problem. For instance, a photographer's foot catches in rocks in a watery cave and the tide rises, threatening to drown him. Putting the bulb of the camera in his mouth, he holds the open end of the rubber tube above water till help comes. This life-saving gimmick was inspired by the similarity between a diving bell and a camera tube. In John Savage's "Lady Overboard," inventor Admiral Cassidy twists a blackmail plot to his own advantage. He's working on a pendulum invention when scheming Madeline Farquhar tries to force him to cancel her lover's naval orders by trumping up a faked love note and threatening to show it to his wife. Cassidy's answer is to get rid of the note she won't give up —by picking her up by her heels and dangling her upside down, out the window of her 25th-floor apartment, till she drops it. This suggests "pendulum as plummet," solves the problem he was working on, and leads to his brilliant invention of the Polycompensator—or plummet pendulum!

2) PSYCHOLOGICAL-PLUS-PHYSICAL ACTION characterizes most slick stories like Arthur Gordon's "Sitting Duck" (*Redbook*), in which attorney Jeff Dixon, in love with Paul Ives' wife Sally, goes on a duck-hunt with the jealous husband. Paul, hating Jeff but being a good sportsman, rigs up a kill-or-be-killed situation, explaining that only one of them will return alive. Jeff plans an ingenious way to shoot Paul first by burying a small mirror in the marsh grass of the duck blind to reveal Paul's position. Reviewing Paul's threats, Sally's worry over Paul's jealousy, Jeff's legal mind convinces him this will be justifiable homicide; that he will therefore be acquitted; and that Sally will be free to marry him. *But* his legal mind "trained in ethics now gave him an evaluation he did not want. If he killed Paul Ives,

coveting his wife, it would not be a simple act of self-preservation. It will be murder." So Jeff cannot kill Paul. Instead he throws his own gun away, knowing that Paul is too much of a sportsman to shoot a sitting duck. He dis-arms Paul, knocks him out, and takes him home, with the conflict solved through *psychological-and-physical* action:

> And strangely, Jeff Dixon felt no regret. There came to him, rather, a tremendous feeling of relief and triumph. Not for his victory over Ives. For his conquest of himself.

"Sitting Duck" has dimension and wide reader-appeal because it adds vivid, colorful physical action to strong psychological action, as you'll find in most slick stories and novels.

3) PHYSICAL ACTION, a "must" in the men's magazines, has a growing importance in the top slick and quality fields because visual, crackling action scenes make a good story more eligible for television, motion picture, and paperback sales.

A recent poll revealed that more men than women attend movies (34 million men to 30 million women in one week) because of increased rugged action in current pictures. If women were polled as to their tastes, I'm sure you'd find them loving the exciting action just as much as the men do! With such a current hunger for action, you'll do well to follow these tips to make your action-writing more profes-sional:

Do's

1) Regulate your sentence rhythm to match the action tempo. Think of the beat and tempo of words as a musi-cal beat.

2) Use active, not passive, sentences, unless the use of passive sentences accentuates the helplessness of the victim as it does here:

> He was buffeted by the ocean, slapped under by giant waves, strangled by the inrushing salt water.

3) To describe swift action, use crisp, quick, words; vivid verbs; strong nouns; a bare minimum of adverbs and adjectives. "The quarterback *uncorked* the pass . . . the end *grabbed* the ball on the 39, *jerked* away from two defensive backs and *hotfooted* 61 yards into the end zone." "He *hurtled* one man, *jarred* past another, *tin-canned* like the great runner he was, *staggered,* and was *jammed* on the goal line." And from Nancy Rutledge's *Alibi for Murder:*

> Rick forgot about the knife. He used his hands, his fists, pitting his strength against Bartholomew's. They rolled over and over on the ground, kicking, gouging, punching. Rick's breath was knocked out of him once. Once his head hit a tree. But he came in again, punching hard and satisfyingly.
>
> Behind him Rick heard shots, but he had no time to think about them. He thought only about killing Bartholomew.

4) Slow action utilizes pace-slowing adverbs and adjectives to create the proper effect: "The snake slipped slidingly through the long bending grasses, and wended its way without hurry." Or, "His horse, fording streams and scrambling down almost perpendicular cliffs, never faltered."

5) You can speed up action by combining two movements in one sentence: "She darted into the bathroom and turned on a drumming rush of hot water" (*Marjorie Morningstar*). Or, "They smothered him and clawed at the ball and kicked him a few times."

✓ 6) Choose graphic similes and metaphors to enliven your action: jaguar-energy, octopus-reach, gelatin-fear, etc.:

> When Caporelli carried the ball, the crowd opened up. It was like a sonic boom from a jet.

Or, again,

> Legs Kelly stepped into the batter's box waving his bat like a cow switching flies.
>
> (William R. Cox, "Playoff Game", *SEP*)

✓ 7) Describe action through first-hand narrative, so that the reader *sees* it happening before his eyes, rather than reported indirectly through dialogue. Be concrete, not abstract:

> Pete growled and came at me with the machete. I turned to run, tripped on the planking and sprawled flat. I rolled over on my back, doubled up my legs, caught him in the stomach with my feet, and kicked. He went up and over my head. He hit hard, shaking the dock with his weight.
>
> (Ben Masselink, in "Killer's Tide")

✓ 8) Utilize suspense and pauses before bursting into action for dramatic effect and contrast. A bull stands, stares, and deliberates before charging.

✓ 9) Integrate action with atmosphere, characterization, emotion, rather than using a separate sentence for each bit of information:

> Faster, faster . . . faster . . . Ahead a highway bridge loomed, the run curving under it. Just as it seemed I must split my skull against the bridge support, the curve shot me through the tunnel, under a railway bridge and into another ice-banked straight. My world was a nightmare of glittering,

blue-white ice, tearing wind, pounding and battering steel. ("Wildest Ride in the World," by Paul Gallico, in *True*)

10) An exciting action scene has *lots* happening, with not just one or two people moving about, but several wanting "to get into the act." Plan this composite action. See how it's done in Maurice Glucher's *Cosmopolitan* story, "Love Song for Quincy." Nancy has eaten a hamburger at a diner before realizing she has no money. Quincy offers to pay her bill, but the irate counterman blows up, insults her and Quincy, who hits him—and then:

> The greasy-capped individual with the buffalo face let out a yell and came running at Quincy. He made the mistake of leading with his beer belly instead of his left. A punch set him on the floor, whooping and gasping for breath. Meanwhile the second counterman had picked up a meat cleaver and was about to use it on Quincy's head when a bottle of catchup, thrown by Nancy, caught him flush on the forehead. He staggered and fell, his face a symphony in red as the catchup ran in a spreading mass.
>
> "Let's get out of here!" Quincy said, grabbing Nancy's hand and running to the door. They were out and racing away when the first counterman reached for the phone . . .

DON'TS

1) Don't stop action to editorialize, describe, emotionalize, or flash back. Since these four devices are pace-slowers, most authors often introduce them with a tangy splash of action, which is finished rather than left in an awkward, suspended stage.

2) Don't let your story progress too long without some sort of action, psychological or physical. Try to have some on every page.

3) Don't use piled-up or repeated action just to put movement into a static story. Action must be meaningful in heightening the principal drama of the plot and in either creating or solving the problem.

4) Don't forget to integrate action with dialogue, emotion, and characterization.

X | THE SENSE OF PLACE

THE PUBLIC'S FASCINATION for travel has affected the literary field so much that there's hardly a successful book, play or short story that doesn't take place in a definite, colorful atmosphere. As you come to feel that all the original ideas and "different" characters have been used up, you may be cheered by the fact that there's a region you know thoroughly and can use as a Plus Factor to make a formula story unique and therefore salable. And, if you learn and apply the techniques of atmosphere writing, you may ride to fame as the interpreter of that place, as Pearl Buck has with China; John Steinbeck with the Monterey Peninsula; and Jesse Stuart with Kentucky.

Before we analyze the technique tricks that make atmosphere-writing successful, let's distinguish *atmosphere* from *setting, local color* and *background:*

1) *Setting* includes the objective, physical facts. As coldly impersonal as the frame of a painting or the setting of a diamond ring, it tells us *where* the story takes place, listing scenic props. It is "the temporal and spacial environment of a play, including the physical surroundings, properties,

buildings, etc., within which the action takes place." It does not actually blend into characters, action or emotion.

2) *Local color* is a more detailed elaboration of the setting, with specific verisimilitude added by characteristic customs, costumes, foods, etc. Keep in mind the definition of color: "A quality of visible phenomena." More specifically, local color is "vividness, picturesqueness, and piquancy; an effect of reality; lifelikeness given by the use of concrete words, graphic description, peculiarities of speech; color derived from the presentation of the features and peculiarity of a particular locality and its inhabitants." You incorporate typical foreign phrases, foods, fads or anything that is peculiar to this place. Kentucky's Harriette Arnow, for example, writes of shingling horses, piggens and froes, bedcord turners, mauls, gluts (tools) and rockahominy.

3) *Background* also indicates scenic description that is in the story but not really part of it. It is "the scenery or ground behind something seen or represented opposed to foreground; an inconspicuous position, as keeping something in the background." We know when and where the story is taking place and the details are sharp and the characters aware of them, but the same story with the same characters *could be* happening elsewhere.

Usually the story action is set in motion by people instead of places. For instance, Edna Ferber writes a human epic about the down-and-outer whose ambition and hard work make him a powerful tycoon but whose success makes him ruthless and thick-skinned. In her book, *Giant,* this story has a Texas background; in her *Ice Palace,* an Alaska background. Again, the basic Faust story appears with different backdrops. Originally it took place in ancient Germany. In *Damn Yankees,* it had a modern baseball background; in *Will Success Spoil Rock Hunter?* Hollywood.

The Romeo and Juliet story originally took place in Verona, Italy. In *West Side Story* it happens in modern New York City with feuding Puerto Rican and New York teen-age gangs replacing the Montagues and Capulets. In the play *Romanoff and Juliet,* the background is a middle European country that is between the Communist and capitalist spheres, with these contrasting ideologies serving as the antagonists. The stories are enriched by background details but are not caused by them—the *who* and the *what* are more important than the *where.*

4) *Atmosphere* plays such an integral part in the emotions, characterization, and plot that the story would not be the same without it. Atmosphere includes time, place *and* mood; setting, local color, background *plus* an emotional rapport between the place, the actors and the reader. Atmosphere is the emotion emanating from a dramatically-delineated setting. In a sense, it becomes part of the characterization, as in George Stewart's novel *The Storm,* in which storms were given women's names (starting our fad for naming hurricanes). It becomes "a surrounding or pervading influence, as the social atmosphere of a place; the aesthetic tone or mood of, or harmony of effects in, a work of art."

Atmosphere is so much a part of the story that it becomes almost a character, a motivating force or in some way such a strong influence that this exact story could not happen anywhere else. Consider, for instance, the 1927 flood that totally dominates William Faulkner's *The Old Man.* It changes the fortunes of the nameless, tall convict protagonist. He would have stayed in prison for many more years, cut off from humanity and hope, resigned, bovine, substituting duty for freedom and obedience for ambition if it hadn't been for the flood which threatened the jail and caused the prisoners to be herded out of their cells to a flood shelter. Because of a shortage of rescue-workers, the convict and his cellmate are given the chance to row a boat out to pick up stranded flood victims. The other man uses this as a means of escape, but the dutiful tall convict follows orders and rescues a pregnant, young woman. He and she are washed away from the shelter, her baby is born, they are given a boat ride in the opposite direction. Throughout several adventures he learns to like companionship, responsibility and normal life. When the flood subsides and he realizes he can enjoy all these, his duty drives him back to the prison. Ironically, he has been thought drowned during rescue operations and has been given an honorable discharge, but the politically ambitious warden sees this as an embarrassment and deterrent to his own standing with the governor and reports that he himself has captured the runaway convict who, poor devil, has ten years added to his sentence! The flood is really the main character here, at first liberating and making a man out of the tall convict, then, after it brings out his noble qualities, punishing him for his very honesty and heroism.

In an atmosphere story, the *where* and *when* totally dominate action and characterization so that the same story could not occur in a different environment—as the confining storm and monotony of Maugham's "Rain" cause the inhibited Reverend Davidson to reverse his asceticism when he succumbs to the overwhelming combination of

Sadie Thompson and the droning, unending rain. In a similar way, the sea has directed such perennially popular novels as Jules Verne's *Twenty Thousand Leagues Under the Sea* and such modern successes as Ernest Hemingway's *Old Man and the Sea*; Hammond Innes's *The Wreck of the Mary Deare;* Nicholas Monsarrat's *The Cruel Sea,* and many others.

And we should not forget short stories like Robert Edmond Alter's "Storm Gamble" in which the hero, David Barron, is failing to make a living as a writer in the Virgin Islands and has decided to sell his beloved yawl, the *Wee Winkie,* call it quits and return to New York a failure. But when he is called upon to transport a boy with appendicitis to a doctor in order to save the child's life, *Wee Winkie* helps him save four lives from the angry storm-wild ocean. The sea wins over the brave little yawl, but the boat wins, too, because her fortitude inspires the hero to keep plugging away and to "keep trying until he either went under or made a strike."

Study stories that are *influenced* by atmosphere and analyze how the techniques are handled. What would Leon Uris's *Exodus* be without the Israeli struggle for independence? Or Sean O'Casey's plays without Ireland's fight for independence? Lampedusa's *The Leopard* without the decay and collapse of Sicilian aristocracy after Garibaldi's conquest of Sicily and the unification of Italy? Or *Gone with the Wind* without Civil War action in the South? *Wuthering Heights* without the bleak atmosphere of the English moors?

After selecting the time-and-place you want to write about and after deciding whether it will be integrated with or independent of the story and characterization, try to use as many of the following professional tricks as possible to insure success in creating atmosphere:

1) *Establish one dominant atmospheric mood immediately.* Any place may seem different to different people depending upon the circumstances and their personalities and moods. Ray Bradbury opens his *Harper's* story, "A Wild Night in Galway," with the mood of sadness:

> We were far out at the tip of Ireland, in Galway, where the weather strikes from its bleak quarters in the Atlantic with sheets of rain and gusts of cold and still more sheets of rain. You go to bed sad and wake in the middle of the night thinking you heard someone cry, thinking you yourself were weeping, and feel of your face and find it dry. Then you look at the window and think, why, yes, it's just the rain, the rain, always the rain, and turn over, sadder still, and fumble about for your dripping sleep and try to get it back on.

Virginia Lee considers San Francisco bathed in cheer in the gay opening of her story, "Too Much Spring":

> Spring was kicking up its heels along the D.L. & W. All along the right of way dogwood was vying with forsythia, buds were bursting in heady profusion, boughs were waving their greenery, and commuters, their buttonholes adorned with flowers, were sporting festive grins.

Choose the mood (or let your character choose it) and build this up like a dominant trait.

2) *Use sensory appeals to sight, sound, smell, touch and taste.* This will add verisimilitude and create a genuine atmosphere experience for the reader. A Scottish scene invariably has the scent of heather in the air and the wail

of bagpipes played by kilt-clad bagpipers in colorful tartans. Winter isn't just white and cold. Its sounds include the lash of sleet against the window, the rifle-crack of deep-freezing ice on a river or pond, the squeaky crunch of snow underfoot.

Nancy Talbert focusses on sounds in her "Noises on the Roof." Doesn't her charming description of sounds make you feel that you are there?

> In spring we can hear the delicate scratching of birds hunting for nesting material and at night, when we hear a muffled thud, we know a prowling cat has leaped from our walnut tree onto the roof to act out the law of the forest.
>
> As we listen to the spirited scurry that follows, we always hope the intended victim got away.
>
> The squirrels that frisk around on our roof gathering nuts make a different sound from the hunting cats or the blue jays who pierce the walnuts with their beaks before dive-bombing over the patio, where they drop the nuts which crack into jay-sized tidbits.

3) *Strive for imagery that is graphic and original.* Use appropriate similes, metaphors and symbolism in order to make the place you are describing vivid and unforgettable to your reader.

Some places naturally lend themselves to more grandiose imagery than others: For instance flamboyant Hong Kong, which John Patrick in *Esquire* likens to "a canvas painted by a slightly demented artist determined to scatter riotous colors indiscriminately"; "a pearl on black velvet"; "an orchid on the brink of a volcano"; "blood on a white handkerchief." Its bay swarms "with kaleidoscopic activity. Small sampans and big black junks skitter amid the marine traffic like skidding water bugs."

4) *Utilize personification.* This means attributing human characteristics to inanimate things or places, like "the trees held up the sky" or "the sunset climbed the hills."

A Chinese funeral procession "winds its way on foot through street and alley as if reluctant to give up the ghost. Two brass bands, each with a high disdain for harmony, blare out dirges. . . ." Any place or season can be compared to a person. Autumn is "an old man in a Mardi Gras suit, an aging woman in carnival clothes, a weaver of entrancing tales falling asleep under a crazy quilt in a darkening garden . . . a woman on whom too much mascara and costume jewelry isn't cheapening . . ."

5) *Make full use of paradox or contrast,* to increase the color, excitement and suspense of the place you are describing. Hong Kong is "a cauldron of contradictions. It sparkles with life and vitality. It shudders with disease and death. . . . It is opulent and poverty-stricken and sports clean laundry in the midst of squalor." Almost any place can be found to have contrasts, even Sicily, where "a hundred generations of occupation, oppression and grinding work have not soured the sunny Sicilian personality."

Sometimes atmosphere is intensified by contrasting the past with the present as in Robert Richards' *Post* story, "The Haunted Room":

> That was a long time ago—October 29, 1877. But I remember it yet. I can still see the ripples of dust that the wind left lying on our front steps and I can still hear the clip-clop raised by a pair of happy grays as they high-stepped past our house. I wish that I could make you see how my father looked that late afternoon because then you would begin to have some understanding of how it was in Memphis on the day that the general died. We have a statue in

Forrest's memory now, and a park named for him, but it's not the same. I'll tell you why. People ride past him in fast automobiles now, always trying to catch the green light, or soured because they have bumped into the red; and they seldom glance over at the big man on the big horse—always facing his beloved South—and likely they wouldn't wink or blink if you talked about Fort Donelson, or Fort Pillow, or even if you mentioned the great victory at Brice's Cross Roads, in Mississippi.

6) *Weave in specific details, interesting information, unknown facts,* without slowing action or movement of story. Be accurate and authentic always, with the proper names of flowers, trees, birds and animals that can be seen in a particular place. In October, New England's hills are "ablaze with crimson maples and golden birches, accented by the dark green of the evergreens and the lighter green of grassy meadows."

If properly integrated and emphasized, realistic details can recreate a scene with striking reality without slowing down the tempo. Often a little research will reward you with a gimmick or a symbol that will be an asset, not a liability to your story. For instance, your characters are watching flying fish at Catalina. The girl envies their carefree playing, the boy (up on his ichthyology) tells her they are not playing, but are flying because they're afraid . . . a researched fact which may help the story by teaching a character to put up a stiff upper lip of courage or cheerfulness the way the flying fish do! If your story is taking place at or near Bodega Bay north of San Francisco, you might work in some interesting historical tidbits including the fact that this is where Russians once invaded our West Coast—they were sea otter hunters and tanners who built Fort Ross in 1814 and occupied it until 1841 when sea otter-hunting became so poor that the Tsar ordered with-drawal, and the entire Russian trading post was sold to Johann August Sutter for $30,000. Or if you're writing about a snobbish, ritzy resort, mention that it was origi-nally settled by pirates and cutthroats or had been a penal colony for exiled criminals. What ironic possibilities here!

After you have chosen the *where* of your story, do not be satisfied just to describe it or interpret it in a surface way, dig into its history just as you delve for the uncon-scious factors in your hero's childhood. The rewards can be enriching!

The use of the above techniques is making atmosphere-writing so intensely popular today that you can find them all used, smoothly integrated with plot, characterization, emotion and action. Where in your own experiences or mental horizons is there a place as vivid and fascinating to you—as inspiring and worthy of painstaking research and emotional thinking?

Start describing it on paper now, utilizing all the tech-niques of atmosphere-writing. Plan to use this background in an original story. Think what you can do when you add specific human problems and emotional conflicts! Keep a file of sketches of places you know thoroughly and keep building these to enrich and professionalize future fiction.

XI | OVERCOMING THE VIEWPOINT BUGABOO

No HUMAN BEING can experience the exact emotions of another. Therefore, we can only surmise another's viewpoint in terms of our own feelings. This may also be why we can never know another real person as intimately as we do a well-delineated character in fiction, and why Oscar Wilde felt that "The only real persons are those who have never lived."

Even after a writer has mastered plotting, characterization, action, dialogue, and atmosphere, he can be tripped up by *viewpoint*.

There are two types of non-selling writers: 1) Those who are unaware of viewpoint and write stories hop-skippity-jump, either switching viewpoint or ignoring it altogether. They never sell except perhaps one rare, wonderful gimmicky success that cannot be repeated. 2) Those who think up a story idea and work out the premise, plot, characters and solution, but get so mixed up about which character should tell the story that they become as panicked as the self-conscious centipede trying to figure out which foot comes after which.

Viewpoint need not be a problem if you *think* your story through before letting the words spill out. Write a one-sentence summary of the story action and ask yourself if the subject-matter will interest men, women, or children. Then select your market accordingly. Remember, men prefer adventure, intrigue, mystery, murder, sports, politics, whereas women are primarily interested in love, domesticity, in-law problems, child psychology, and conflicts between career and marriage. Children like to read about experiences that happen to a child or animal—they are all like the little boy who came to the children's library every day to "sit in the little chairs and read about fierce things."

The surest way to make your reader feel emotion is to make him *experience* the story through the viewpoint of the character who is the most emotionally involved. *Empathy* is the key word here, the "imaginative projection of one's own consciousness into another's being." The Mexicans call it being "simpatico." It is more subjective than sympathy, which merely means feeling sorry for someone with *your own* feelings. Empathy enables the author to *become* the character.

Establishing a viewpoint rapport is a triple-feature deal in which understanding flows freely between author, reader, and protagonist. Your reader will feel closer to your hero if you give him a chance to delve into his point of view—this is why you need to be sure you choose the right viewpoint character—one who has things in common with the reader of the magazine for which you slant your story.

In a court trial under oath, different witnesses will swear to the truth of opposite stories about a crime or accident. Adults see things one way—teen-agers or children another.

You'll find antipodal viewpoints between children and adults, the rich and the poor, capital and labor, farmers and city folks, Russians and Americans, etc. It's a cinch your story can be told quite differently according to which viewpoint you choose. No matter how flat a pancake is it still has two sides. Your story is like a pancake and should be turned over and over before you decide on one side or viewpoint. Then, after you have selected the one you will use (preferably the person most emotionally involved) ask yourself "Shall I tell the story in the first person? Second? Third? Which will be most effective?"

Basically, a story can be written objectively or subjectively. Here's a list of the possible viewpoint-presentations—*Objective* and *Subjective:*

I. OBJECTIVE VIEWPOINT

This is emotionless and presents a straight job of reporting. You are permitted no editorializing, just facts. You are outside the deeper feelings and thoughts of the main characters. Objective stories fall into two categories:

A. NO VIEWPOINT AT ALL. This technique states bald facts with no editorializing, no opinions, no emotions. A character's age, size, name, weight, coloring, and sex are given, but you cannot say he or she is "virile," "feminine," "handsome," or "beautiful," because that expresses an opinion. The reader is not given an emotional evaluation of the character, nor does he ever know what he is thinking or feeling. Here's a no-viewpoint opening from my story, "Come, Bomb My Kailing":

> Crickets had almost chirped themselves out for the night and the little Kailing river was quiet of the frolicking splash of fish. But old Chao Fei-Yen worked sleeplessly at the bam-

boo barge beyond the bombed willow tree. The char-black night, the muffling fog concealed her betel-toothed smile, her sharp, night-seeing eyes, and the task her wrinkled fingers trembled at. The task of stuffing papers, hemp, and other combustibles into the crevices of the bamboo poles.

There's no viewpoint in this passage from Graham Greene's "The Destructors":

> Next morning the serious destruction started. There were two casualties—Mike and another boy whose parents were off to Southend and Brighton in spite of the slow, warm drops that had begun to fall and the rumble of thunder in the estuary like the first guns of the old blitz.
> "We've got to hurry," T. said.
> Summers was restive. "Haven't we done enough?" he said. "I've been given a bob for slot machines. This is like work."
> "We've hardly started," T. said. "Why, there's all the floors left, and the stairs. We haven't taken out a single window. You voted like the others. We are going to *destroy* this house. There won't be anything left when we're finished."

A no-viewpoint story creates the cold, lifeless effect of a marble statue and is dangerous in the average yarn where the reader's interest is held only as long as he *cares* about one or more of the characters. In the no-viewpoint story, the writer manipulates his characters from the outside like a puppeteer, and no sympathy is created for any one of the characters in the story.

Objective viewpoint is rarely used in fiction and only when the author has excellent reasons for lack of emotion or for withholding the protagonist's feelings. Graham Greene wanted to show the heartless process of destruction and violence on the part of characters with sub-human insensitivities. In my story, I did not use viewpoint for purposes of surprise. Here was a friendless, rejected and ridiculed old woman building crude bamboo rafts and setting them on fire when enemy bombers flew over. The reader believes this to be sabotage but the ending reveals that her motive is not revenge but patriotism: her fires attract bombs away from the village into the river, thereby churning it up and providing fish for the starving children whom she wants to have a better life than she has had.

B. OBSERVER VIEWPOINT. Here, the dramatic action is related by a narrator or observer who takes no real part in the story. Often a "frame" is drawn around the yarn itself, an introductory scene before the main drama and a concluding scene after it.

Sometimes the observer is on the scene, however, as in William Sambrot's "Barrel-Roll Finish." Here a radio technician watches the drama of gray-haired Air Corps Colonel Aldershot checking the diving maneuvers of a jet pilot. We never know what the colonel is thinking or feeling, the only emotion being expressed through the observer, the tech who calls the old man "Old Ice-Water Himself" as he marvels at his emotionlessness. The wallop-ending reveals facts that would not have been surprising if the story had been told from the main actor's point of view:

> The radio technician turned to his partner and picked up the stopwatch. "That guy's got a heart of brass," he murmured. "Chewing out his son—his own son—after a dive like that."
>
> They stood looking at the stopwatch, its crystal crushed at the precise moment the colonel's son regained consciousness and pulled out of the dive. . . .

Observer-viewpoint stories told in a frame are rare for two reasons: The reader cannot delve into the inner emotions of the main character most deeply involved in the drama, and there is an inclination to invest interest in the characters who are first introduced, therefore when the major story action shifts to someone else, disappointment may occur.

II. SUBJECTIVE VIEWPOINT

This is the only way to give your reader an emotional experience, which, according to Faith Baldwin, is the purpose of fiction. Even after you have decided on the more popular subjective viewpoint, you still have several choices of presentation:

A. FIRST PERSON. If you're writing for most confessions or other markets requiring first-person narrative, you have no choice, but for many of the general magazines, first person is optional and should depend upon your material and how facilely you handle it. First-person style creates intimacy and increased emotional impact and makes it easier for the writer to stay in one viewpoint.

The main advantages of the first-person viewpoint are that it 1) gives an "I was there" or "it happened to me" authenticity to strange happenings; 2) personalizes the narrative, since the inner protagonist is usually "talking out" the story with the warm eagerness of someone confiding a deep secret; 3) it increases sympathy for the narrator, and it colors all action and events with inner emotional reactions.

There are also some disadvantages in using the first-person viewpoint: 1) It may be awkward to handle, requiring a monotonous excess of "I's," "me's," and "my's"

(appropriate for a conceited narrator like some of the
swain-heroes in Max Shulman's collegiate stories). 2) All
action and characterization must be limited to the knowledge and emotions of the narrator. 3) There isn't much suspense about survival, since the "I" character obviously
lived to tell about it (unless you use a "twist" ending
where the narrator winds up in a death cell or on cloud #9
in heaven or stoking furnace #9 in the other place). We
are constantly reminded that the action is over by now and
the narrator is telling about stale events in retrospect. Description of the narrator is hard to achieve without self-consciousness or the hackneyed device of looking in the mirror.
Some professionals achieve it smoothly as Harriet Frank,
Jr. does in a *Saturday Evening Post* story, "The Girl With
the Glow":

> I'm not saying that I'm a raving beauty or anything like
> that. As a matter of fact, I'm only medium pretty. To be
> absolutely honest about it, I'm concave where it would be
> nicer to be convex, but I buy blouses with ruffles, so who
> knows the difference?

Others, like Kate McNair in her *Ladies' Home Journal*
story, avoid the egoism of first-person by being almost self-
deprecating:

> I do not look high-styled and leisurely, as though I spent
> most of my time at the country club. My family loves me,
> so when I ask them if I look all right, they say yes every
> time.
> I'm not very bright, either. I always figured that I.Q. test
> they gave me when I entered college was graded by a no-
> expert type. I got in and I got through, but that is about it.

Sometimes it is expedient to write most of the story in
the third-person, but to switch to first-person in dramatic

moments of decision or innermost thought, almost as if the character is talking to himself, as Nancy Rutledge does frequently in her *Post* serial, "Alibi for Murder":

> Rick stood up. His dark young face was very grim. He was angry, but not as he had always been angry before. Those had been hot outbursts of temper, flaring suddenly, soon forgotten. This anger was cold, waiting, deadly.
> *They think I've committed two murders, but I haven't. Yet. I'm going to commit one now. If it's the last thing I ever do, I'm going to kill the man who killed Antek.*
> Rick did not now feel the despair he had previously felt about finding the killer or proving his own innocence. His own innocence had become a comparatively minor matter. He was obsessed with only one idea, that of avenging Antek.

B. SECOND PERSON. This viewpoint is rarely used in fiction. It is even more intimate than first person and is used chiefly to force the reader to identify and sympathize with a person whose experiences or characteristics are very different from those of the reader: a Martian, Chinese Communist, unwed mother, or the poor devil who is human contraband in *True's* "Through Hell's Passage," which opens:

> Your name is Woloski, Arthur Woloski, one time of Poland. Right now you're just another piece of human contraband lying in the thin gray darkness on the slime-wetted planks of a dirty *goleta* tossing sluggishly along somewhere off the coast of Cuba.
> You wear the number 166,773 tattooed on your arm. It was put there by Nazis at the Auschwitz concentration camp even before your parents were killed in the gas chambers. . . .

C. THIRD PERSON

1. *Single, steady, unchanged.* Most published short stories are written entirely through the emotions of one main

character—the person with the problem to solve or the goal to reach. The reader becomes identified with this protagonist throughout the story, seeing all actions through his eyes, thinking all thoughts through his brain, evaluating all people and places through his prejudices. The reader is kept informed of any changes as in the following viewpoint excerpts from a story of mine, titled "Push-Button Brain." Krissta is an information librarian who answers telephone questions. Mr. Q is her favorite questioner.

> "You're quite welcome," she said, sedate as her own grandmother back in Bardstown, Kentucky.
> She clicked the receiver sharply, and sudden loneliness made her wish she were in Bardstown, too. She was tired of the glary gaudiness of Los Angeles . . .

Later, when Mr. Q phones in:

> "Can you tell me how to fry liver?" He'd been apologetic. "I really tried this on my own," he said. "I even studied two cookbooks."
> "That's the trouble," she said in her Bluegrass drawl, "too many cookbooks spoil the cook."
> "You can say that again!" . . . .
> Krissta's fingers tightened on the telephone and for a crazy moment she wished she could zip through the wire to his kitchen and preside over his skillet. . . .
> "Just simmer it in shortening or oleo a few minutes on each side. Or you can just plain broil it."
> Then they were discussing exotic ways to cook spaghetti. . . .
> When Krissta hung up that time, California was lovely, not lonely. She felt as if he'd called to invite her somewhere instead of to ask how to cook liver. Maybe that would come —or so she had thought until yesterday.

2. *Multiple or changing.* This takes the reader into two, maybe three viewpoints to convey vital information not known by the hero. Viewpoint is often changed to show an action, character or object as considered by different observers. Shifting viewpoint is difficult for beginners although they are often intrigued with the idea that each person is really several people: one to his parents, one to his spouse, one to his co-workers, children, etc. It is not advisable to change viewpoints unless absolutely necessary, as in J. J. Godwin's story "The Breaking Point" which proves that oppressive heat can cause a loving couple to quarrel and make each other miserable. The author uses each viewpoint to blame the other person:

Wife

She gazed stonily at the wall. A girl goes trustingly into marriage . . . only to find herself enmeshed in a ghastly mockery with a barbarous oaf.

Husband

A man has to pick his chin out of the gravel sometime. Obviously, the girl had no reason, kindness or generosity. This should hardly have surprised him. You find out about women when you marry one.

3. *Omniscient viewpoint* plunges into the thoughts, feelings, and emotions of all the characters in the story. It must be handled skillfully to avoid jerkiness when the point of view is changed. Jumping around can be disconcerting and deprive the reader of the profound and unified emotional experience he receives when a story has a single viewpoint. There must be one common denominator which all the characters share. In Gertrude Schweitzer's story, "A Bunch of Roses," the roses provide the unifying

thread. Hero Mike Tyler awaits his girl Amy in the station with a bouquet of roses. She doesn't come and he gives the roses away one at a time until there's only one left. Each rose changes the life of the woman he gives it to, and we share each emotional event by delving into all viewpoints: young Kathy, feeling unloved and unimportant, is about to join a girl-gang to have a sense of belonging. The rose from a stranger makes her feel attractive and she decides against a life of crime. The fading, trying-to-be-young Candace sees pity in the rose, abandons her strenuous dieting and straining to hold her young lover and decides to be her own grandmotherly age—and relax. Mary is tired of being taken for granted by the man she loves, but the rose solves her problem by making him jealous enough to propose. The final rose helps Mike when Amy arrives late and sees in one perfect rose evidence of his imagination and romance!

TIPS ON VIEWPOINT

Just because your story characters have different opinions of or attitudes towards a subject, you do not have to use the omniscient viewpoint. Naturally, thinking people will not agree on everything and the disagreements of people whose harmony is necessary for their happiness will provide the conflict of your yarn. The best thing for you to do is to work out their opposite viewpoint-attitudes as if you were writing the arguments for both sides of a debating team, consider how the story will be if it follows one viewpoint, then how differently it will work out if you write it from another viewpoint. Then, before actually writing the story, study the following tips carefully:

1) Plan your story for one specific magazine and choose for

your viewpoint character the person who has most in common with the reader, the viewpoint with which you can readily identify.

2) If it's absolutely necessary to shift viewpoint, plan the change ahead, using a smooth transition, perhaps changing the scene so that one viewpoint is maintained throughout the scene.

3) Introduce your viewpoint character at the beginning of the story, before confusing your reader with the names of minor characters. When using first person, you must establish the identity of the "I" narrator immediately.

4) Do not give the reader any information the viewpoint character doesn't see, feel, know, hear, or think according to the traits, education, and cultural background you have given him. All knowledge of the other characters must come from their action, dialogue, or your viewpoint character's conjectures.

5) In writing foreign-background stories that include foreign and American characters, it'll be easier to sell your story if you tell it from the viewpoint of an American. (Reader-identification again!)

6) A novel usually presents more dimension and a broader scope than a short story; therefore it presents many viewpoints, but usually maintains one consistently in each chapter.

7) Toughest of all is the "looking-back-viewpoint," like the nostalgic stories in *The New Yorker,* where childhood experiences are relived after the narrator has grown up, and confessions which must relive past-action with suspense and expectancy. Here you need special

spurs to stir curiosity and keep the reader's attention: a "little-did-I-know-then" or "how-could-I-realize?" touch.

8) In choosing a viewpoint it is usually unwise to select one too remote from your own.

In one of my writing classes, a soft-spoken lady artist inserted her feminine personality into a belligerent, hard-drinking, uneducated man; a Hollywood burlesque dancer told a religious story through an aged priest; an aristocratic lady became a delinquent boy escapee from an Honor Farm without changing her refined thought-processes one iota; while a robust aircraft riveter insisted on writing from the viewpoint of a little girl in starched organdy. None of these produced believable characters.

There are men who understand the woman's point of view (James M. Cain in "Mildred Pierce" and Christopher Morley in "Kitty Foyle") and women like George Eliot and Isak Dinesen, who write good men's viewpoint, but in general it is safer for beginning writers to choose a viewpoint closer to their own.

9) The ideal viewpoint character is the one with emotional involvement, the one who is hit squarely by the plot problem and does his best to solve it. He also appears in the most scenes, has the best dialogue and action, and therefore earns his top billing.

Just as a gunman or archer closes one eye when he sights his target for direct, accurate shooting, you, too, will hit your target of unified emotion and single effect if you write from one viewpoint rather than several. And choose that one with care according to the effect you wish to create. It can make a difference. As the little girl watched the cat wash its face her mother said "See how clean kitty is, always washing her face and ears." But the child retorted: "No she isn't! She's washing her feet and wiping them on her face!"

XII | WHAT'S NEW IN CONFLICT?

LIFE'S TROUBLES ARE CAUSED by too much conflict, whereas fiction troubles result from *not enough* conflict. The solution is to transfer life's struggles to fiction and work them out in a clever resolution. First of all, you must realize the difference between them. According to the dictionary, the verb "conflict" means "to clash . . . to contend; to strike or dash together; fight." The noun "conflict" is a "contest, strife, antagonism; a fight or struggle for the mastery; a battle, a violent collision. . . ." Life conflict, then, means physical action—people, animals or things in active opposition. It could be a knife-fight or fist-fight between two people; two boxers, wrestlers, or teams struggling to win; a dog-and-cat fight; children knocking each other about; jets colliding in mid-air or any oil tankers, boats or trains crashing; an earthquake leveling a town; a mine explosion, etc. But this type of collision-conflict constitutes only one-third of the Total Conflict that you must develop for fiction.

Life conflict just happens. Fiction conflict has strong cause and effect. Think of story conflict as a sandwich, with the bottom piece of bread representing motivation or cause; the "filling" or middle being the active conflict itself; and the top slice of bread symbolizing the dramatic results of the conflict-action. You can find exciting conflict in any court trial, divorce action, lovelorn column or newspaper headline, but that's just the beginning! Develop your own fiction characters to act out the conflict to a conclusion, and use ingenuity and purpose in building valid reasons for it and significant results that affect characters and reader. Keep in mind that the dictionary-meaning of conflict is merely the *middle* part of fiction conflict which consists of:

1) Sound motivation or cause. Sometimes the reasons or motivation for the conflict are kept secret at first (for reasons of suspense); sometimes they are explained immediately. But they must be in the story sooner or later. A man barging into a dance-hall, beating up several men on the dance floor, and stomping out or being tossed out may be dictionary "conflict" in the sense of action, but it is not a story until there is motivation. If his motive is A) avenging his brother's destruction through narcotics, B) avenging a girl's reputation, or C) warning them to clear out for another reason, it has DRAMATIC SIGNIFICANCE. Otherwise there is no story value.

2) The physical, psychological, or philosophical conflict as it is presented on stage in the story. Be sure you make your reader see and feel it, not just be told about it.

3) Repercussions and results of the conflict . . . within and between each participant of the conflict. It must change and move the story and the character.

Your first job in creating story conflict out of life conflict is to fill in the gaps in order to create three-dimensional Total Conflict. If a young couple with a baby are quarreling over the wife's wanting to work, first of all you should build convincing motivation: wife wants more money toward down-payment for a house with a yard for the baby to enjoy freedom, or a college trust fund or to buy nicer clothes or furniture which she thinks will improve her husband's chances of advancement. Husband's motivation: feeling of inadequacy if he can't support his family on his own, plus too much pride to let their friends know they need the money. Results: Wife understands and respects her husband's pride, insists that because he has bought her so many labor-and-time-saving devices she has too much time on her hands and suggests advertising for typing clients through a newspaper-box number, not using their name. Of course there are many other resolutions, but the one you use must be clued in by the active conflict (for instance the husband dropping hints of his pride in their arguments leads the wife to a solution that upholds his pride).

In addition to making the conflict total and complete, you must make it significant and meaningful to the reader. How do you do this? By making the CONCRETE conflict represent the clash between ABSTRACT values which concern all people of all time. The abstract values represent the *hidden* conflict entities, whereas the physical factors in conflict are immediately obvious and recognizable. But no story is complete unless both abstract and concrete forces are there, battling it out suspensefully from the beginning to the end. Every story, from the ancient tale of Beowulf fighting to deliver the Danish Kingdom from the monster Grendel and his terrifying monster-mother, to the most sophisticated modern story or science-fiction yarn of the future, must have this double conflict between abstracts as well as concretes, and the opening curtain must reveal GOOD fighting EVIL so clearly that the reader immediately takes sides and desperately wants one to win.

TYPES OF CONFLICT

This is true of all the different types of conflicts featured in today's fiction. Once upon a time in the dim, dead past, writers were told there were three kinds of conflict to write about: character against nature, character against another character, and character against himself. As life has become more complex, the list has increased to seven, and you have a better chance of bucking competition and producing a fresher story if you include one of the "newer" conflicts, such as,

✓   1) *Man* versus *Machine.* This conflict keeps abreast of our current emphasis on automation and the machines that successfully teach students, answer exams, give medical diagnoses, write plays and stories, select people to be fired or hired, shoot guns, and actually reproduce themselves. Whether it focusses on the struggle against something as small as a zipper or a washing machine that "whips the sheets into Boy Scout knots and steals socks" or the frustrating appliances which gang up to destroy Barrett Finchley in the play *The Thing Against Machines,* or is the fight of workers to hold onto their jobs against automation, or a human fight against overpowering robots, this conflict type is becoming more popular and also more timely and realistic.

2) *Character* versus *Fate* is perhaps the oldest fiction conflict, and the earliest literature of every race features ghost stories, fantasies, or a hero fighting Old Age, Satan, or Death. *On Borrowed Time* and *Death Takes A Holiday* echo ancient Catalan legends in which a character locks Death in a cupboard or keeps him up a tree, but eventually decides there are worse things than dying. And every generation produces a new version of the old Faust story in which man sells his soul to the devil.

3) *Character* versus *Society.* Here, the individual battles organized social traditions and prejudices. Hester Prynne forced to wear the brand of the adulteress (*The Scarlet Letter*); the inventor or artist who's ahead of his time and is persecuted for his originality (*The Fountainhead*); the struggles of a member of a minority group (*Gentlemen's Agreement, Grapes of Wrath, The Dollmaker;*) a paroled prisoner seeking a job and place in society that rejects him because of his past, etc.

4) *Character* versus *Situation.* The antagonist here is overpowering, probably impersonal, seemingly invincible, like a corrupt political regime, over-industrialization, depression, war, poverty, concentration camp, as portrayed in *Stalag 17* and *The Snake Pit.*

5) *Character* versus *Nature.* Man fighting an earthquake, typhoon, blizzard, forest fire, flood, the desert, frozen wastelands or nature in the form of disease, always has and always will make suspenseful drama, from Noah's flood on through the sea stories of Jack London to Hemingway's *Old Man and the Sea.*

Whitworth College Library
Spokane, Washington

6) *Internal Conflict.* The major battleground is within the protagonist himself:

a) Two traits fighting for control (*Dr. Jekyll and Mr. Hyde*); pacifistic religion vs. patriotism (*Friendly Persuasion*); cowardice vs. conscience. Or you might use a conflict between loyalties, like that in the Civil War novel, *Sycamore Tree,* in which Anne Rogers is torn between her love for her younger brother who is a Rebel soldier and her older brother who is fighting with the Union army.

b) Character fights a habit like narcotics, drinking, gambling, etc., as in *Lost Weekend* and *Man with a Golden Arm.*

7) *Character* versus *Character.*

a) Opposite character traits: A liberal vs. a reactionary; a religious missionary vs. a libertine. Or any opposite personalities: fastidious vs. sloppy; tightwad vs. spendthrift; serious vs. comic; naive vs. sophisticated; brave vs. cowardly; spiritual vs. carnal; etc.

b) Intellectual or ideological conflict: Here, the inner beliefs of the hero and heroine are irreconcilably antagonistic, at least apparently so, unless love, perhaps, is the catalyst. The Salvation Army lass vs. the gambler (*Guys and Dolls*).

c) Out-to-get-each-other conflict: Here the boy and girl belong to enemy factions, thus their hatred is kindled even *before* they meet. They could be members of hostile races, religions, nations, or the detective vs. the gangster's sister, etc. (There could be a light-touch or comedy out-to-get-each-other conflict—the vice squad officer or judge vs. strip-tease queen.)

Most well-plotted stories feature a composite of conflicts, not just one type. *After* planning your conflicts, but *before* writing the story, decide whether you are dealing with *hostile* or *friendly* conflicts, and choose your style accordingly. The former is a fight-to-the-finish struggle between hero and villain, with one triumphing over the other. The *friendly* type, on the other hand, usually ends "in a draw" with a compromise or reconciliation. In the *friendly conflict* yarn, there are differences between two people who have one thing in common: love, kinship, work, neighborly proximity, a common enemy, family, etc. The conflict is caused by opposite character traits, backgrounds, or ideological differences between sweethearts, parent-and-child, in-laws, buddies, co-workers *whose harmony is necessary to the success and happiness of each.*

Before starting your story, plan the conflicts you will use and line them up into pros and cons as you would plan the arguments of both sides of a debate. Be sure that each conflict develops, bounces back and forth, and affects future action. For instance, if you stress racial prejudice between a white and black member of a robbery-gang, it must have important repercussions, perhaps the white man's distrust of the Negro wrecks their success because he won't trust him with the keys to the get-away car and they are caught.

In the very beginning be sure to present the major conflict that will dominate the whole plot and be the last to be resolved, or at least open with a promise or foreshadowing of strong conflict-to-come. Do not keep your reader in the dark as to what the conflicts will be; who is the protagonist, the antagonist, and what are their chances of ultimate success. In the happy-ending, hero-triumphs story, give the advantage to the villain and the sympathy to the hero—who is obviously greater and more admirable when he conquers truly tough obstacles!

Test your plot by asking the following questions:

1) Are all the characters engaged in some form of conflict?
2) Are the opposing entities clearly defined and introduced quickly?
3) Are they evenly matched?
4) Is there suspense as to the outcome?
5) Is the conflict sustained in a smooth, easy-to-follow manner instead of jerking and jumping confusingly?
6) Is the solution surprising and yet logical and credible?
7) Are the dialogue and action dynamically alive?
8) Are the conflict entities concrete representatives of abstract human values?
9) Does one symbolize good, the other evil?

XIII | THE PROBLEM

WILLIAM FAULKNER once wrote that "the problems of the human heart in conflict with itself *alone* can make good writing because only that is worth writing about, worth the agony and the sweat." This may be true of soul-searing tragedies, but fortunately the scope of problems that are appropriate for fiction is much larger and includes humorous, casual and little everyday problems with which the reader can readily identify. In fact, the unestablished writer is better off concentrating on these and leaving the heavy drama to the Faulkners.

Your best bet is to think of the reader. Everyone has problems; that's why most of them become readers. In non-fiction they find information and solutions to their problems; whereas they turn to fiction either to escape their own dilemmas in sheer entertainment or to become involved with situations that are so much worse that it's a relief to return to their own.

A story can be only as interesting and salable as its problem, which Webster defines as "a perplexing question, situation or person . . . a question proposed for solution."

Everything depends on the problem—the type and tone of the characters you develop, the style you use, the incidents or actions that occur, and the premise which is always the working out of the basic truth or philosophical lesson learned as the problem is solved.

Franklin Delano Roosevelt once said, "When you come to the end of your rope, tie a knot in it and hang on." You can even use that knot in the rope to pull yourself to the top of the mountain. And writers can use life problems, their own and others, with similar success. Start jotting down and collecting problems from everyday life, conversations, newspapers, television, radio, etc. Work out solutions, switch them about, but most important of all, learn which are usable for fiction and which are taboo or worthless to develop.

Problems that are timely and universal, that have reader identification—masculine problems for the men's magazines, feminine problems for the women's markets—are popular. As one slick writer says, "In women's magazines, the men don't have the problems, they just cause them." Generally, everyone is interested in specific problems related to basic human emotions and experiences: love, friendship, health, self-improvement, earning a living, and integrity.

Dr. Norman Vincent Peale's survey of the most commonplace everyday adult troubles lists: worry, marital drifting apart, health, irritability, tension, loneliness, alcoholism, fear of empty retirement, resentment, finances, grief over death, disapproval of children's friends, older relatives living in the home, and children's failure at school.

Teen-age problems of today (according to the poll of H. H. Remmers and D. H. Radler) center around popularity, loneliness, getting a driver's license, self-consciousness, fear of non-conformity (being an odd-ball), weight and height, physical attractiveness, sensitivity, stage fright, fear of making mistakes, guilt, embarrassment, daydreaming, temper, sex, worry over little things, and so on.

Corny and trite problems with no new twists or trimmings are unpopular. Also, avoid problems that are too easily solved by coincidence, those that are controversial, taboo, bizarre, freakish, or too specialized for general reader appeal. (Servant problems for low-income readers, etc.)

There are trends and styles in problems just as there are in fashions. Study them; take your cues from life and adapt popular problems to your writing.

Always use the principle of the Problem Paradox. Briefly and objectively, work out the main problem and solution so that one is simple and familiar and the other is fresh and intriguingly original. Readers lose interest if both problem and solution are either too usual or too unusual.

Let's look at the *general* problem of violence, hostility or the destructive instinct which should be balanced with a *specific* solution.

For instance, let's take the general problem of violence or destructiveness in children. One specific solution might be a definite punishment. But there are many other possible solutions.

1. In Hatfield, England, the Town Council set up a Mischief House to be used as an outlet for pent-up violent instincts. This actually reduced delinquency.
2. In San Fernando, California, boys made trouble for the police and the Edison Company by constantly throwing rocks at street lights and breaking the globes. *Solution:*

Replacing the glass with plastic nose cones, which protect the lights.

3. Animal study or care of a pet. In a magazine article a sadistic boy was cured of his death-dealing instincts and humanized by his hunting dog which, after losing her own litter of pups, refused to kill baby woodchucks and mothered them instead.

4. Reciprocity or retaliation. In a teleplay, two brothers who killed fish belonging to a despised foreign-born garbage collector were forced by their father to replace the fish, even though it meant fishing all night and all day in the hot sun.

5. Another parent might provide a place for violence (a special fighting field, "screaming" or "crying" room; a punching bag, etc.)

6. A therapist might solve the violence problem with art, music, literature. Sir Herbert Read's recommended solution is Education through Art. He says that our technological civilization increases feelings of suppressed frustration without providing any satisfactory outlets. He quotes the nihilist Bakunin who claimed that destruction is also creation. Sir Herbert adds that destruction is a substitute for creation and if we give a child sufficient opportunities for artistic creativity there will be no serious violence.

Above are just six of many possible *specific* solutions to a *general* problem. You can reverse this sequence by starting with a *specific* problem of violence and working out a *general* solution. Plan an original, unique problem of violence, then let your hero solve it in a general or abstract way. The religionist might resolve it by turning the other cheek or returning good for evil; the militarist would fight fire with fire and subdue violence with stronger violence; the intellectual would figure out a clever way to outwit brawn with brain. An example of a specific problem might be the method of saving the lives of eighty-two men on a sinking submarine; the general solution might be the way in which strict discipline and training bring about automatic response, immediate action, and ultimate rescue.

Study the problem paradox in published stories. See how the *usual* problem is solved by an *unusual* gimmick. On the other hand, an *unusual* problem, involving an exotic setting or specialized situation (a safari, an attack by a wild animal) not common or familiar to most people, may be solved by *usual* or *familiar* devices (ingenuity, faith, courage, self-control, or some other example of recognizable resourcefulness).

The problem must be significant, worthwhile (much ado about something), and emotionally important to a great number of readers as well as to you. It should be credible and realistic even though unusual, and it must seem insoluble. Throughout most of the story, the solution seems impossible, certainly unguessable. It always represents the conflict between good and evil.

The solution to the problem must express author viewpoint. The final premise must be a philosophy you believe sincerely. Take, for instance, the problem of Career versus Marriage. One writer will prove the superiority of one; another author will work it out from the opposite viewpoint. In *Macbeth,* Shakespeare proves the evil results of ambition; another author may work out the tragedy of lack of ambition (Erskine Caldwell's *Tobacco Road*) or the real virtues of ambition in a Horatio Alger success story.

It is advisable to use a time limit to force the solution of the problem by a certain day, hour, or month, to intensify drama and tighten the unities. Thus time itself becomes an additional villain or obstacle to be overcome.

Problem Don'ts

Don't wait too long to introduce the pivotal problem, and never confuse your reader by mentioning a secondary problem first. In a story, the main problem appears in the first fifty to one hundred words.

Don't let yourself or your characters get excited about a problem that doesn't really exist, except in their overworked imaginations. There's a current editorial prejudice against the story with a problem involving a false suspicion of infidelity, or a supposed villain or a threat that turns out to be a real blessing. Readers want a real problem cleverly solved.

Don't drag out the solution artificially when any normal conversation between reasonable characters would reveal it immediately. Only in a ridiculous farce or operatic melodrama can you use mistaken meanings, identities or misconstrued acts and words to prolong the finale.

Don't fail to give convincing *motivation* for the problem. If a man incites the fury of the town boss by refusing to drink with him, you must eventually explain why. Is his objection to the drink a religious one? Is he just being ornery? Is his refusal related to a sacred deathbed oath? Does he purposely want to antagonize the other man? Is it because long ago while intoxicated he killed someone? In addition to giving strong motivation for the actions of your main character, build up strong motivation as to why the other man makes such a big issue of their drinking together.

Don't bite off more problem than you can chew and digest for your word length and market. Total character development is too vast for a short story, but is just right for a full-length novel. You can't fight a crusade or change the world in a short-short; nor should you use too trivial a problem in a book length.

No builder, craftsman, or designer should spend time, talent and energy working with materials that won't hold up. The problem and solution are the basic materials of everything you write. Be sure to test your materials thoroughly before working with them.

XIV | PLOT BLUEPRINTS

PLOTTING IS the planning, the blueprinting, the pre-battle strategy, the road map, or recipe that must be thoroughly worked out and kitchen-tested before you begin writing the actual story. No matter how dramatic, original, and splendid your story idea is, its eventual success or failure depends on how you work out the plot.

The original idea that inspires you to write a story in the first place may be an unusual character, gimmick, premise, idea or incident. Once you have this seed, you must plant and cultivate it. You must be willing to work hard until you have developed it into a problem—i.e. a strong conflict that has many valid obstacles standing between the presentation of the problem and its eventual resolution into success or failure. The strongest obstacle is the CRISIS which always presents the opposite stage from the ending or CLIMAX. Thus, in a happy-ending, commercial story, the Crisis shows success—always the opposite of the Climax.

After you have charted the story line, examine it critically to see if you have a "whole plot" which must include the following:

1) Abstract values representing good versus evil in the major conflict situation.
2) An urgent *must* with its obvious *cannot*.
3) Contrasting characters in action—each one strongly motivated in his efforts to achieve a definite goal.
4) Apparent insolubility of the problem but with an ingenious solution that is credible even though surprising.
5) A moral theme or premise to which the story action serves as a parable, proving a definitely worthwhile philosophy.
6) Some featured attraction or X-Plus Factor that gives your story a fresh angle and color.
7) An individual style that expresses you and yet fits the subject matter, the era, area and characters of the story itself.

When you get an idea for a story, think of it *not* as a mighty conflagration, but as a mere spark capable of igniting greater fires. Be sure to test it objectively, not subjectively and ask yourself not what meaning it has to you but what meaning will it have to your reader.

The most effective plot material is that which concerns mankind at all times and has emotional impact, drama, freshness, and credibility. To escape the hackneyed, you must strive to evolve new arrangements or culminations of life's familiar elements. Your first step is to select significant plot material. Then you should arrange the story action into a professional plot. The third step is to pyramid all incidents and ideas to an effective climax and premise.

Decide on the most effective viewpoint (preferably that of the character who is most involved and does most to solve the problem), and plan your time order, which can be:

1) Chronological—works smoothly ahead from start to finish of action.
2) Flashback—starts with a dramatic high point of interest, works back.
3) Composite—mixes chronological with flashback method of telling story.

The plot marches from a clearly-defined problem to a specific solution that will have universal meaning to the readers. The march must not be too smooth or there will be no suspense and conflict. You should plan increasingly difficult obstacles which the protagonist overcomes until the toughest obstacle blocks his path at the crisis, which contains the solution to the whole problem. For example, when Cinderella's fine clothes turn to rags at the ball, this is her humiliating crisis, but it leads to the climax because in her hasty departure she loses the glass slipper which later enables the prince to find her.

Think of the obstacles as "fictional frustrations." If you give your protagonist several of these strong, well-planned fictional frustrations and work out clever ways for him to overcome each one, you'll be on the right plot track.

The Fictional Frustrations must: 1) have universal application and strong reader identification; 2) involve the characters and reader emotionally; 3) criss-cross the obstacles of other characters; 4) alternate with the temporary triumph; 5) be related to each other (each step growing out of the preceding one and developing into the succeeding one); 6) represent the antithesis of the hero's goal or desire. If the hero wants approbation or love, each Fictional Frustration points to rejection; if he wants riches, the Fictional Frustration points to poverty; 7) crescendo in intensity, building up to one supercolossal Fictional Frustration which forms a major crisis of the story, and paradoxically enough, reveals the premise or theme.

One of the secrets of professional plotting is that the impossibility of the crisis makes the climax possible. We've seen how it worked in Cinderella. How many other examples can you think of? In the old-fashioned melodrama the villain ties the hero in the abandoned shack. To make matters worse, he sets fire to it as he leaves. But this makes things better because the hero holds his tied hands to the flame and burns himself free. Or perhaps the fire attracts help—at any rate, whatever constitutes a king-sized threat at the time becomes the means of a happy ending.

It is wise to plan the crisis that contains the solution before writing the story. Also synopsize the story, then work out the plot blueprint like this:

1) Write synopsis of story

2) State the problem

3) List the obstacles (fictional frustrations) with the alternating temporary triumphs, all leading up to:

4) The crisis or super-obstacle; and finally:

5) The climax which resolves the problem.

6) State the premise.

There are eight different formulas or plot types editors are buying today. Analyzing published examples of each type will enable you to plan and write better-plotted stories.

1) HERO GAINS HIS GOAL or PURPOSE ACCOMPLISHED

The protagonist here is sympathetic and has a worthwhile goal which seems impossible to attain. After many valiant efforts to conquer ever-worsening obstacles and setbacks, he achieves the goal and solves his problem, *always through his own efforts.*

EXAMPLE: James Thurber's "The Catbird Seat" (later made into movie, "The Battle of the Sexes.")

> *Problem:* Hard-working Mr. Martin wants to keep the status quo in the office where he works, and retain Mr. Fitweiler's high esteem of him.
>
> *First Obstacle* (Fictional Frustration): Loud, meddlesome Mrs. Barrows is hired as special adviser and starts making radical changes.
>
> *Temporary Triumph:* She stays away from his office.
>
> *Second Obstacle* (F.F.): She invades his domain and questions his need of so many files.
>
> *Temporary Triumph:* He gathers enough courage to "rub her out"; goes to her apartment.
>
> *Third Obstacle* (F. F.): He can't think of a way to get rid of her; there is no weapon available.
>
> *Temporary Triumph:* She offers him hospitality and he drinks a highball and smokes a cigarette (both habits being alien to him).
>
> *Crisis* (Super F. F.): When he threatens violence against Mr. Fitweiler, she orders him out and promises to report him to the boss.
>
> *Climax:* When she tells Mr. Fitweiler about Mr. Martin's smoking, drinking and threatened violence, this sounds so ridiculously out of character for Martin that Fitweiler thinks that she needs psychiatric care. He dismisses her and the old status quo that Martin longed for is resumed.
>
> *Premises:* The end justifies the means. You've got to be dumb like a fox and fight fire with fire.

2) VILLAIN IS FOILED OR BITER-BIT

This is a reversal of the preceding Hero-Gains-His-Goal. The main actor is a hateful heavy with a negative goal which will bring disaster to a sympathetic character. Throughout the story, his obstacles or fictional frustrations are the hero's efforts to block him and his triumphs are the hero's fictional frustrations. At the crisis, he enjoys a triumph that seems final, but it reverses to defeat at the climax. All action must grow from his character trait, and he must receive the same punishment he has planned for the hero. If he planned to poison, he is poisoned.

Henry Slesar is a master of the biter-bit story. Here is a plot blueprint of his biter-bit story, "Insomnia":

Problem: Charles Cavender wants to cure his insomnia.

First Obstacle (Fictional Frustration): He hasn't been able to sleep for so long that he has lost 3 jobs in 8 months.

Temporary Triumph: He goes to a psychiatrist and unburdens himself of the fire that claimed the life of his young wife, Linda. He says that in his dream she is at the top of the stairs smiling when the flames grab her from behind and pull her back. He tells the doctor that it happened differently; that he was awakened by the fire to find her already dead, so he fled in order to save himself.

Second Obstacle (F. F.): He keeps receiving accusing letters from Linda's brother, John Fletcher, first from a veterans' hospital, then, (after he leaves the hospital), he keeps tormenting Charles with midnight phone calls.

Temporary Triumph: Charles gets Fletcher's forwarding address from the hospital, goes to have it out with him.

Third Obstacle (F. F.): He finds a cripple in a wheel chair, belligerent, incapable of being appeased since Fletcher is convinced Charles caused Linda's death. They fight. Charles kills Fletcher.

Crisis: Charles realizes that he's free—free from Fletcher's threats, accusations, letters and phone calls. He celebrates by buying beer and going to his room for his first sound sleep in ages.

Climax: Faulty heater in his room starts a fire that guts the entire building, but insomnia-free Charles sleeps right through all the commotion and burns to death—as his cowardice has caused Linda to die.

Premises: You may escape the world's vengeance, but never that of your conscience. Conscience is its own accuser and punisher. He who diggeth a pit shall fall into it.

3) DECISION

A sympathetic character must decide between two courses of action. He makes the choice that he thinks will solve problems and lead to happiness, but the opposite happens: it leads to new set-backs and a strong negative crisis, all of which he conquers in order to achieve a happy ending. There's no limit to the type of decisions that make a dramatic story: In Roger O. Hirson's "Drop-out," 16-year-old Jerry Dahlquist has to decide whether to keep struggling through high school or quit and become his father's business partner. He drops out but soon realizes he's ill-equipped and reverses his decision to discontinue his education.

William Holder has had some splendid decision stories in *The Saturday Evening Post.* In his "Pay-Off Bout," almost-through boxer Eddie Miller's decision is whether to accept $2000 for throwing a fight with a younger fighter who'll probably beat him anyway or refuse it and do his best to win an honest fight.

Problem: Eddie Miller, 31-year-old boxer, wants to be happy.

First Obstacle (Fictional Frustration): He faces a big fight with younger, better boxer. His manager, Fenton, urges him to throw the fight for a much-needed $2000 bribe.

Temporary Triumph: Eddie's conscience rebels. Is reinforced when he meets Helen Casey, a singer who can't sing well but keeps plugging on courageously.

Second Obstacle (F. F.): Pressures to take the bribe. Insults. Temptations, etc. plus genuine need of the money.

Temporary Triumph: He refuses the bribe. Has good, clean fun dating Helen, fishing, picnicking. They like each other.

Crisis: The big fight arrives and he is losing. He realizes he'll lose everything, the fight, money, etc., but the thought of Helen's invincible courage spurs him on to do his best.

Climax: He wins, although he knows he's not good enough to continue. Neither is Helen. They'll marry and build a future together instead of chasing rainbows.

Premises: There are different kinds of courage: Sometimes it is brave to keep plugging away against odds, other times it is wiser to quit. The decision must be your own and must be conscience-free.

4) HERO ABANDONS HIS GOAL OR PURPOSE ABANDONED ✓

A sympathetic character has a negative goal—usually revenge, destruction, hate or something that is out of kilter with our moral standards. There must be strong motivation (or he would not be sympathetic). At the point of the story where success is in sight, he realizes the harm he will cause to others and he unselfishly gives up his original goal, usually reaping richer spiritual satisfactions. Be sure that he abandons his purpose for unselfish reasons, not just because he changes his mind or no longer wants it, or you'll have a disappointing "white elephant" plot, and your hero will lose reader-respect because he wasn't smart enough to know what he wanted. The goal should be as strong as the Count of Monte Cristo's desire to destroy the man who framed him, ruined his life and stole his sweetheart. And his abandonment of that goal should be as noble as the Count's when he chooses not to destroy his enemy because this would also destroy his innocent wife and children.

Here is a blueprint of Louis Auchincloss' Purpose-Abandoned story, "The Trial of Mr. M.":

Problem: Retired headmaster of Chelton School, Mr. Minturn, wants to keep alive the rigorous old discipline of the school as it was in his day.

First Obstacle (Fictional Frustration): The present headmaster is Arthur Knox, who is younger, more liberal and modern.

Temporary Triumph: Mr. Knox seems anxious for Mr. Minturn's advice in disciplinary matters.

Second Obstacle (F. F.): Although in agreement with Mr. M. in principle, Mr. K. has methods of his own, which Mr. M. can neither understand nor sanction.

Temporary Triumph: Mr. Collins, Latin teacher, expresses his distaste for the new administration and his allegiance to Mr. M.'s ways of thinking. Supported by this, Mr. M. again approaches Mr. Knox regarding a specific incident.

Third Obstacle (F. F.): His opinions are politely but firmly rejected.

Temporary Triumph: Mr. Collins and Mr. Prince of the English department openly express their desire to reinstate Mr. M. and his policies. Although he tries to keep an open mind, he cannot help but succumb to their mutinous, but flattering, ideas. Egged on by Collins and Prince, he plans to seize control on Founders' Day, when the alumni, parents and trustees will be present.

Crisis: He is shocked to learn that many of the Founders' Day guests agree with the new policies. And Mr. Knox has known of his plan from the beginning!

Climax: He abandons his plan in the sudden realization that: his time is past; his vision was circumscribed by his own ideals; Mr. Knox is carrying out those same ideals in his own way. Now he can peacefully retire.

Premise: Each man has his inning and should not overstay or steal another man's chance.

5) COME-TO-REALIZE

A sympathetic character is in a negative state of mind brought about by frustration, envy, self-recrimination, grief, anxiety, failure or some other minus situation. Because of a changed set of moral values, he realizes his blessings and is satisfied, perhaps even grateful at the end. This is the only plot type with a passive protagonist. That is, the main actor does not have to be actively trying to solve a problem. The changes are spiritual and psychological, not physical, since the external situation may be the same at the end as in the beginning, even though the hero has changed in his evaluation of it.

In Lawrence Williams' "Rich Man, Poor Man," (*Good Housekeeping*) Gino, a sincere, young Sicilian stonemason, is dissatisfied with poverty and wants to lavish wealth on his bride and her family. When he realizes his dream by finding ancient statues and selling them to a greedy crook (against the law), he sees how this new-found wealth is corrupting them all and that honest poverty is better than dishonest wealth. *Redbook's* short-short, "Premonition," by Michael Shaara, dramatizes a young father's fear of his own death, but he comes to realize that we have to think we're losing something in order to appreciate it. He says:

> "All it was— Listen, life was going by too fast and I wasn't paying it any mind. You see? Nothing goes on very long— not the house or us, not anything—but we hurry along and we don't pay attention. As if there were all the time in the world. . . . And that's what the weird feeling meant."

An interesting variation of this idea appears in Paul Horgan's *Post* story, "Wall of Flame":

> *Problem:* Professor Ford Michaelson wants to save his home, animals and possessions from the Malibu fire.

First Obstacle (Fictional Frustration): He is miles away, teaching a class at UCLA when he learns of the fire; his wife is away; the house is unprotected, empty, except for the pet horse, Lady Fox, and pet dog, Maisie, and her new pups.

Temporary Triumph: He dismisses class and tries to drive home.

Second Obstacle (F. F.): Traffic is congested, with the roads clogged by rubberneckers. Inability to make headway gives him more time for frustrating reflection of the precious possessions endangered: the living creatures and the irreplaceable sentimental and cultural treasures.

Temporary Triumph: He circumvents roadblock at his usual route and takes a shortcut.

Third Obstacle (F. F.): Car-radio reports that the fire is racing in the direction of his home. As he comes into the fire area he sees the homes burning.

Temporary Triumph: Traffic slackens enabling him to get closer to home.

Fourth Obstacle (F. F.): Police won't let him drive closer.

Temporary Triumph: He parks his car and walks through the brush to his property.

Fifth Obstacle (F. F.): The fire is almost to his stable where horse and dog with her new pups are trapped.

Temporary Triumph: He frees the terrified horse which races toward the ocean to safety.

Sixth Obstacle (F. F.): The fire jumps downhill, collapsing the hillside wall of the stable. When he searches for the dog, Maisie, he finds her gone, but two pups are left.

Temporary Triumph: She has carried two to safety. He bundles the others in his coat and tries to leave stable, but:

Seventh Obstacle (F. F.): The blazing door is riveted shut. He can't get out.

Temporary Triumph: Frantically, he kicks and pounds the door open, finds Maisie safe.

Sub-Crisis: In opening the blazing door he is painfully burned. The agony makes him fall forward.

Temporary Triumph: His wife has returned. He's no longer alone for the terrible crisis of watching their beloved home burn. He has freed the living things.

Crisis: Their home is apparently the next victim of the voracious fire. Helplessly, they stare at the spectacle of their lifetime of treasures about to be destroyed. His wife tearfully asks: "Ford, what shall we save?"

Climax: A spiritual revelation and maturity spring from the test of the tragedy. He realizes that: "Well, as we loved the things that we were about to lose, they mattered less than what they stood for, nothing could really deprive us of what we loved. And so before they were wrested from me, I gave up voluntarily the things which the fire came to take. . . . We were free, and I think free forever from the tyranny of things—even the most dear things. . . ." An ocean wind blows back the fire-spreading wind and the house is saved. In the author's words: "It was as if the fire said to me, *Very well, now that you are free of your possessions, you may keep them.*"

6) CHARACTER REGENERATION

A character with a negative dominant trait or who is controlled by a bad habit is shocked by a strongly-minus crisis into rehabilitation. A misogynist becomes a humanitarian; a misanthropic Scrooge, kindly and generous; a sinner regenerates into a saint; an alcoholic, dope addict, compulsive liar or gambler breaks the chains of habit and rises to usefulness and happiness. "The Hanging Tree" relates the character-improvement of an embittered, officious, hated and feared tyrant to a softened, humane leader who tempers justice with mercy. Many confessions have character regeneration plots.

7) CHARACTER DEGENERATION

Here, the protagonist deteriorates morally, spiritually or mentally. At the crisis, there is a flicker of hope—a hopeful upward trend, but it is only temporary and he slides downhill after that, as does the minister in Somerset Maugham's *Rain,* Jet Rink in *Giant.* The character has some good qualities and some hope of redemption; therefore the reader's hope is stimulated to want a happier ending than finally occurs. This type of plot is found more in quality stories and plays than commercial yarns which end more satisfactorily.

8) PURPOSE DEFEATED OR PURPOSE LOST

This is also quality rather than commercial, with even a sadder ending because the protagonist is thoroughly sympathetic and we want him to achieve his goal, which is also sympathetic. But "life isn't always like that" and this sad-ending Purpose-Lost story emulates life often at its grimmest. *Winterset, West Side Story* and *The Diary of Anne Frank* are examples of an undeserved fate dealt out to more deserving people.

THE DON'TS OF PLOTTING

1) Don't be victimized by inspiration—that "intellectual overheating." Don't start writing a story until you have worked out the mechanics of the design or plot.

2) Don't write a story just "because it really happened." The truth is too dull, humdrum, libelous, full of coincidences, or incredible to pass for fiction. Fiction is an improvement over life—it makes sense, presents order out of chaos and must be *planned.*

3) Don't overlook the prime necessity of taking a moral stand in your story. This will be expressed through the Premise which is always worked out before you begin writing the first scene.

4) Don't think you have a plot if there's just an intriguing assortment of incidents and characters. Plot has Problem and Solution plus Crisis.

5) Don't overcomplicate the plot of a short story or oversimplify that of a long script. Novels and plays have intricate crisscrossing of plot types. Recognize the Plot Types you will use and follow the given formula.

6) Don't forget to pyramid your incidents to a Crucial Peak, at which point your reader cannot guess the ending. As the producer requested: "Begin with an earthquake and work up to a climax!"

7) Don't use hackneyed or incredible plots which frustrate the reader: Cinderella, Sleeping Beauty, Robin Hood, Hidden Animal-Identity (you think you're reading about people, but they're animals!), Beauty-and-the-Beast plots. These are so trite and tired; give them a rest (unless you have a whizbang up-to-the-minute angle!) Also avoid paper-dragon plots in which all the action, excitement and mental turmoil is stimulated by an imagined situation. A problem that takes up the reader's time and attention must be *real*. You do not have a story if the wife thinks her husband is unfaithful to her because he was seen lunching with another woman and at the end we learn it was an innocent meeting which will actually benefit the wife or improve the husband's position.

XV | YOU DON'T HAVE TO BE ORIGINAL

HAVE YOU EVER WONDERED how prolific professional writers get so many ideas, especially the slick writers whose by-lines appear in the magazines almost every month? Often it's not genius as much as adaptability: adapting the plot structures of classics to modern situations.

Most professionals consciously or unconsciously "borrow" classic plots—especially those in public domain like the works of Chekhov, Poe, Shakespeare, etc. To the original skeleton, they add fresh body and features: characterization, atmosphere, dialogue, and sometimes premise or moral—anything that will increase Reader Identification and timeliness.

For instance, Steve Fisher cleverly revamped Guy de Maupassant's "Ball of Fat" into a "Have Gun Will Travel" script. In the original, the French girl of easy virtue is snubbed by her co-travelers until they are captured by a German officer who will kill them unless she surrenders to him. They beg her to, promising her acceptance and friendship, but afterward they look down on her more than ever. Fisher converted the French girl into an Apache princess on her way East to marry a cadet, and the snobs of our Old West scorn her because she is Indian. At the crisis, Paladin saves her from a fate worse than death, but de Maupassant's premise of ingratitude and intolerance is maintained.

Is this stealing or plagiarism? No. In fact the audience is comfortable with a tried and true formula and is delighted with the originality of your adaptation. It's as if you followed a smart clothing pattern or blueprint but used different materials, sizes and details. This procedure of building on ready-made foundations reaps such rich rewards that one top author-critic told writers: "If you have just two hours a day to write, spend one of them reading!"

Because so many classics have everything (especially the necessary ups and downs) it's worth your while to study them for two reasons: 1) to test and perfect your plot sense even if you're one of those lucky people who have more plot ideas than time to write them down; or 2) to utilize a time-tried successful structure as a base when your own plot-well runs dry.

The greatest best-seller of all time is so rich in reader identification that its stories are as applicable today as when they happened to Biblical characters long ago. All people everywhere have known temptation and have either conquered it or succumbed to it—therefore they can understand and identify with the anguish of Judas, who yielded to mercenary temptation and suffered all the agonies of conscience leading to suicide; with King David who gave in to carnal temptation for Bathsheba and was also punished in addition to losing the respect of his people; and with Adam and Eve who paid the price for not resisting temptation. Daniel and Jonah, on the other hand, resisted temptation even when their very lives were the reward for denying or turning against God and they enjoyed happy endings in keeping with their loyalty. Moses was honored for his fidelity to the Lord by being privileged to lead his people to the Promised Land, but he was punished for his insubordination and impatience by being deprived of the right to enter it. And who has not at some time or other been called upon to sacrifice one principle for another, as Abraham was ordered to sacrifice his son?

Reader identification is so strong throughout the Bible that many of its plots that dramatize human values and emotion in conflict have been successfully adapted to more recent settings, characters and situations. Isn't Leon Uris' *Exodus* an up-to-date version of Moses leading his people through the wilderness into the Promised Land, uniting the disunited and restoring faith to those who have lost it? John Steinbeck's *East of Eden* harks back to the Old Testament situation all the way down to the names of the rival brothers, Caleb and Aaron, which are similar to Cain and Abel. Every story of a fallen woman regenerated echoes the rehabilitation of Mary Magdalene, and each plot in which a valiant, virtuous individual conquers a giant (the "giant" may be a human enemy, an evil force like a crime syndicate, an abstract villain like prejudice or disease, or even a fear of defeat or electrical storms) is a rehash of David and Goliath.

Choose the type of plot that best meshes with the philosophy, characterization and specific atmosphere you want to write about, one that has timeliness and pertinence to contemporary problems.

There's no end of stories, books and plays built on classical plot structures, just as many popular songs echo classical music. Doesn't Homer Price's automatic donut machine that can't stop making donuts remind you of *The Sorcerer's Apprentice?* And isn't Daphne Du Maurier's *The Scapegoat,* in which the rich Frenchman and humble British professor who look alike, change places like Mark Twain's *The Prince and the Pauper?* This plot idea involving look-alikes keeps popping up, and reappears in Michael Redgrave's first novel, *The Mountebank's Tale.* Here the doubles are a European actor, Joseph Charles, and Paul Hammer, a man whom he trained to be his twin in a play and who thereafter lived in his shadow. Joseph Charles loses his desire to act and persuades Hammer to impersonate him on an American tour and never to reveal the deception. At the end, we are as in the dark as to which is who as we are at the end of *The Scapegoat.*

My Fair Lady is based on G. B. Shaw's *Pygmalion* which goes back to the ancient Greek legend about the woman-hating sculptor, Pygmalion, who created an ivory statue so beautiful that he fell in love with it and pleaded with Venus to bring it to life. The Broadway musical features speech expert Henry Higgins as the Pygmalion equivalent who transforms cockney flowergirl Liza Doolittle into an elegant lady, and in more automation-conscious stories the scientist creates a lady robot whom he loves. Occasionally this love story is reversed into a Frankenstein type, in which the human being manufactures a creature for different reasons (perhaps to be his slave, to attack others, or to prove his powers); then the created overcomes the creator. Mythology inspired many plays like O'Neill's *Mourning Becomes Electra* and Jean Anouilh's *Antigone,* which had strong meaning when it was written and produced during the Nazi occupation of France. Creon, the evil king who overturned all human values, was obviously Hitler. The play frankly appealed to its French audience to rebel, insisting that only the individual acting against mad tyranny and injustice can be saved. In Sophocles' original tragedies, *Antigone* and *Oedipus at Colonus,* Creon forbade Antigone to bury her brothers. She defied him and conducted the burial rite. In punishment Creon buried her alive. In the French play, she also defies the tyrant and tells the audience: "What a person can do, a person must do."

Another phase of the Oedipus myth was probably the springboard for the modern play *The Visit.* When Oedipus realized his own responsibility for the tragedies suffered by his people, he offered himself as a sacrifice. In the recent story, a wealthy woman returns to her hometown in Switzerland from which she was exiled years before because of her pregnancy by a man who denied his paternity. After she sets the village up economically and accustoms the townsfolk to luxury, she demands the death of the man who has betrayed her. They all love him and are horrified at first, then, selfishly, they agree to sacrifice him. More pleasant is Jacob Hay's reversal of the old Trojan Horse legend in his satirical story "Exploit of the Embalmed Whale," in which a ton of new type rocket propellant is smuggled out of a warehouse in Pilsen, Czechoslovakia, in an embalmed whale.

How many modern works can you trace to a borrowed structure? Aren't there echoes of the King Midas legend in Robert Wilder's novel, *The Sun Is My Shadow,* in which money-loving Mark Hillyard is a modern Midas whose mercenary ambitions affect his daughter, Carol, making her as hardboiled and materialistic as he and causing her to turn against him and wreck her own life? Ibsen's *A Doll's House* was recently rebuilt into a contemporary play about a politician who considers his wife a convenient toy and refuses to share mutual confidence and mature decisions with her when the crisis arises. The politician's fashion-plate pretty wife duplicates Nora's character, emotions and actions, and walks out on her husband just as Ibsen's heroine did. Shakespearean structures keep reappearing: *Kiss Me, Kate,* based on *The Taming of The Shrew;* the underworld story of ambitious *Joe Macbeth* following *Macbeth;* and Elmer Rice's *Cue for Passion* frankly admitting its indebtedness to *Hamlet.*

The old Faust idea of man bargaining with the Devil to get what he wants keeps cropping up with intriguing variations. In addition to dozens of operas from Gounod to Ferruccio Busoni's *Doktor Faust,* here are other examples in literature: 1) *The Devil and Daniel Webster* takes place in early 19th century U.S. and the hero exchanges his soul for mundane wealth and prestige. 2) In *The Day the Yankees Lost the Pennant* (or *Damn Yankees*), the older man sells Satan his soul for the chance to be a young, long-ball hitter who helps his baseball team win the pennant. 3) *Will Success Spoil Rock Hunter?* uses Hollywood for its target of satire and depicts the mediocre hack-writer who bargains with the Devil in order to become a top screenwriter and Hollywood success. 4) Irwin Shaw's novel, *Two Weeks in Another Town,* reverses the Faust and Mephistopheles roles and it is the former who must save the latter. 5) Comedy saturates Ira Levin's Faust variation, *The Devil, You Say,* which was adapted for TV by Jameson Brewer. Nick Lucifer doesn't want the soul of an elderly male Faust, but instead tries to win a young

American housewife who bakes divine (oops! "hellishly" good) devil's food cakes. He charms her and tempts her with wealth, fame and every possible lure but she remains faithful to her husband (who is really an angel who came down to earth to marry her when she won a cake-bake contest for an angel food cake!)

The genealogy of the Romeo and Juliet story is equally as fascinating and varied. Shakespeare himself borrowed it from earlier sources: Arthur Brooke's poem "Romeus and Juliet" (1562), Girolamo dalla Corte's "L'historia Di Verone" (1594), Luigi da Porto's novella of 1530, Bandello's 1554 novella, Masuccio's 1476 novella of a similar story, and/or others going back to 1303! How many modern versions can you recall? All dramatize the plight of lovers representing factions that are dedicated to hate. In Arthur Laurents' *West Side Story*, the scene is changed from old Verona to contemporary New York, and the family feud of the Capulets and Montagues gives way to the gang-war between the Puerto Rican "Sharks" and the American "Jets." Maria is the Puerto Rican Juliet who loves Tony, the American Romeo, although tragedy results from the violence engendered by hate. Maxwell Anderson's *Winterset* also had a New York background, with slightly different characters in a lovers-can-be-the-casualties-of-haters theme. This Romeo's father has been executed for a crime he did not commit and the son wants to avenge his father's death. This Juliet's brother is part of the crime syndicate that represents the evil that love cannot defeat. In *The Hatfields and McCoys* the setting changes to the Kentucky mountains and involves feuding families who constantly feed their hate with real and imaginary grievances they *must* avenge with killing. As usual, the lovers from the hostile families are as determined to end the feud as their folk are to continue it. One of the few happy endings to the lovers-fighting-hatred story is Peter Ustinov's *Romanoff and Juliet,* a comic-satire on prejudice and political protocol. Because the Communists and the Americans are trying to draw a neutral, peace-loving little country into their hostile blocs, the President-General helps the lovers marry and also promotes tolerance between enemy ideologies. Instead of the classical premise that "Hate destroys Love," Ustinov promulgates the idea that tragedy can be averted if and when people think for themselves instead of letting politicians rule them. And that Love and Peace not only *can* triumph over Hate and War, but *must* if we are to survive nuclear annihilation.

As long as you make an old story-idea meaningful to people today you may borrow to your heart's content, perhaps following the original with only slight changes in setting and characters, or perhaps reversing and altering it considerably. Jerry Lewis' *Cinderfella* reverses the sexes as Cinderella becomes the orphan-boy, Cinderfella, with a fairy-godfather instead of a godmother. Incidentally, don't overlook fairy tales as springboards. *Once upon a Mattress* is based on Hans Christian Andersen's tale about the lady who was so sensitive that she could feel a pea through a mattress, and so passed the test of royalty and was considered eligible to marry the prince. Such fantasies as *Mr. Peabody and the Mermaid* and *Prince and the Mermaid* hark back to the ancient Undine legend and are popular because of current stress on youth and virility. So many Ugly Duckling, Red Riding Hood and the Wolf, and Beauty and the Beast stories have been written that they're considered clichés. But nothing's dodo-dead or impossible if you enliven it with your original style and feeling, a colorful setting and universal meaning that gives insight into the reader's problems.

Lord David Cecil claims "The most interesting human dramas are those in which unusual and remarkable individuals are involved in issues that have a universal application." Whether the personalities are unusual or exactly like the folks next door, the second part of the statement is *always* true: *involved in issues that have a universal application*—situations in which the reader can see himself or someone he knows.

Reader identification is the alchemy that makes the specific general, and the objective, subjective—thus widening reader appeal and salability.

XVI | THE BEST PLOTS IN LIFE
ARE FREE

The most popular, most quoted author who ever
lived never actually *wrote* a story. Yet he knew so much
about plotting, premise, satire, and characterization, that
playwrights, screenwriters, and all penpushers today are
still parroting his themes and plots after 2500 years.

You can't go through a day without running into one of
his "original" gems that have become clichés from over-
use: "Spare the rod and spoil the child," "A friend in need
is a friend indeed," "Honesty is the best policy," "One
good turn deserves another," "He laughs best who laughs
last," "Half a loaf is better than none," "Misery loves company," "Pride goeth before a fall."

The perennial best-seller, of course, was Aesop, who
used tightly-plotted, innocent-seeming animal allegories to
poke fun at human foibles and to convey political satire
that was often strong enough to influence public opinion
and change history. One of his tales actually averted mob
rule at Corinth; and he helped Pisistratus keep his throne
at Athens by telling the people the fable, "The Frogs De-
siring A King," in which dissatisfied frogs asked Jupiter for

a king and received a stork-king who promptly gobbled them up. MORAL: "Let well enough alone"—and the Athenians did.

Aesop's fables have enough gimmicks, themes, and allegorical plot situations to save your stories. They are public domain, stimulating, applicable, and balanced plot-patterns. Drop a few into your mind and let them blend with your own thoughts, experiences, peeves, and philosophy. This is how it works:

Let's pretend you're a Hollywood animated cartoon writer. You need a snappy new *Tom and Jerry* plot, so you read the Aesop's fable, "The Mice in Council":

> For many years the mice had been living in constant dread of their enemy, the cat. It was decided to call a meeting to determine the best means of handling the situation. Many plans were discussed and rejected.
>
> At last a young mouse got up. "I propose," said he, looking very important, "that a bell be hung around the cat's neck. Then whenever the cat approaches, we always shall have notice of her presence, and so be able to escape."
>
> The young mouse sat down amidst tremendous applause. The suggestion was put to a motion and passed almost unanimously.
>
> But just then an old mouse, who had sat silent all the while, rose to his feet and said: "My friends, it takes a young mouse to think of a plan so ingenious and yet so simple. With a bell about the cat's neck to warn us we shall all be safe. I have but one brief question to put to the supporters of the plan—which one of you is going to bell the cat?"
>
> MORAL: *It is one thing to propose, another to execute.*

This is a good example because it poses a problem but no solution and this gives your imagination a chance for exercise. You set up a mouse college, whose featured course is "How To Get the Best of the Cat." The pedantic professor goes through elaborate shenanigans to teach the dumbish, itty-bitty mouse how to get the bell around the cat's neck, but each time he fails. The mouse uses his own idea: he ties the bell on a fancy ribbon, gift-wraps it magnificently, and marks "Do Not Open." Tom, the cat, naturally tears it open, puts it around his neck with the joy of a woman trying on a $30 hat, and wears it proudly. Here the author added to a 2500-year-old fable the modern principle of reverse psychology. Result: an amusing and satisfying plot solution. The writer added other incidents to round out the script and leave the audience happy. Happy because the underdog (itty-bitty, dumbish mouse) triumphed over Enemy Cat *and* Pedantic Professor Mouse (representing authority).

Aesop's fables have thousands of uses and can inspire you along many lines. How about all the promises politicians make to win votes? Don't they remind you of the fable, "The Angler and the Little Fish," where the caught fish says "Let me go now and I'll let you catch me next year when I'm bigger and better eating"? ("Beware of the promises of a desperate man.")

"The Trumpeter Taken Prisoner" tells of a trumpeter captured during a battle. When the enemy was about to kill him, he argued: "I do not fight and indeed carry no weapon. I only blow this trumpet and surely that cannot harm you. Then why should you kill me?" But his captors replied: "You may not fight yourself but you encourage and guide your men to fight." MORAL: *Words may be deeds.*

Isn't this the Tom-Keefer-subplot of *The Caine Mutiny?* Wasn't "Word King" Keefer the real instigator of the mutiny, even though he, like the trumpeter, swore innocence and ignorance at the court-martial? Keefer was the ring-leader of those hating Captain Queeg. Keefer planted all the suspicion and the seed of mutiny, then kept his own hands clean. He was as innocent as the trumpeter, and Greenwald was right when he told Steve, "Your sensitive novelist friend is the villain of this foul-up all right." This same Aesop fable could be the basis of a story in which a small boy starts things then blames others, or a story about a court dispute or a war between people, neighbors, or nations. Think up your own.

Dreaming up your own characters, locale, and situation, see what you can do with this one, "The Dog and the Shadow." A dog was carrying a piece of meat home in his mouth. Crossing a plank over a brook, he looked down and saw his own shadow reflected in the water below. Thinking it another dog with another piece of meat, he made up his mind to have that also. So he snapped at the reflection, but as he opened his mouth, the meat fell out, dropped into the water, and disappeared. "Beware lest you lose the substance by grasping at the shadow."

Pause a while to think through your own story with this pattern. . . . Suggestions: a flighty, flirty young girl tries to collect more and more boy friends, with the result that she loses all of them, including her old stand-by. Or a protagonist who's dissatisfied with a marriage partner, divorces for selfish reasons, and loses all companionship and happiness. In an Adela Rogers St. Johns story, a man and woman in love divorce their respective spouses and leave their children and marry each other, thinking they have found the perfect love which everyone seeks. After their first quarrel (he objects to her squeaky singing), they realize they've lost everything: friends, position, prestige, self-respect, and now even that transitory treasure, physical love. At the end the heroine is speeding madly in her car toward???

Likewise, *The Man Who Watched the Trains Go By,* which appeared as the movie *Paris Express* some years ago follows the lose-the-substance-for-the-shadow allegory. The middle-class Dutch office clerk leaves his homey, middle-class wife and family for money, glamorous Paris, and a French wench. He winds up losing everything, including his sanity.

Friendship or the "one good turn deserves another" touch is a vastly popular theme today. Maybe you can think of a fresh version as you remember Aesop's "The Lion and the Mouse," the moral of which is, "Little friends may prove great friends." Any situation involving intrigue, war, enemy occupation, or even romance could follow this basic pattern. Paul Annixter varied it somewhat in his story, "Last Cover," in which a G.I. saves his own life in the jungle by remembering from his boyhood a fox's trick of hiding under the leaves in a pond. (He didn't kill the fox then, and the memory saves him now.)

Or take "The Ant and the Dove," in which the ant drinks in the spring, falls into the water, and almost drowns. He is saved by a friendly dove who throws a leaf into the water for him to climb on and float to shore. When the hunter is about to catch the dove with his net, the ant bites the hunter's foot, causing him to drop the net while the dove escapes.

"The Goose with the Golden Eggs" (MORAL: *Greediness overreaches itself*) is a most popular and prevalent theme, with fresh accessories, of course, like those used in Michael Gilbert's recent story, "The Secret of the Missing Will." Before rich old Tobias Buckley died, he told his greedy relatives, Gertrude and Ambrose, "If you keep the garden, the garden will keep you." Avariciously, they dug up the garden in their search for the missing will (in England, if there's no will, the estate goes to the crown). Thus they destroyed the will itself, which Tobias had trickily planted in flower seed (*Zinnia Florata*).

All things and all plots are possible in Aesop, even direct contradictions. If one good turn deserves another, one *bad* turn also deserves another, as in the case of "The Fox and the Stork." Here, the practical-joker fox invites a stork for dinner, but serves only soup in a shallow dish which the poor, hungry stork can't possibly manage with its long beak. At the end of the meal, the fox regrets that the stork ate so little, but the stork retaliates by inviting the fox to a banquet served in a long-necked jar with a mouth much too narrow for the fox's snout. A balanced biter-bit that sets your brain perking along humorous or serious wrong-doer-gets-done-in lines.

Old Aesop was a shrewd biter-bit plotter who would have cleaned up in our current commercial markets. Just a few of his biter-bits are: The lazy donkey who developed the habit of falling into the stream with his master's loads of salt so they'd melt away and he'd have no burden (He was foiled when the man loaded him with sponges which were much heavier after the dunking). The similarly lazy pack horse who forced his teammate to carry most of the load until the poor creature died and the lazy horse had to carry his corpse.

Other biter-bits also suggest plots:

"The Wolf in Sheep's Clothing"—The wolf dons a sheep-skin in order to hide in the flock and kill some sheep. But the shepherd, hungry for lamb, grabs him and kills him for dinner. "Appearances often are deceiving."

Similar story structure: Sol Lesser's TV play, "The Firebird," in which the jealous ballet dancer puts a razor blade in the star's toe-slippers and is forced to wear them herself, slicing her own toes to ribbons.

"Jupiter and the Bee"—Jupiter, grateful to an industrious bee for her gift of honey, promises to grant any wish she makes. She asks for a sting that will kill anyone who tries to rob her hive. Surprised at the bloodthirsty wish, Jupiter says: "Your prayer shall not be granted in exactly the way you wish. But the sting you ask for you shall have. When anyone comes to take away your honey and you attack him, the wound shall be fatal. But it shall be fatal to *you*, for your life shall go with your sting." Moral: *He who plays hard against his neighbor brings a curse upon himself.*

Similar: From Kamikaze pilots to other revenge-ridden characters. In Jules Archer's excellent story, "Holy John's Chimney," the villain steals so much firewood for his hideous chimney that his victim plants explosives in the wood, with the result that the thief destroys his own property.

As you read the fables, classifying them into plot-types, see how many of their story-lines you recognize in contemporary fiction. Take "The Fox and the Goat":

The fox fell into a well, couldn't get out, and would have been permanently stuck if a goat hadn't come along to see what was the matter. The fox told him there was a great drought. "Just as soon as I heard, I jumped down here where the water is plentiful. You'd better come down, too. It is the best water I have ever tasted. I have drunk so much I can scarcely move."

The goat jumped into the well and immediately became the stepladder which the fox climbed to get out of the well. His farewell words to the trapped goat were "The next time, friend goat, be sure to look before you leap."

MORAL: *It is not safe to trust the advice of a man in difficulties.*

This fox-and-goat formula is always good with a pretty girl luring a gullible man (or vice versa) into covering up her or his own crimes of any possible nature. You can think of dozens of variations.

For our commercial markets, the foxy character can't succeed in victimizing the innocent one, so the structure is altered to give the "hero what he desires, the villain what he deserves." The fox must be punished or the goat rewarded. But if your sense of reality cringes at fairy-like falsification of truth, you can find tailor-made quality stories throughout Aesop's fables. Here are just a few for you to think about. See what you come up with:

"The Wolf and the Lamb." A wolf was lapping at a spring on a hillside where a lamb was beginning to drink lower down. "There's my supper," thought he. "If only I can find some excuse to seize it." Then he shouted angrily at the lamb "How dare you muddy the water from which I am drinking?"

"Nay, master, nay," said the lamb. "If the water be muddy up there, I cannot be the cause of it, for it runs down from you to me."

"Well, then," heckled the wolf, "why did you call me bad names this time last year?"

"That cannot be," said the lamb, "I am only six months old."

"I don't care. If it wasn't you it was your father!" And he rushed on the lamb and ate her up. Before she died, she gasped: *"Any excuse will serve a tyrant."*

What does this inspire you to plot? A story of aggression (or even an article)? An intolerance piece in which any type of prejudice is justified? A political campaign? A love story in which intolerance is directed against a rival? In *Johnny Guitar*, Emma made up all kinds of excuses to get rid of her hated rival, Vienna. Think up a fresh situation in which a character will do anything to rationalize irrational acts.

What kind of quality stories do the following patterns remind you of? A Hollywood or Broadway yarn? Labor-capital? Army? Fraternity or sorority story? Racketeers? What?

"The Lion's Share"—A lion went hunting with a fox, jackal, and a wolf. After they caught and killed a stag, the question of dividing it arose. The lion said, "Quarter me this stag." The other animals skinned and quartered the stag, then were told by the lion: "The first quarter is for me in my capacity as king of the beasts. The second is mine as I am arbiter. Another share comes to me for my part in the chase. And as for the fourth quarter, I dare anyone to lay a paw on it!"

"Humph," grumbled the fox as he walked away with his tail between his legs. "You may share the labors of the great, but you will not share the spoils."

"The Wolf and the Crane"—A wolf had a bone stuck in his throat and screamed through his agony: "I would give anything to have it taken out!"

Pitying him, a crane put his long neck down the wolf's throat, loosened the bone, and saved the wolf.

"Will you kindly give me the reward you promised?" asked the crane.

The wolf grinned, showing his teeth, and replied, "Be content. You have put your head inside a wolf's mouth and taken it out again in safety. That ought to be reward enough for you."

MORAL: *Gratitude and greed do not go together.*

Reread old Aesop for new ideas and plots. Most great writers admit basing their significant stories on an allegorical framework and here are plenty for the taking: story-patterns that can be slanted to any market, commercial, quality, juvenile, or what-have-you. Be sure to add your own ingredients: refreshing locale, interesting characterization, motivation, theme, and original gimmicks. Your stories will be better built, pithier, and more vital and salable.

It'll be worth a trip to the kiddies' bookshelf or the public library to restock your plot-shelf. See what fine story ideas are inspired by "The Bald Man and the Fly," "The Fox and the Crow," "The Falconer and the Partridge," "The Porcupine and the Snakes," and "The Boasting Traveler." Don't forget "The Miller, His Son, and Their Donkey." (MORAL: *Try to please all and you end by pleasing none.*) This fable serves as a warning to the writer who tries to please everyone: the publisher, editor, reader, advertiser, friends, relatives, and himself.

THE BEGINNING AND THE MIDDLE OF YOUR STORY

BEGINNINGS

THERE ARE so many ways you can begin a story, and since the opening is the crucial section where you either win your reader or lose him forever, it is necessary to think through your yarn before deciding where to start. Most non-professionals overwrite their beginnings, laboring conscientiously to pack everything in and to get the machinery going. But your reader doesn't want to *see* the machinery oiled up and wound up clankily in his presence. The writer can and must do all this ahead of time by planning the story, characters and incidents thoroughly before writing an opening, and then cutting and pruning that opening before being satisfied with the final draft.

Your story opening must win your reader away from any competing attractions. How can you do this? By including only essentials and omitting all non-essentials which slow your story down. Be sure that your story opening:

1) Captures reader attention with a fresh, original hook (even if you must startle or jolt your reader to accomplish this).

2) Stirs suspense, arouses expectancy, promises more to come, or poses a question. (Why won't the girl marry the man she loves? Why is Jim going to kill Jayne? Why does the mother reject and hate her new baby?) Why? What? Where? When? Who? Prick curiosity to make the reader continue.

3) Clarifies the WHO, WHAT, WHEN, WHERE, WHY and includes plants as to how the problem will be solved.

4) Sets the mood for the story. The opening must be the overture to the whole story, preparing us for the type of yarn that will follow. An action opening prepares us for an adventure, action, or sports story; a characterization opening advertises the fact that we're in for character-development; and a philosophical opening hints that we will be stimulated to think and increase our areas of awareness on some phase of human behavior.

Decide which of the following seven types of opening will be the most appropriate for the story you are going to tell:

1) CHARACTER OPENING

The first words vividly paint a portrait and we know the chief concern of the story will be characterization, with all the dramatic plot action stemming from the main character.

I didn't like Don Nicola, he frightened me. Not because he was a gangster, or had been one back in America, but because he shouted so loud. He spoke two languages, English and Italian, both of which he rendered incomprehensible to me. His Italian was not Italian but a glorious hodge-podge of all the varied dialects the immigrants brought with them to America. And his English was no English I had ever heard before. Like so many immigrants, he had ended up not being able to speak any language coherently. During the fifty years he had spent in America, he had lost his familiarity with his native tongue, and during the eight years he had been back in Italy, the English he had learned had slipped away from him.

("Don Nicola," by Mollie McCush, *The Atlantic Monthly*)

More than one person may be delineated in a Character Opening:

Orlando Cruz made up with brain what he lacked in physical assets. He was short, thin and mild-mannered, but as a Filipino lawyer in Manila was well known and respected.

The one cross in Orlando's life was his brother-in-law, Bogado. Bogado, a farmer, was a big reticent man, always carrying a grudge in life and usually taking it out on his wife Melana.

Little Orlando resented much the way his sweet-mannered sister put up with Bogado's cruelty. If she had more sense —no, she wouldn't. Love is a very strange thing. No matter how badly Bogado treated Melana, she never ran away. Though Orlando was a single man himself, he could understand this. Women—some of them—loved their husbands even while getting beaten up too much.

("A Man Withdrawn," by Leonard J. Guardino, *The Saint*)

2) EMOTION OPENING

The quick, waste-no-time opening of modern TV dramas is not new, but was featured over a century ago by E. A. Poe, who advised the writer to decide on "a certain unique or single effect to be wrought out" and to dedicate every word, character and idea to heightening that effect. The whole story fails if "the very initial sentence tends not to the bringing out of this effect." Here is an *emotion* opening that plunges the reader into the protagonist's viewpoint immediately and powerfully:

> I was sick—sick unto death with that long agony; and when they at length unbound me, and I was permitted to sit, I felt that my senses were leaving me. The sentence—the dread sentence of death—was the last of distinct accentuation which reached my ears. After that, the sound of the inquisitorial voices seemed merged in one dreamy indeterminate hum. It conveyed to my soul the idea of revolution —perhaps from its association in fancy with the burr of a mill wheel. This only for a brief period; for presently I heard no more.
>
> ("The Pit and the Pendulum," by E. A. Poe)

3) ACTION OPENING

This beginning wastes no time. It plunges straightway into action, always promising more to come. Examples:

> The pony came running through the Rivermere suburb between two and three in the morning. Andrew Garth woke to the sound of drumming hoofs coming from way over on Canberra Road. He followed the sound from wonder and a mounting dread as the pony turned off Canberra onto McIver, and when he heard it make another turn onto Cavanagh, he jumped from his bed and ran to the front door. He rushed out on the stoop as the pony turned down Gramercy Lane, his street.
>
> ("The Runaways," by Leland Webb, *Playboy*)

> Fresh out from the New Zealand port of Auckland in bright and dancing weather, the old bark *Jessie Seydon* wheezed and wallowed across the Tasman Sea, and young Amarillo knew that this, his first voyage in her, would also be his last.
>
> ("Treachery's Wake," by Olaf Ruhen, *SEP*)

Mental action (or the action of a lively imagination) flavors the opening of Elizabeth Spencer's *McCall's* story, "Moon Rocket":

A cone of light fell on the open tablet, its page blank except for the formula $x = \pi/r^2$ printed on the top line. He looked up from his desk at the white wall before him. An equation no longer than this one had divided the atom. It had lifted huge rockets from their launching pads, roaring flame, their noses true upon the zenith, with the great oiled cylinder below, turning, turning, turning into the certainty of power. . . .

4) ATMOSPHERE OPENING

This emphasizes the fact that the specific *Where* and *When* of the story will dominate it, affecting plot and characters:

A bleak gust of wintry Korean wind cut through the thatch-roofed little city of Kim-Muk-Chu, drying one more layer of mud and plastering the fine red dust over the olive-drab paint of several dozen assorted Army trucks neatly parked in a bombed-out square near the center of town. A weathered sign on a tiny shack at the square's entrance said this was the motor pool and salvage dump of the _____th Infantry Division's ordnance company. A smaller sign said, SGT. R. WILLIAMS, DISPATCHER. A satisfying aroma of coffee trickled from the shanty's stovepipe when the wind died momentarily, and from within came the occasional flip of a comic-book page, followed by a grunt of bored appreciation. Otherwise the motor pool appeared deserted.

("The Affair of the Wayward Jeep," by Bill Mauldin, *SEP*)

Or

The hospital waiting room was an island of inefficiency in the long echoing and white-painted and silenced stretches of the hospital. In the waiting room there were ashtrays and crackling wicker furniture and uneven brown wooden benches and clearly unswept corners: the business of the hospital did not go with the intruders waiting restlessly.

> ("A Great Voice Stilled," by Shirley Jackson, *Playboy*)

5) PHILOSOPHICAL OPENING

Prepares the reader for the fact that ideas are in the offing and the story will make him think. Here are some examples:

> The principal trouble with being married is that being single never prepares you for it. The initiated members never tell you beforehand; no college course provides a proper introduction. . . ."
>
> ("The Uninvited Guest," by Eileen Herbert Jordan, *McCall's*)

A Philosophical Opening may be facetious or humorous as in "You Just Can't Kill a Skinny Girl" by Alex Austin:

> The trouble with trying to murder a fashion model is that she looks dead before you kill her.

Or it may be profound as in Katherine Anne Porter's "Holiday" (*The Atlantic*):

> At that time I was too young for some of the troubles I was having, and I had not yet learned what to do with them. It no longer can matter what kind of troubles they were, or what finally became of them. It seemed to me then there was nothing to do but run away from them, though all my tradition, background, and training had taught me unanswerably that no one except a coward ever runs away from anything. What nonsense! They should have taught me the difference between courage and foolhardiness, instead of leaving me to find it out for myself. I learned finally that if I still had the sense I was born with, I would take off like a deer at the

first warning of certain dangers. But this story I am about to tell you happened before this great truth impressed itself upon me—that we do not run from the troubles and dangers that are truly ours, and it is better to learn what they are earlier than later. And if we don't run from the others, we are fools.

6) SITUATION OPENING

This places situation or problem above all. Examples:

Much to everyone's astonishment, the young Chinese juggler, Han, severed his wife's carotid artery with one of his heavy knives in the course of a performance. The young woman died on the spot. Han was immediately arrested.

At the scene of the event were the director of the theatre, Han's Chinese assistant, the announcer, and more than three hundred spectators. There was also a policeman who had been stationed behind the audience. Despite the presence of all these witnesses, it was a complete mystery whether the killing had been intentional or accidental.

("Han's Crime" by Shiga Naoya, in *Harper's Bazaar*)

7) DIALOGUE OPENING

This type of beginning indicates that it will be a story of human communication, often, but not always, light, yeasty. Examples:

"I don't mind staying after school," I says to Professor Herbert, "but I'd rather you'd whip me with a switch and let me go home early. Pa will whip me anyway for getting home two hours late."

"You are too big to whip," says Professor Herbert, "and I have to punish you for climbing up in that cherry tree. You boys knew better than that! The other five boys have paid their dollar each. You have been the only one who has not helped pay for the tree. Can't you borrow a dollar?"

"I can't," I says. "I'll have to take the punishment. I

wouldn't mind . . . You don't know my father . . . He
might be called a little old-fashioned. He makes us mind him
until we're twenty-one years old. He believes: 'If you spare
the rod you spoil the child.' I'll never be able to make him
understand about the cherry tree. I'm the first of my people
to go to high school."

("Split Cherry Tree," by Jesse Stuart, in *Esquire*)

THE TEN COMMANDMENTS FOR PROFESSIONAL OPENINGS

1) Start either *in medias res*—right plunk in the middle
of things—or just before a crisis, or just after a crisis,—
never on a dull plateau of interest.

2) Introduce the main actors before bringing in secondary characters, either by direct on-stage action or reference
to them and spotlight the major problem before attracting
reader-interest to minor problems.

3) Establish a definite emotional reaction to each character and clarify their emotional attitudes toward each
other. Strive for variety, so that the reader doesn't *like* or
dislike everyone. Use action, dialogue and character clues
to help the reader identify with the main character and
decide which team he's rooting for.

4) Do not open with a character alone just thinking,
reminiscing or worrying about that first gray hair she's
staring at in the mirror. If there must be one character on
stage alone, show a dramatic struggle with a momentous
decision or place him in mysterious or interest-arousing
action.

5) Plant any gimmicks, characters or information that
will be important later on.

6) Rewrite, prune and polish your opening sentence and
paragraph, so that it is the very best way you can think of

to rivet the reader's attention and pull him into succeeding happenings.

7) Be sure there is at least one unsolved mystery in the beginning, and a definite cliff-hanger at the end of the first scene. Never solve an introductory problem, unless you immediately replace it with a knottier problem. Keep asking yourself, as Catherine Drinker Bowen does: WILL THE READER TURN THE PAGE?

8) Be sure you open with the appropriate overture for the particular type of story and with a quicker pace for a short story than a novel.

9) Never telescope the ending or give the impression everything's going to be fine before the actual solution is reached. When your reader stops worrying and guessing he'll stop reading. Keep pricking his curiosity and use various methods of suspense to whet his appetite for more.

10) Plan your ending ahead so that the opening is written in the same style even though the ending may reverse the beginning situation.

THE MAGIC OF THE MIDDLE

A story middle that's flabby and unattractively oversized or undersized, or boring or poorly written can scare away your customers and defeat the whole story. The middle has its own techniques and requirements which are as important as those of the beginning or end. Among these requirements and techniques are suspense, tension, character development, theme, and plot.

Remember that the story opening intrigues attention and states the problem. The ending is primarily concerned with the solution of that problem; and the function of the middle is to dramatize the development of action, incidents and character changes that occur between the opening and the ending. It contains ups and downs in the hero's efforts to attain his goal. There are new hopes established with a fear accompanying each hope. In this way maximum suspense is achieved.

Minimizing the importance of the middle can at worst wreck an entire story, at best deprive the yarn of its major significance. In a women's slick story, "Cross Your Fingers," the opening shows young housewife-and-mother Tina wanting to be taken into the socialite-women's group, the Junior Assembly, so that her husband will have the "right" contacts to make him a success in the insurance business and her daughters will grow up with the "right" friends and be taken into the "right" dancing classes. The opening also shows her *not* making it the first year she tries, even though her college chum has been trying to help her. The story ends a year later, when Tina is accepted. Goal Gained, Purpose Accomplished. Hooray for our side! But the story values evolve in the middle. Tina is advised to do more welfare work to impress the socialite group, and it is her voluntary service at the charity children's hospital, working with doomed, crippled tots, that makes her realize her own blessings in the health and happiness of her own family. Unselfish service has replaced selfish ambition; gratitude has taken the place of griping, and Tina is a more mature, worthwhile and happier wife and mother. Her comment upon being accepted is "I couldn't care less," although she has definitely learned to care *more* about significant human values. Here, as in most stories, the greatest reader-values occur in the middle. The beginning carves out the problem and the ending resolves it.

But the middle is equally important, not just because it develops complications, increases action and expands emotional experiences of the characters in the story, but because it clarifies universal human values.

In the story body, you must not change the hero's goal, his major characteristics or introduce any important person who will aid or hinder him in solving his problem. Do not let a minor character, a secondary plot line, or a new thematic interest take over the spotlight or create detours from the trip promised in the beginning.

The middle is the *Continuation* of all you have set forth in the opening—an expansion and increasing of already-established conflicts. It augments emotional suspense without changing the emotions or anything else—yet it adds incidents and ideas that are not in the beginning or end. It never merely repeats what has been said. It shows the protagonist *actively* overcoming an obstacle; after which his success is reversed dramatically by the villain force, which always gains as he loses, teeter-totter-like.

The actual number of triumphs and failures depends upon the word-length of the story and the market you are writing for (some preferring more complications and more twists than the slicks or quality stories). But in all types, the story body never bogs down; it always keeps the reader guessing. If it answers one question, it asks a new one—always keeping the reader's curiosity fresh and alive.

It moves steadily toward a suspense-filled Crisis which is always the exact opposite of the Climax. In a happy-ending story, the Crisis is the black moment of bleak failure and catastrophe. In a sad-ending, biter-bit yarn or tragedy, the Crisis spells out temporary success for the Main Actor.

The tantalizing secret of the story body is to keep things moving—dramatically, dynamically—breathlessly rushing toward the outcome—and yet, still at the same time, holding your reader back from it.

XVIII | STORY ENDINGS

MANY STORIES which start out with a sparkle have been ruined by bad endings. These fizzle finales can be avoided by planning and writing your ending first. Top-flight professional fiction writers have often used the write-it-backward method. Adela Rogers St. Johns, for example, writes the last paragraph of a story and pins it on the curtain in front of her typewriter.

Mickey Spillane once said that the *only* reason people read a story or listen to a joke is to find out how it ends. Of course a script must also have living characters, intriguing incidents, gripping emotions and conflicts to make the reader hang on *until* the end—always *hoping* that one thing will happen and *fearing* that it won't (or vice versa).

The End solves the problems and answers the questions that have intrigued the reader throughout the story; it is also what stays with him after he has finished the story. For this reason the ending of a story must top all of the drama of the entire story. It is the reader's earned dividend for his time investment. Be sure you give him a story ending that *satisfies* (it must never cheat or frustrate your reader as life often does); *has an element of surprise* (no matter how small, your ending must contain a twist of some kind that the reader did not foresee); *is logical* (Even if the ending is a great surprise, it must be credible and convincing. You will have planted subtle signposts along the way which lead inevitably to the final solution.)

These are the three must's which all story endings have in common. In other ways, of course, they are *not* alike; variety and suspense are achieved by the use of different types of endings. You must decide which type of ending will best suit your story and will produce the emotional reaction you want to inspire in the reader for whom you have planned it. Most modern stories have one of the following endings:

1) FINAL, SUMMATION ENDING solves the problem with firm finality and a neat, prim period—as all stories did in the past. Whether a happy ending with virtue rewarded and vice hissingly defeated, or the sad ending like the operas and Shakespearean dramas with the characters dead or dying, the end was The End.

There is a "you can't go home again" finality in the ending to George H. Freitag's *Atlantic* story, "The Burial of a Friend." The narrator recalls and savors a childhood experience in which he and his cousin Judith played in an abandoned cemetery:

> We walked out of the yard of the dead, the leaves of all the trees dripping with the spent rain, the sun glistening on the old white church and poking into the opening at the window. We walked out through the iron gate and had gone two or three yards or so when Judith stopped. She unlocked her arms from around me and without looking at me she turned back and fastened the gate securely, and then

shook it to see if it would come open. When it didn't, she turned and joined me, but all the way home we walked just a little apart, together but making two separate shadows, together but in a lonely kind of together, and somehow, without Judith's telling me or without my telling her, we knew we would never return and that if we did it would not be in the same way ever again!

Elizabeth Spencer's short novel *The Light in the Piazza* presents a dilemma of wealthy Margaret Johnson, whose mentally retarded daughter, Clara, is rejected by her financially successful father. To escape the tensions at home, Margaret takes Clara to Florence, Italy, where Fabrizio Naccarelli falls in love with the girl, and Margaret decides not to tell him and his family about Clara's mentality. The day before the wedding, Fabrizio's father tries to call it off because he has learned that Clara is 26 and the boy only 20, but Margaret reverses his decision by saying that her husband's latest letter said he wanted to give the couple $15,000 instead of $5,000 for a wedding gift. The marriage takes place and the book ends with Margaret saying:

> "I did the right thing . . . I know I did."
> Signor Naccarelli made no reply. "The right thing": what was it?
> Whatever it was, it was a comfort to Mrs. Johnson, who presently felt strong enough to take his arm and go with him, out to the waiting car.

Whether or not you approve of Margaret's decision, this ending contains a triple summation; Clara attains marriage to the man she loves; Margaret eases tensions in her own marriage; and the Naccarellis attain the wealth they want.

The Boy-gets-Girl or Girl-gets-Boy story usually has a summation ending. Will Stanton's excellent *Post* yarn, "A

Sentimental Subject," is about a girl who wants a boy who wants to learn to play the piano. The goals are merged when she teaches him music, using flattery and other feminine lures to lead him to the altar. In the end each attains his goal, and the husband says:

> "Marriage and piano playing have a lot in common. It depends on whether you listen to the mistakes or the music. It isn't the polished performance that's important, it's the feeling you put into it."

Summation endings are decreasing as the reader's taste turns toward sophistication, variety, and realism. In life, nothing is absolutely final or solved or conquered or ended. Once in a while we flee into fiction to find this security, and editors balance each issue with different endings to keep us guessing.

2) ANTENNAE ENDING sends feelers into the future, promising more to come after the problem itself is solved. The story action has tangled and untangled threads of interest, the major question has been answered. But we're made to feel the magic promise of new beginnings. One of the most famous antennae endings in literature is Scarlett O'Hara's worry-about-Rhett-tomorrow philosophy at the end of *Gone with the Wind*.

You must know when and why to use this type, and how not to abuse it. Give a brief promising peek into the future, but don't drag the reader there and draw out the story ramblingly.

In many confession stories, the reader has been on such intimate terms with the sins and sufferings of the protagonist, he's not in too much of a hurry to take an abrupt leave. Antennae endings peek into the future when the protagonist has done too terrible a thing to deserve a happy ending, yet we sympathize with his repentance and permit him the "someday hope"; or when the main actor has sinned, suffered, repented, and been forgiven, yet his own transgression will always haunt him.

> He looked up and she was gazing at him curiously. "What's the matter, honey?" she was asking. This was the woman he loved, that he could not help loving, and she was looking at him apparently in innocence and candor. "Aren't you pleased? Aren't you interested?" But beneath the other, smaller voice went on still, inexorably, as he knew it would go on in the years to come: ". . . hate you, hate you, hate you."

3) IDEOLOGICAL ENDING is the opposite-pole brother to the summation. The author has posed a problem, developed it dramatically, but leaves the solution up to the reader. More popular in the intellectual quality market, this type annoys the unimaginative reader who wants the writer to do all the work.

This is the most intriguing and troublesome of all endings and should not be used unless there's a very specific reason. You can be tricky, cute, or cleverly mystifying; you can avoid a controversial subject like divorce or illicit love or a taboo subject; or you can give the reader a chance to choose between fact and fantasy.

This type of ending poses questions for the reader to answer. Be sure it pleases him and gives him a chance to be pleased with you for making him do your work!

The ideological ending can serve as a rhetorical question, giving you a chance to say what the character should do to solve his problem. Example: *Redbook's* "Daddy's Day," in which an ex-husband takes his little boy out for the day. When he returns the child to the remarried mother and knows the strain of dividing the boy's love between two fathers, the real Daddy wonders if the child will be better off if he never sees him again.

Henry Beetle Hough's *Post* story, "The Legend of the Rose," tells about the beautiful girl who was frozen in Swain's icehouse like a rose in a block of ice for almost sixty years.

4) ANTI-CLIMAX or BONUS TWIST is a double-helping ending that adds an *extra* twist, emotional wallop, or added incidents. Although the story could end before it, the anti-climax improves it.

In *This Week's* "Panic on Strawberry Hill" the father worries so about his daughter's safety on her first baby-sitting job, that he drives to the house to check, is terrified when he sees all blinds up, drapes open, no sign of daughter. Strong arms seize him, and he learns how sensible and mature his daughter is: she's left blinds open as a safety-measure, detected a prowler and called police! End. Daughter can be trusted, has been properly reared, even though husband thought his wife wasn't worrying enough. Anti-climax: He is on his way back to the car when he hears rustling in bushes. Ah! he was right . . . but the "prowler" is his wife, who's also been concerned about their daughter even though she concealed it.

Your anti-climax must solve something, re-emphasize a premise, or turn a new light on characterization. It must be purposeful, never used just because you love your characters so much you can't let go!

5) REVERSAL ENDING is the exact antithesis of the opening. If the boy and girl start out feuding and fighting

they wind up loving; if the villain is on top at first he is defeated at the end. The main danger here is obviousness. If there's a miserly misanthropic Scrooge squeezing shillings and hating humanity at Christmas you know he'll change into a veritable Santa Claus. The suspense is achieved in dramatizing how and why he changes.

In Alex Austin's "You Just Can't Kill a Skinny Girl," the jilted boy friend breaks into the model's apartment at night to shoot her, but pumps bullets into her life-size cardboard image (one of her most popular ads). Sylvia Dee features clever gimmick endings in her stories like "Kisses That Click" and "Ask Me No Questions," which satirizes marriage questionnaires by showing that the happily married wife flunks the quiz that is passed 100 per cent by the couple who are getting a divorce.

6) GIMMICK ENDING uses a tricky device to solve the problem and offers an extra surprise as Hitchcock stories usually do.

Start collecting gimmicks that solve problems. For instance, you know how engineers can change the course of a river and redirected the Colorado River to form the Salton Sea. A similar gimmick served to get Alexander Botts out of a tight spot when he was ordered to build a bridge on the Alaska Highway over a frozen river in midwinter. The snow was so deep that not until spring did the poor hero learn he'd built the bridge over a dry wash several miles from the real river. Impossible to move the bridge in the brief time before the tough C.O. arrived, so the hero moved the river under the bridge with a bulldozer. Author William Hazlett Upson says "These things are easy if you work them *backwards.*"

The Ten Commandments for Professional Endings

1) Be sure to spring a surprise which the reader and hero have not been able to predict, one that is logical, credible and satisfactory.

2) Tie up all the loose ends and harvest all the dramatic and emotional seeds which you have planted in the beginning and cultivated in the middle.

3) Always show the How, Why, and When everything turned out as it did, satisfying all phases of reader curiosity.

4) Dramatize the hero's emotional reaction to the way things turned out.

5) Decide definitely on one of the specific ending types popular today: Summation, Antennae, Ideological, Anti-Climax, Reversal or Gimmick.

6) Avoid endings that are skimpy and leave too much for the reader to figure out.

7) On the other hand, don't overload your climax with too much pedantically presented information.

8) Don't ramble on and on after solving a major problem or focus on minor characters telling what happened to the principal actors.

9) Be sure the characterization and philosophy have changed, but that the style is consistent and all changes convincingly motivated.

10) Don't telescope the solution before the end or give the reader the impression that your problem is only temporarily solved.

XIX | MOTIVATION: THE *WHY* BEHIND THE *WHAT*

MOTIVATION IS IMPORTANT in every phase of life, although it often appears under different names. In medicine, the doctor has a better chance of curing a physical disease if he knows the causes, just as a psychiatrist seeks *reasons* for a psychosis, often digging all the way back to childhood. In law, criminals are often caught through a discovery of the *motives* behind their crimes. In advertising, human motivation is the target, and motives here are referred to as "appeals," "lures," or "bait," to induce the public to buy certain products.

A thorough understanding of human motivation is helpful in life and absolutely necessary in writing. People turn to fiction to escape the frustrating, irrational injustices in life. Fiction gives *causes* for *effects,* motivation for action, but only after the reader's curiosity has been aroused by a dramatic act or situation that makes him wonder *why.* For curiosity is the most universal trait, the secret of successful learning, writing, and living. It can be your most valuable tool because:

1) The writer's curiosity will prompt you to dig out the

facts behind the facts and usually lead to your best story-ideas.

2) You can count on the reader's curiosity to lure him into a yarn and hold his interest as long as there is a mystery to be unravelled. In fact, he'll keep hanging on *only* as long as there are questions to be answered, some point of curiosity to be cleared up. As soon as he loses his curiosity, he'll stop reading.

Being motivation-aware has many advantages for the writer:

1) It stimulates ideas and inspires gimmicks and information for future writing.

2) It sharpens suspense and helps hold the reader's interest. If you describe an intriguing situation, fact or characterization and then stimulate curiosity as to the Why? When? Where? How? the reader will stay with you until all the questions you've aroused in his mind are answered.

3) Knowing and eventually explaining motivation will add depth and dimension to your characters. The late Bernard De Voto said the hardest thing for him in writing was to create bona fide villains. How true! By the time you delve into motivation, you begin to understand the brute, and then you find yourself in sympathy with him. Soon it's difficult to hate him and make your reader hate him, too. For example, the hated medical school prof who gives such tough exams and grades them so severely that most of his students flunk. Motivation: his beloved wife died on the operating table, a victim of medical incompetency, and he doesn't want this to happen to anyone else. Or the tough sergeant or drill instructor who is humorless, vindictive, sarcastic and merciless with his men. Motivation: he knows

that by making them angry, he toughens them for battle and they are better equipped to hate, fight, kill, survive and win the war.

"Why are people's actions like great rivers?" asks a riddle. The answer is "because you can see the course they take but not the source whence they spring." Perhaps this describes the limitations of the average layman, but not the writer, who must always be aware of the "source whence actions spring." Only when you are armed with an accurate knowledge of human motivation are you ready to write about people. You can professionalize your writing by studying motivational psychology. Analyze motivation with a view towards understanding human nature, creating true-to-life characters, and triggering plot ideas.

Conflict is often generated by opposite characterization instead of contrasting desires. But you can also achieve suspenseful drama by planning opposing desires in two people with something in common. One is spurred by the gregarious urge and wants to be with other people, the other needs hermit-like solitude. One is motivated by acquisitiveness, the other by generosity. One is devoted to traditional beliefs, the other to progress and change. One is motivated by a wish to conform, the other, to be an absolute individualist. One, by fear, the other, foolhardy courage. How many professional stories can you think of where two members of a marriage, family or team have opposite desires, like *The Sundowners* in which husband Paddy is motivated by the migratory propensity, whereas wife Ida and son Shawn want to settle down?

A character's motivation can change within a story just as the incentives that spur you to action in childhood or youth are not the same as those that motivate you in adulthood. Revenge or lust can drive a person to a criminal act, and then later remorse or guilt impel the culprit to confess or perform a noble deed. In *Room At The Top,* Joe Lampton is originally motivated by a driving *ambition* to succeed socially and financially; later this motive changes to *love,* and he is willing to abandon material success to marry Alice; after this desire is thwarted and they separate, the *sex urge* leads him to seduce Susan; and finally when he learns of her pregnancy, *duty* motivates him to marry her even though he does not love her.

In C. P. Snow's *Time of Hope,* Lewis Eliot's background is similar to Joe Lampton's: he is lower middle-class in stratified British society. *Ambition* plus *superior intelligence* are his incentives to study law and begin a promising career. *Love* for Sheila, the neurotic daughter of a wealthy Anglican clergyman, even though she doesn't love him and is too psychopathic to make him a good wife. Throughout the marriage, she is a drag on his career and an obstacle to his happiness; but when he finally has a chance to be free from the bondage and he no longer loves her, he cannot leave her because he is now impelled by a stronger motive than physical love: *moral responsibility.* Eliot says:

> "I could not send her away. I could not manage it . . . (if I did) she would move from hotel to hotel, lonely, more eccentric as each year passed.
>
> "I could not bear to let her. Whatever our life was like, it was endurably better by the side of what she faced. I must stay by her."

In all his works, Snow is brilliantly aware of the complexities of human motivation. He feels that "Jealousy and the animal instinct for self-preservation can go appallingly far toward explaining the history of the race," but there are deeper, finer, truer motives that people respond to.

Do not pack too many different kinds of motivation in one story, nor have jerky transitions between the changes. One strong motive may be exploited thoroughly: *loneliness* stimulates different responses from all the different characters in Terence Rattigan's *Separate Tables*.

Just as self-seeking ambition has motivated characters from Macbeth and Lady Macbeth through the gray flannel heroes of our business novels, lack of ambition, apathy, disillusionment and despair motivate the protagonists in several novels written in our nuclear age. For example, Herbert Lobsenz's *Vangel Griffin* (Harper $10,000 Prize novel of 1961); Mario in Robert de Maria's *Carnival of Angels;* the daughter who commits suicide in Jean Rikhoff's *Dear Ones All*; and Joshua Bland, the fallen-genius, ex-prodigy hero of Merle Miller's *A Gay and Melancholy Sound.* Each reflects the negativism and pessimism of our post-human, technological climate although each character's motivation is dissimilar, and each has different motives behind the motives. For instance, Joshua Bland's reason for wanting to end his life is his sense of failure and inability to love or communicate. These are caused by his unnatural childhood as an intellectual genius, and by his ambitious mother who conspired with a monstrous society to push him to the wall and prevent him from living a normal, private life.

Always look for the motive behind the motive. Build both of them strongly so that they have emotional intensity, and reveal them in a way that best fits the story and heightens the drama. Emotions themselves can motivate or lead to specific actions; since the primary function of fiction is to create vicarious emotional experiences, you should know how these operate.

The *asthenic emotions* are the dynamic, energetic, explosive emotions like fury, hate, revenge and panicky fear. They propel a character toward a goal that promises either huge rewards or dire punishment. The situation is exciting and may be irritating, risky—a life and death matter: A cowardly person beats a rattlesnake to death; the pacifistic Quaker girl grabs a gun and shoots the killer who is after her husband or child.

The *asthenic emotions* are often characterized by passive enjoyment at the phase of satiation or achievement of the goal: The mountain climber thrills at the view from the peak; the oil driller experiences his first gusher; or the lover enjoys the presence of his loved one.

The *anxiety emotions* are those of indecision: "What should I do?" "What's going to happen now?" "Where can I go?" There's always tension rather than relaxation: The man caught in a flood, tidal wave or forest fire deciding whether to risk his life trying to save someone who may be either dead or already gone away; the son of a pacifist-religious sect debating whether to fight for his country or side with his family and church; or a character forced to make a choice between two different jobs, vacations, neighborhoods, fraternities or marriage partners.

The above emotions motivate *normal* people in average or superdramatic situations, but for weird, psychological stories and whodunits, you'll probably use the abnormal motivations that have appeared in literature since ancient Greek tragedies.

The offbeat motivations can range from exaggerated

emotions like Othello's obsession-like jealousy, to delu-
sions, illusions or phobias of various kinds such as: acro-
phobia—morbid dread of heights; monophobia—morbid
dread of solitude; necrophobia—exaggerated fear of death.

Consider these as "starters" to give you an idea what a
multitude of ideas you can get if you sharpen your motiva-
tion-awareness and continue your analysis of WHY people
are as they are and WHAT makes them act as they do. Obviously, the normal motivations should be used in typical
stories for the average markets, whereas the negative, subnormal motivations will be used in offbeat, "literary"
quality-type fiction or Tennessee-Williams-like drama and
melodrama.

Occasionally human actions are so vile and inhuman that
motivations must be sought in prehuman animality. A
popular theme today is that man's animal brutality is
called forth in the case of war to make him kill and rape
and commit inhuman atrocities, and that, once the mon-
ster-destroyer, Mr. Hyde, submerges the good man and
healer, Dr. Jekyll, there is no stopping him. This is the
animal-motivation in Glen Sire's *The Deathmakers,* and
the motivation is always the preview to the premise. Mr.
Sire says "when you train a man for war and put him in
the front ranks, you are feeding him the same potion that
releases the brute that is Mr. Hyde" . . . that motivates
him to take human life and destroy it. The whole point
of Sire's book is to awaken man to the realization that if
we can use science to destroy man, we can also use it to
examine the human heart and save mankind.

In addition to the subnormal and animal motivations,
writers also use reversed motives, often topsy-turvying
accepted premises like "It's better to give than receive"

and "Cast thy bread upon the waters. . . ." Many quality stories recognize the reversed truth of "do unto others" or "cast thy bread upon the waters:" that many people cannot bear to be grateful or indebted to another for kindness, that they can continue a relationship as long as they are condescending toward someone else, but they abhor kindness from that person, especially if it can be interpreted as pity.

Whether motivation is normal and wholesome, subnormal and neurotic, or reversed, be on the lookout for any characterization, situation or action that pricks suspense as to WHY? Add a motivation section to your Idea File, perhaps in question form, or else divided into "serious" or "humorous" and "true-life" or "fiction." The really good ones will grow into more complete ideas and eventually into salable scripts.

Here are a few starters that might have been nucleus starting-points of professional stories. See what answers or motivations you can think of before you peek at probable explanations given at the end. Then, make up your own rather than using other people's.

1) *Why* does the general lie to his men and say "We're in a shooting war!" and order the bombers to drop H-bombs on Russian targets?

2) *Why* did the bank teller put money in the till (instead of taking it out)?

3) *Why* does the fat lady demonstrate vacuum cleaners house-to-house?

4) *Why* was the usually polite bank teller rude to the sweet old lady, insisting that her small deposits waste the bank's time and patience?

5) *Why* does the woman go to the launderette every day

to read the magazines as she sits against a washing machine?

6) What's the *Why* behind the three beautiful homes in San Bernardino where no one ever answers the door, entertains or goes in or out? Nor are they ever for sale or rent even in housing shortage-eras.

7) *Why* are blackberries considered pure poison on St. Michael's Day in September?

8) *Why* did the well-dressed man in the grocery store pass up all the good fruit and pick inferior-quality, marked-down cantaloupes?

9) *Why* did the wealthy, healthy, happily-married young mother-to-be commit suicide?

10) *Why* does the fat couple try to lose weight by a certain date?

11) *Why* was the devoted wife unfaithful to her husband?

There are several possible reasons or motives for each of the above. See how many you can guess. It will be interesting to see if, among your own several explanations for each, you coincide with the motive a professional author has used for the same situation. Here is at least one professional reason for each:

1) In Peter Bryant's *Red Alert,* Brig. General Quinten is impatient with civilian leadership and the stalling of his military superiors. He wants to destroy Russia before it can destroy us.

2) In John Hess' *The Wicked Scheme of Jebel Deeks,* revenge against the bank that has overworked and underpaid him for 27 years; ambition for gain; self-assertion since this will cause financial confusion which he'll straighten out, thus gaining attention.

3) She hates exercise, but this way she's paid to bend over and reduce.

4) The teller knows the bank is going to fail and doesn't

want the sweet old lady to lose her savings. He insults
her into closing her account.

5) She could have a back ailment which the vibration
helps, or perhaps she's collecting gossip, evidence for a
court case, story material.

6) They were built as decoys to cover oil wells too ugly for
this ritzy neighborhood.

7) Superstitious folk swore the devil put his foot on every
blackberry, poisoning it. (They had to blame something
for their hangovers and tummyaches after St. Michael's
Eve when everyone imbibed!)

8) He's a scientist studying penicillin and other molds
that form on decaying melons.

9) In Daphne Du Maurier's *No Motive,* a red-haired furniture salesman awakened a hideous memory from her
childhood, reminding her of rape and her illegitimate
child and making her feel unworthy.

10) A Reseda couple wanted to adopt a baby they've reared
since its birth, but he weighed 320 pounds, and she 250,
which the County Adoption Bureau thought threatened
their life expectancy. The Superior Court Judge said
they could have the baby if they lost weight consistently
within three months.

11) In *Strange Interlude, Lady Chatterley's Lover* and other
works, the motive is the husband's desire for a child
and his inability to have a healthy-in-mind-and-body
heir.

XX | SUSPENSE

SUSPENSE FLAVORS many moments in our everyday lives and is, therefore, an important element in fiction. Life often asks questions which it refuses to answer. Let your imagination help you transfer life's tantalizing question marks into fiction where you will fork out satisfying answers and relieve the suspense pressures of your readers.

Fiction is an improvement over life because it goes a step further and after presenting a well-motivated problem, it solves it sensibly and satisfactorily. Police files are filled with frustrating unsolved mysteries—over eighty per cent of the total number of crimes committed remain unsolved. In commercial fiction, on the other hand, every crime is eventually explained, motivated, solved and punished. (Perhaps that's why we still have fiction.)

The only way an amateur author can become a professional is to recognize his readers' suspense hunger and to satisfy it. Too often the amateur ruins all chances of success by overlooking suspense opportunities because he's so eager to tell all incidents and events with naive, truthful enthusiasm. The beginning writer tells all—neither realizing nor exploiting the suspense in little things. The amateur starts out by telling you, for example, exactly why Rufus became a dope addict. The professional writer dramatizes the effects, makes you curious about the causes, then eventually reveals them in an intriguing way.

Again, the amateur usually tends to tell all right away, while the professional uses the same information to play games: He starts to give the reader a fact, then interrupts it or pauses in a dramatic way before completing the information. The professional is a holder-outer, but never a cheater or deceiver. The amateur might tell you: "Karen and Tom wanted a baby, and when they couldn't have one of their own they tried to adopt an infant. When they couldn't get a new baby they agreed to take five-year-old Ricky. At first there were awkward incidents and feelings and it looked as if they weren't going to get along together; but finally they worked it out and all liked each other."

How would the pro handle the same story materials? He would use suspense-pauses to make the reader think, wonder, and guess what would happen next. In planning your story, you can express these suspense pauses in questions—either implied or stated somewhat like this: What was the one thing that kept the marriage of Karen and Tom from being idyllically happy? Only after a teasing pause for considering several possible answers does the professional let us know that their happiness was marred by their inability to have a baby. Why won't they adopt one? . . . Same process. Will Tom be able to persuade Karen to adopt? Yes. Can they get a baby? No. Why not? What should they do? Can the social worker convince them they should apply for an older child? Yes. Do they get one?

Yes. Do they like him? Does he like them? What seems to be the trouble? How do they remedy it?

In working out your story before writing it, plan the questions as if they were interesting hurdles that the story will leap over or alluring mountain peaks to scale for a better view. If you prefer, consider your story an out-rigger canoe-ride: the suspense pauses are the waves that add thrills to the ride and move your story to a definite destination.

An amateur often fails because he omits chances for suspense even in major dramas by telling us right away who killed Cock Robin and why and how he was caught. The professional, on the other hand, builds tiny, humdrum incidents into high drama merely by using suspense.

Here are some of the opportunities you have for adding the mystery factor that feeds the suspense interest of your reader:

1) By creating a character whose traits make the reader wonder what's going to happen next. After you know Auntie Mame, you're sure she'll get into scrape after scrape and you wonder how she'll get out of them. In our age of gold-bricking, there's suspense in an overly-conscientious draftsman who works harder than anyone else in his engineering office, without vacations or other privileges. When the reason comes, it must be convincing (for instance, the overly-conscientious draftsman has an inferiority complex because he's the only man in the office without a college education. He tries to substitute dependability for a diploma, but only succeeds in becoming a doormat).

2) By opening with a situation that features a mystery factor and makes us want to read on to know more and

answer the questions implied in the beginning. Often this opening mystery situation combines with characterization. Example: Why did the painfully honest anthropologist suddenly develop kleptomania and why were his colleagues delighted? Why did the apparently devoted bridegroom desert his lovely bride on their wedding night? What made the man who had never lost his temper angry enough to kill? Why was the couple offered $2500 a month rent for their mediocre home on condition that they ask no questions and never see the mysterious tenant? Why does the insignificant little private volunteer for a suicide mission that braver men tremble at? Why does the girl run away from the man she loves, and after he finds her, why does she reject him and never see him again? Why does the screen star refuse the success he has worked all his life to obtain? Why? What? Who? Where? When?

3) By continuing all-over suspense throughout the story and creating as many cliff-hangers (or "What'll happen next?") as possible. Daphne du Maurier is excellent at this in all her stories. In *Scapegoat* the tantalizing question continues throughout: Why does the rich man want his double to live his life so completely? Finally, when we learn the reason—that he needs a substitute fall-guy to take the blame when he murders his wife—we are left with another question mark at the end: which of the two men survives the showdown shooting?

Of course every whodunit is packed with suspense: Who committed the crime? Why? How and when and where will he be caught? There's even more suspense if we don't know whether a person was murdered or not. Clever authors keep readers guessing by pointing clues in the directions opposite to the truth. *Rebecca* is rife with suspense-questions. Was the first wife so wonderful? How did she die? If she was murdered, did the husband really kill her? Did the husband love Rebecca so much that he'll never be able to love his second wife completely? What does the housekeeper's hostility have to do with the whole thing? And many more. Throughout a story, in the beginning, middle, and end, hold your reader's interest with implied questions: Will the protagonist achieve the love or approbation he craves? Will the chased victim escape? Will a person survive a medical crisis or a war? Why did the man hold-up the bank for ten dollars? (He wanted to be arrested and go to jail to receive medical attention he couldn't afford.) Why did the man try to be seen stealing military secrets to give the enemy? (To attract newspaper publicity, prove his innocence—then sue the paper.)

4) By using intriguing words and the principle of "suppression," that is, you, the writer, know what's going to happen, but instead of telling the reader right away, you deliberately tease him with mysterious words. For instance: "at that moment there occurred the grimmest episode of the day"; "then I learned something I'd rather never have to know"; "when I woke up that Tuesday I didn't know that would be the most exciting day in my whole life"; "then he saw something he'd never forget"; "the news they brought was the reverse of what she expected"; "it kept happening again and again and he knew he couldn't stand it."

5) By setting up *roadblocks*. This merely means that as the hero rushes toward a certain goal, he is detained by unexpected events and characters which sometimes hinder,

often help him (perhaps by making him miss the plane that crashed or by introducing him to a character who later helps him solve his problem, etc.). In Leon Ware's *Post* story, "The Friendly American," Harry Evans takes his "Goodwill Ambassador" letter from the President seriously and tries to be helpful to everyone he meets in England, to the chagrin of his rather impatient, snobbish family. His trip to the pub, his stopping to help two ladies with car trouble, his befriending a swarthy stranger he meets at Westminster Abbey—cause conflict with his wife, but later pay dividends by giving the Evans family entree into higher society which they would not have had without the road blocks.

Use every opportunity to create a feeling of suspense, a sense of anticipation that holds the reader's interest until the mystery is explained. The secret of suspense is one of the secrets of writing success. So live up to the dictionary definition of "suspend": "to hold fixed in wonder, contemplation . . . to hold in an undetermined state, awaiting fuller information." And make that information worth waiting for!

XXI YOU NEED FLASHBACKS!

FLASHBACKS USED TO BE CONSIDERED necessary evils, but now they can be necessary attractions if you use the cliff-hanger technique to intrigue reader interest with the present action and promise the reader continuing drama following close on the heels of the interruption. For instance, the hero's child has fallen into the well and while he's trying to get him out, he remembers . . . Or the hero is horseback riding to save his brother from hanging or he is riding to the Governor with evidence for a pardon.

In Hamilton Basso's novel, *The Light Infantry Ball,* John Bottomley is on his way to duel villain Ules Monckton when he flashes back to the motivations for their conflict. In this case, extended flashbacks build up characterizations, themes, and tensions so that the reader is engrossed with the pre-story happenings while looking forward to the life-and-death excitement of the duel that is to come.

Jo Sinclair's novel, *Anna Teller,* begins in 1956 with the flight passengers of a plane flying from Munich to New York curious about an old woman who had been one of

the Hungarian freedom fighters and was now going to
make her home in America. The entire book consists of
flashbacks of Anna's past life, and what is more natural
than reminiscing on a long flight when the mind is lulled
by the droning of engines and the monotonous rhythm of
flying.

The first two rules concerning flashbacks, then, are 1)
introduce present action that promises future excitement
before lapsing into the past, and 2) make your flashback
natural, occurring when the character really has time to
think. For instance:

> In the plane, Anna floated with memories of the long-ago
> dead in her life, trying to give them back their meaning. It
> was easier here, in the mists between worlds. No streets, no
> soon-greening fields, no shape of river.

In a short story flashbacks are fewer and briefer than in
a novel, in keeping with the definition: *The flashback is a
short interruption in the sequence of the plot to introduce
events prior to those last presented.*

Make any flashback rewarding to the reader, who is
primarily interested in the sustained excitement of a story
moving quickly from its problem to the resolution. A yarn
that "lives in the past" is as much of a bore as people who
do!

If the past scenes and incidents are more dramatically
significant than what happens later, perhaps you started the
story too late and you should have revealed the past action
as if it were occurring *now,* making sure that the living
story has immediacy, identification, and the happening-
now flavor that makes the story real. Avoid unnecessary
flashbacks; never use a flashback-within-a-flashback. Always

ask: "Is this flashback necessary?" "Will it slow down story action?" "How can I use the best flashback method to keep the story palpitatingly alive?"

Keep in mind the fact that many editors frown on flashbacks as deadweights and torpid tranquilizers especially in short stories. But they can add suspense, if handled correctly. In fact, flashbacks are necessary, since you cannot write a well-rounded story with the entire spotlight on the present only. Somehow and somewhere you must bring in antecedent material which contains motivation, character-foundation, and full explanation for what happens later.

Before beginning to write a yarn, work out pre-story character sketches and pre-story happenings. Then select for the actual opening a strong moment of decision or crisis or question—one that poses a mystery. Only if your reader is intrigued by this mystery and interested in the persons involved will he stay with you, so you should *suppress* vital, pre-story activities until you reach satisfactory places for revelation or discovery by the hero, as a never-fail method of insuring suspense. The best story is the one that keeps the reader guessing and then satisfies his stimulated curiosity at the end.

Whodunits are the most obvious examples. In these, you start with a crime already committed, with the subsequent story action and hero-efforts dedicated to solving the crime by unravelling the motivating factors and important facts *that have happened before.* Often there are various levels of antecedent material with a reverse revelation of information of the near-past coming to light before those of the longer-ago past.

Let's look at George Sumner Albee's *Post* story, "Desert Death." State trooper Matt Wheelock and villain Sheriff

Hoffner find a dead blonde on an abandoned desert road, her husband collapsed in an expensive car one-and-one-half miles away. Even though she was obviously killed by a rattlesnake, the sheriff (for political reasons) wants to convict the husband, Bullock, of murder; and the grief-stricken husband is ready to confess, since he feels that his quarreling with his wife did cause her death. Matt doesn't feel that Bullock is guilty and he delves deeply into the case to prove his innocence. Since the present story tops a series of past events, naturally flashback methods will have to be used to dig up the past and to clarify and solve the present problem, as in most whodunits.

Through questioning, research, and putting two and two together, Matt solves the mystery. Here is an excerpt of his questioning Bullock about the details of the day leading up to the tragedy:

> "That's right . . . And I had another reason. With Lynn dead it doesn't seem important. It has no connection with this ghastly thing that's happened, so I don't think it would interest you."
>
> "It might."
>
> Bullock shrugged dispiritedly. "I'm interested in juvenile delinquents," he said. "For a good reason: I was one myself when I was in my teens. Two weeks one summer at a charity camp—just two weeks!—cured me. I've had the idea, ever since Lynn first mentioned coming out here, I might buy a ranch and turn it into a reclamation center for tough kids from city slums. Those that wanted to stay out west I could give jobs in my plant . . .
>
> ". . . Saturday, Lynn showed me around town. On Sunday morning she said she wanted me to see the desert. I thought we were just going for a ride, but we drove all day —here, there, I don't remember the names of the towns. Along toward evening we passed through this place on our

way back to Fort Vernon. Lynn said it would be an experience to watch the sunset from the open desert. I was a
bit tired—we'd had a picnic lunch at noon, but Lynn forgot
the vacuum jug and we hadn't stopped since lunchtime—but
we turned off on a side road. We drove in toward the mountains, climbing, and parked. I was feeling a little dizzy by
then—just thirsty, I guess, or else too much sun. I told Lynn
I thought we ought to go back but she kept saying, 'Just five
minutes more.' Then I must have fainted."

"It was more than a faint," said Matt. "The doctor says
they worked on you half the night at the hospital. They were
afraid you were gone. Do you have a chronic ailment of some
kind—diabetes, or anything like that?"

"No."

"You couldn't accidentally have taken an overdose of
medication of any kind?"

"Once or twice a week I take a pill to trim down my
weight, but that's all."

There are other details, but this is enough to reinforce
Matt's faith in Bullock's innocence and to cause him to
question the townspeople about Mrs. Bullock. This requires more necessary flashback material which is also
expressed in dialogue since our hero must learn the past
facts from others. He learns that she was a conniving cheat
who at the time of her death was planning to leave her husband for another man. Matt keeps putting together the
separate sets of pre-story facts: the actions of the fatal day
plus Lynn's urging Bullock to take reducing pills plus her
preventing him from drinking any liquids in the hot
desert.

"Mr. Bullock," said Matt, "it was Mrs. Bullock who
wanted you to come west, you say, and it was her idea to go
sight-seeing last Sunday. She didn't take along your vacuum
jug. You were thirsty—didn't you stop anywhere for a
drink?"

"Lynn went into a roadside stand, yes, and asked for water. She came out making a face. She said the water was alkali, wasn't fit to drink."

"Didn't you try anywhere else?"

"We went into another place, yes, and tried to buy beer or soda. They didn't have any."

"That time, too, it was Mrs. Bullock who went in and asked. She had you wait in the car?"

"Yes, I was tired."

"It was your wife who insisted you drive with the top down?"

"On account of the scenery."

"And it was Mrs. Bullock who suggested turning up the mine road? Is that right?"

"Only one more question. It was Mrs. Bullock, sir, who told you she thought you were overweight, several months ago, and got you a prescription for diuretic tablets? Dry-out pills, boxers and jockeys call them. . . ."

Later he explains:

"Last winter, we had a tragedy out this way. A family of four—father, mother and two kids—were driving on a back road down by the border. They had a blowout. They weren't carrying a spare, so they waited in their car for help. A trooper found them that night, hands folded on their laps, smiles on their faces, dead of dehydration. It doesn't happen much any more because we've licked the desert with drilled wells, but ask the old-timers about dehydration. There's no warning. You just drowse off. The item about the family was in the papers last February. Your wife read it, I think, Mr. Bullock. That's when she laid out her plan— located the abandoned road, decided to nag you into coming out, even thought of starting you taking dry-out pills just to make sure."

The news item from the far past (which the author saved until last) *inspired* Lynn's plot to kill her husband—

a plot that boomeranged, thanks to Matt's ability *to use the past to solve the present crisis.*

This is the ideal structure for all fiction, short and long. Even non-whodunits intrigue readers with a mystery opening, then delve into the past to explain or solve it. Peg Bracken's *Post* story, "What Husbands Don't Know" opens with, "Sometimes you have to lose your figure to find your husband." Soon we have a comic reverse situation: Wife Marj Bidwell tries to gain weight by overeating and succeeds. She sums up the whole flashback idea of the present resting on the past when she says: "I say that's when I started to lose my figure. But, of course beginnings are never that simple. They go way back. Trace the cause of anything and presently you're face to face with Eve."

Marj's motive is jealousy of beautiful but fat Mavis O'Toole, to whom her husband is paying too much attention, in line with his job as advertising man for Venus Triumphant Figure and Charm Salon. There are further-back flashbacks of Marj's beauty-queen figure before she married Andy. But the flashbacks—near and far—are used as scantily as spices and never bog down the here-and-now story of Marj eating on twenty-seven pounds to win her husband's total attention; then abandoning the whole project by patronizing Venus Triumphant and helping his advancement in business.

Flashbacks must never overshadow forward-moving events even though contemporary action does have seeds in previous happenings and every interesting character is the sum total of past experiences. No one is born full-grown at the time of the story like Aphrodite, Eve, or Galatea. The secret of integrating and presenting all pertinent material is to plan the chronology of your story carefully. Start at a high point—the protagonist's dramatic date with destiny. A suspense-filled moment that challenges with a problem, decision, or conflict. When you find it necessary to introduce prior-to-the-story incidents or information:

1) Plan to do it briskly, briefly, interestingly.
2) Be sure to use smoothly flowing transitions between the present and past.
3) Use a variety of methods of presenting flashback material. You do not always need to reënact the whole scene from the past.

Flashback Techniques

1) *Narrative statement of past events.* Merely tell what has happened long ago, but don't ramble on and on. Keep the writing vivid even if nostalgic. For example:

> George Crowder had been an important man. He had been a successful lawyer and State's Attorney; and he was headed for the Governor's Mansion, many people said. But in his capacity as public prosecutor, George Crowder had, inadvertently, sent an innocent man to the electric chair . . .
> ("Murder Throws a Curve," by John Harris)

This information is necessary to explain why a sympathetic character, Uncle George, has become a recluse and a drinker, although his young nephew can depend on him to emerge from his hermit's solitude to help solve a murder.

2) *Dialogue* is the shortcut means of telling what happened before. (Here you must be careful to be natural and not have characters tell others what they already know.)

In Hugh B. Cave's excellent *Post* yarn, "The Mission," the opening mystery is *why* is the six-year-old Haitian girl, Yolande, walking seventy-five miles to the capital without food or money? See how briefly and simply dialogue gives the flashback-motivation and knits together the past, present, and future, as she explains:

> "I have to. My Papa lives there and I have to find him. Maman died yesterday."
>
> "Oh, oh. Where do you live?"
>
> "Nowhere now. I did live in Aquin. Maman kept house for some people there."

3) *Comparison of past with present,* in which the two are smoothly blended:

> Then he saw that Matilda Bollin Binghan's face had assumed a calm, a detachment, a dignity. The twisted strain seemed to have gone out of it, it was smooth as evening water, and he thought, with a strange, fleeting twinge of the heart, that her face would look this way when she was dead . . . Then he knew, viewing the face in that instant of calm and dignity . . . that what he was looking at was the face of Matilda Bollin when she was a girl, a sickly girl who had quoted poetry to him and held hands with him in the leafy side streets of the West End section of Nashville . . . Looking at her now, he felt time flee away from him, and for one split second he thought that they might now take hands again. . . . (*The Cave,* by Robert Penn Warren)

4) *Reverie.* Deep in viewpoint, the character remembers . . .

> Arthur reflected that he had first noticed Clarissa when, hardly more than a child, she had begun to make herself a name by her remarkable tennis playing.
>
> (*By Love Possessed,* by James Gould Cozzens)

5) *Reminiscence* is reverie spoken aloud to someone else, although it often turns out to be more like monologue than back-and-forth dialogue.

> . . . The man raised his forefinger and there was something about him that held the boy and would not let him go away.
> "Twelve years ago I married the woman in the photograph. She was my wife for one year, nine months, three days, and two nights. I loved her. Yes . . . I was a railroad engineer. She had all home comforts and luxuries. It never crept into my brain that she was not satisfied. But do you know what happened?"
> ("A Tree, A Rock, A Cloud," by Carson McCullers)

6) *Self-Analysis,* insofar as it reevaluates something the character has done or thought or been in the past. Although having a person look in the mirror is a verboten cliché, it is used effectively by Agatha Christie in *Appointment with Death:*

> Instead of writing letters, Sarah sat down in front of her dressing-table, combed the hair back from her forehead, looked into a pair of troubled hazel eyes in the glass, and took stock of her situation in life.
> She had just passed through a difficult emotional crisis. A month ago she had broken off her engagement to a young doctor some four years her senior. They had been very much attracted to each other, but had been too much alike in temperament.

7) *Objects used as symbols to bring back the past.* You can use snapshots, toys, jewelry, keepsakes, old clippings, theater programs, heirlooms—anything that triggers memories and makes a person or incident of the past important to the present or the future. Like the dolls in *Raintree County* or the watch in *Of Time and the River.*

8) *Letters and diaries* are used to bring in flashback information like Wally Wronken's diary in *Marjorie Morningstar*. The diary often incriminates its writer, as in Samuel Elkins' short story, "Survival of the Fittest." Here two wealthy sisters are suspected of killing handsome Paul Sheparton, and his diary explains his nefarious plan to cause one of them to kill the other, so that he would get their wealth. Here is a sample:

> . . . No matter which one is killed, I'll marry the other —even in jail as she is being tried for murder. And if convicted—fine. If not, then—well, one way or another, sooner or later, I shall come into the Brampton fortune. A perfect plan. And only a unique person could accomplish it—a man without a foolish conscience, a survivor of the fittest.

9) *Repeating the whole scene.* For instance, in Peter Ustinov's *Atlantic Monthly* story, "The Loneliness of Billiwoonga," George, a former prisoner in a Nazi concentration camp, is starting a new life in Australia. His best friend and business partner is Bill Schoemaker who, when questioned about the war, says he was a medical orderly. But in a scene where Bill loses his temper and shouts furiously, "A great vein, like a tree, rose and throbbed on his temple." This recalls to George a horrible scene from his own past:

> George had never heard Bill speak German before, let alone shout it. Medical orderly? He saw a room full of naked people, men and women, some of transparent thinness, others bloated by hunger, and he smelled the odor of decomposition. The voice carried him back into the half-light, the white coats of doctors, the parchment yellow of the naked flesh, the glint of glasses, the routine of the night-

mare. Stout Dr. Tichte, loading his hypodermic dispassion-
ately, swabbing with cotton wool, holding out his pudgy
hands for implements. "Cough. Cough. Breathe. Deeper.
Take him away. Unusable." A quiet, rational voice. And
behind him, in brown, under a brown cap, shouting hysterically, a great vein, like a tree, throbbing on his temple,
another man. *"Still stehen! Schweine! Schweine!"*

Whichever flashback method you use, consider the
meaning of the word "flashback" . . . "A brilliant outburst; to break into one's mind; to light up; to send out
speedily . . ." Minimize the "back" and stress the "flash."

XXII | TITLE APPEAL

A GOOD TITLE will not sell a bad script, but the assumption is that an author clever enough to write a humdinger of a title is probably clever enough to write a humdinger of a story. The title is your first attention-getter, and you know how important first impressions are! Do not make the mistake of slapping a quick title onto a script that you have spent time and energy on. Learn the craft of title-making as you learn the other ingredients of writing technique. You need every advantage and a good title gives a definite editorial advantage, whereas a bad title is a distinct disadvantage.

A good title is original. It has definite eye-appeal, even if it stands alone. It sets the mood of the story, arouses curiosity, has color and excitement, clarifies the story action to come, establishes the emotional tone of humor or tragedy fairly and unmistakably. James L. Hanyen put it this way: "A good title is a little like a good strip tease act. It's honest, but not candid. It's provocative but not revealing. It has a come-hither look." In other words, it gives a clue to the plot without revealing too much.

A good title is appropriate. That is, its style fits the subject matter. Just as *Flower Drum Song, Teahouse of the August Moon,* and *Inn of the Sixth Happiness* suggest poetic Oriental works, *Battle Cry, Beachhead, Attack, Paratrooper* and *Up Periscope* promise war action. A good title is slanted to a definite market and a specific reader, just as magazine titles hint at their content: *Boys' Life, American Girl, Humpty-Dumpty, Wee Wisdom, Mademoiselle, Ingenue, Playboy, Esquire, Mr., Sir, Good Housekeeping, Democratic Digest, Wisdom, Scientific American, Life, Newsweek, American Heritage, Charm, Vogue, True Detective, American Scholar, Outdoor Life, Skindiver* and *Boats.*

A bad title falls into one of several categories:

1) too stale, corny, or archaic ("Maiden's Prayer," "Roses Are Red," "All that Glitters Is Not Gold," "To Be or Not To Be")

2) tells too little ("Anytime," "At Last," "The Man")

3) tells too much and telescopes the climax, giving away story action and eliminating suspense ("Larry Lands the Job," "Sue Rockets to the Moon," or "A Little Child Shall Lead Them")

4) is profane or controversial

5) misleads by giving the wrong impression (A tragic title for a hilarious yarn or vice versa). *View From Pompey's Head* suggested to many readers a giant excavated Roman statue instead of the prejudice problems of a southern small town. *The Country Girl* mistakenly sounds as innocent as *Alice in Wonderland* or *Rebecca of Sunnybrook Farm.* Misleading titles have led to a parlor game of categorizing titles by what they suggest with ludicrous results. For instance, Adams' *Tenderloin* under "Cooking"

and the *Quiet American* under "Mythology." There was truth in the cartoon showing the little monk returning *From Here to Eternity* to the library, saying "This isn't what I thought it would be."

Some of these bad features are the reasons why original titles are often changed. Let's look at a few and analyze possible causes for the switch. *The Constant Wife* was a play that opened in Europe, drew no crowds, and soon folded. Later it was released with a new title, *Do You Think Constance Was a Loyal Wife?* and immediately became a sensational hit. The first title is dull and drab. The second contains suspense, the intriguing element of doubt, and a question pointed straight at the audience, giving it a chance to guess and participate.

Motion picture producers often change titles and for obviously good reasons. The title *The Long, Hot Summer* has more pull suggested by barometric tension than William Faulkner's *Barn Burner* and *The Hamlet,* on which the story was based. The latter might mislead by promising a British locale or a Shakespearean character. Faulkner's novel *Pylon* was changed to *Tarnished Angels,* probably because *Pylon* is too technical, specific, non-human and intellectual and not too many movie-goers know that a pylon today is an aviation field flight post or marker, while in ancient Greece and Egypt it was used to mark the entrance to pyramids. But most imaginations are intrigued by the incongruity and sin-promising of *Tarnished Angels.* Perhaps spiciness is the reason for the movie title *The Mating Game* instead of the old-fashioned-sounding play title, *The Darling Buds of May.* On the other hand, censorship often necessitates a title change as the switch from the novel title *Magnificent Bastards* to the alliterative

The Proud and the Profane. Alliteration is so attractive that Grace Metalious' publishers changed her title *The Tree and the Blossom* to *Peyton Place* utilizing easy-to-pronounce, easy-to-remember word-sounds.

Try to think of other title-changes and ask yourself why they were made. Was Dreiser's *An American Tragedy* changed to *A Place in the Sun* because the former sounds epic, national, or political with insufficient human interest? Was *Outward Bound* changed to *Between Two Worlds* because the latter sounds more spacelike and modern and also suggests conflict and a dramatic predicament?

Study current title trends like the following categories which dominate today's market:

1) NEGATIVE TITLES: Strangely enough, these are prevalent. Perhaps the old melodramatic song: "No, no, a thousand times no" started something! Arthur Miller was asked to change the *Death of a Salesman,* but he refused, perhaps realizing the drawing-appeal of the negative. (Is it a reversal of the saccharine *Power of Positive Thinking* philosophy?) And how many people would be attracted by *The Life of a Salesman* or *Life in the Afternoon* instead of *Death in the Afternoon? The Day Christ Died* is somehow more dramatic than *The Day Christ Was Born.*

2) SHOCKERS: *Honeymoons are Hell, Stop Hanging the Insane, How Doctors Gyp You, How to Make a Monster, Child Monarchy in America.*

3) BOOBCATCHERS: *Babies by Appointment, The Head I Almost Lost, The Banana Was Pink, God Is Good to a Jew, I Died Twice.*

4) QUESTIONS: *Is Your Husband Becoming a Bachelor?, Why Babies?, Are Californians Crazy?, Has Inflation Become a Way of Life?, Can This Marriage Be Saved?, Where*

Do We Stand?, Where Did My Money Go?, How Should We Pray?, Who Knocks?, Can Men Be Such Fools?, Are Women Sheep—or Are Men?

5) SYMBOLS: *The Hanging Tree, A Doll's House, The Sugar Pill, Glass Menagerie, Fountainhead, The Window, The Amethyst Cat.*

6) CONVERSATIONAL TITLES: *"I Rise in Flame," Cried the Phoenix; Where Did You Go? Out. What Did You Do? Nothing; Please Don't Eat the Daisies; Walk Softly, Stranger; Goodbye, My Love; Don't Just Stand There!*

7) ALLITERATIVE TITLES: *Sad Sack, Winthrop Woman, Sheltering Sky, Perils of Promiscuity, The Galloping Grandpa, A Domestic Drama, Lust for Life, Dumb Dog, Miss Under the Mistletoe, Wind in the Willows, Secret Snow.*

8) MYSTERY TITLES: *What Every Woman Knows, What Men Won't Tell, The Land Where Time Stands Still, Behind Locked Doors, How Doctors Use Hypnotism, The Truth About Love.*

9) PUN TITLES: *No Place Like Rome, Once Upon a Dime, A Bed of Neuroses, Under the Spreading Atrophy, Girl Boys Ship, The Awful Sleuth, Yukon Have It, Icicle Built for Two, Heir Restorer, Televicious Circle.*

10) PARADOX TITLES: *Sweet Smell of Success, The Good Thief, Roots of Heaven, Crash of Silence, Beloved Infidel, Friendly Persuasion, A Majority of One, Kiss Me Deadly, I See With My Ears, The Happy Cardiac, Blue-Eyed Grass, Fatherhood Without Fear, Young Man of 90, White Mother to Negro Twins, Angels in Bobbysox.*

11) KEYWORD TITLES: *Exodus, Sapphire, Psycho, Warlock, Vertigo, Compulsion, Dollmaker, Tempest, Underwater, The Scientist, Giant, Ransom, Nightfall, Rain-*

maker, Joyride, Hitchhiker, Stagefright, Wetback, Jilted, Kismet, Sinners, Bullwhip, Reprisal, Skeleton, Carousel.

12) SITUATION TITLES: *The Man Who Stole the Jet, Storm Center, Crash Landing, The Man With My Face, The Girl Upstairs, The Man Who Came to Dinner, Yourself When Young, Duel With the Witch Doctor, Pig in a Barbershop.*

13) PREMISE TITLES: *My Brother's Keeper, You Can't Take It With You, Paths of Glory, You Are Not Alone, Where There's a Will, People Are Here to Stay, Good Cooks Start Early, He Profits Most Who Serves Best, It's Later Than You Think, No Easy Way, Children Are Bored on Sunday.*

14) SUPERLATIVE TITLES: *This Is My Best, Toughest Man Alive, Greatest Story Ever Told, My Most Unforgettable Character, The Best Advice I Ever Had, France's Greatest Scandal.*

Also popular are Atmosphere, and How, What, When and Why titles which must have more of an element of intrigue than was necessary in the past. Always study contemporary title trends and give each script a moniker that can compete favorably with the best in the field.

TITLE DON'TS

1) Don't imitate or plagiarize a title that has already been used. It's impossible to check *every* published title, but you can check book titles in card catalogues in the library; article titles in *Reader's Guide to Periodical Literature.* Even though authors cannot copyright their titles, you may get into legal trouble, and you'll cloud your own reputation by being a copycat in *any* way.

2) Don't give away any plot surprises in your title.

3) Don't use profanity.

4) Don't use parodies of popular song titles, gags, or expressions. They become dated and stale too soon.

5) Don't feature a minor detail while ignoring the main situation, theme, character, or subject matter.

6) Don't be too cute or forced.

7) Don't be too erudite, mysterious, exhibitionistic (*The Peregrinating Prestidigitator*) or ambiguous or abstract (*Ever Thus To Be*).

8) Don't feature foreign, unfamiliar, or unpronounceable words.

9) Don't use archaic quotation titles for a modern story.

10) Don't forget to *slant* your title for the proper magazine, giving the specific readers what they want. Intellectual magazines like *Scientific American* like titles on the order of "Nuclear Fuel Reactors," "Angiotensin," "Barriers in the Brain," "The Absorption of Radio Waves in Space," "Ballistocardiography," "Isotope Economics," "Agammaglobulinemia." *True* likes hairy-chested titles: "Who the Hell Is Hemingway?," "The Case of the Compulsive Killers," "The World's Greatest Matador," "A Gun for Your Son?," "Make My Coffee Strong" (implying a virility that shuns all weakness, even in coffee). The confession magazines like personal revelations titles: "I Couldn't Say No," "Love Starved," "Trapped In Another Man's Arms," "I Distrusted My Daughter."

In *The Inn of the Sixth Happiness,* when the two English lady missionaries wanted to spread the gospel in northern China, they did not hire a hall and put up a sign:

"Come in and be saved." That would have accomplished nothing. Instead, they opened a cozy inn to attract weary mule-drivers, who were the circulating newspapers of the area. They called it "The Inn of the Sixth Happiness" because every Chinese knows that the five happinesses are wealth, health, longevity, virtue, and a happy death. Everyone would be curious to learn what the sixth happiness is, and thus lured in by mystery and curiosity, they would be fed Bible stories with their food—and eventually converted. Of course it worked. So will your title if it satisfies that curiosity. (In the case of *The Inn of the Sixth Happiness,* the sixth joy is the one each person must find for himself: love, work, religion, etc., depending on the individual.)

Try to choose a title that arouses curiosity, lures the reader into the script to find the answer to the question implied in the head. Grinoff's exposé of a Soviet Babbitt, *Tale of the Whistling Shrimp,* takes its title from a 1955 speech of Khrushchev: "We will abandon Communism when the shrimp learns to whistle." In the story, one character says: "They whistle all the time, but only for each other."

"The Surest Thing in Show Business" (Jesse Hill Ford's *Atlantic* "First") adds superlative to the curiosity appeal and you must read on to learn that the surest thing is not love, sex, human tragedy, or humor, but snakes. Why? Because, says the hero:

". . . there ain't a single living American that ain't had a great-granddaddy or a stepuncle or some connection like who was swallered whole by a rattler. Understand, they never *knew* him, but Granny told them about it, which makes the rattlesnake the surest moneymaker in American show business. They will pay to see what swallered Grand-daddy every time."

T. S. Matthews explains his non-fiction book title *No Sugar Pill* in these words: ". . . the press is not our daily bread, but our daily sugar pill. I should be the first to admit that the pill is habit-forming. Whether it is also harmless is another question."

There are thousands of other curiosity-pricking titles that act as barkers to lure the reader into the showman's tent, where his curiosity is satisfied. Study them and start building your own file of intriguing titles. Always remember, your title is your script's good-will ambassador!

Whitworth College Library
Spokane, Washington

XXIII | STYLE

EVERY SUCCESSFUL WRITER has an inimitable *style* that distinguishes his work because it projects his own personality, philosophy and ability into his writing. Clever plots, characters, backgrounds and gimmicks will not make you a professional unless you express them in a distinctive style, which has been defined as the author's individuality, trademark, flair, signature, hallmark, personal viewpoint and creative expression. Your style becomes the essence of the real you, the sum total of your outlook on life, your character, your conscious and subconscious thoughts—your personality on paper.

You cannot think of an important writer without being aware of his style which is in a sense his label: Hemingway —concise, brittle, terse, direct, clear, striving for honesty and eliminating deception and ostentation; Thomas Wolfe —rolling, rhythmic, rhetorical, poetic prose, with unrestrained, ecstatic sensory appeals that kindle nostalgia; Michener—rapturous, descriptive narrative of colorful people and places electrified with his own enthusiasm; Tennessee Williams—psychoanalytical probing into the lowest neuroses and vulgarisms of degenerate characters.

As vital to literature as it is in the fashion world, style can be the main springboard to writing success. Since individuality of style differentiates the pro from the amateur, and because some pros claim "it comes naturally," new writers are often deluded into thinking that writing style goes with genius and that you are either born with it or you'll never have it. But this is not true. Even "geniuses" with native talent admit to hard work and conscious study of techniques. They agree with Sean O'Faolain who admits: "When I got down to the business of writing, I found that half the art of writing is rewriting, and I would be happy if I achieved two hundred words of lapidary prose in a day." The "Spontaneous Me" that sparked Whitman's uninhibited poetry cannot be depended on to carry the fiction writer to soaring success. If he writes as an outlet for inner inspiration, his work can be as ridiculous as Billy's composition when his fourth-grade teacher told her class "Do not imitate what other people write. Simply be yourself and write what is in you." Obediently, Billy wrote: "We should write what is in us. In me there is a stomach, heart, liver, two apples, one piece of pie, a lemon drop and my lunch." A style that *seems* spontaneous is the result of infinite study, experience and conscious planning. Before writing your story, plan the style carefully. Ask yourself, "What style should I develop?" And answer it according to:

1) *The emotional mood or reaction you want your reader to feel.* For pathos, you'd choose a serious, perhaps sad, sentimental style. For ridicule, a sardonic, satiric style.

2) *You yourself, your sophistication or naïveté.* This depends upon your intellectual development, education, sense of humor, cynicism, disposition, etc.

3) *The time and place you are writing about.* The style must faithfully reflect the flavor and color of the era and the area. Avoid anachronistic expressions in historical stories and archaic expressions in modern ones.

4) *The subject matter.* Choose terminology and imagery pertinent to the profession or topic at hand. If you are writing of music and musicians, you might flavor the philosophy accordingly. For example:

> If you fall flat in mid-morning like a sour note from a short-winded tuba player, you, like him, are suffering from power loss. You give an off-key performance, have a weak fortissimo, and uneasy breathing in the works. Your power loss can come from too little breakfast or too much.

5) *The nature of the person you are writing about.* Faith Baldwin's "Romance of Penelope James" is written from the viewpoint of Poppet, a cat who directs her mistress' love-affair, and the terminology is appropriately flavored with such sentences as, "She'd always liked Penelope, and now this person belonged to her . . . But it was evident that Penelope needed a guiding paw."

6) *The market slant.* Even pros who have an inimitable style vary it for different markets. Philip Wylie's strongly original style changes according to whether he writes an essay type think-book (*Generation of Vipers*), a science-fiction novel (*The Disappearance*), a stylized idea-novel (*Opus 21*), a whodunit (*Ten Thousand Blunt Instruments*), or light, commercial fishing stories for the *Post*. Paul Gallico's style is factual and virile in his sports stories but sentimentally idealistic in his *The Snow Goose* and *Mrs. 'Arris Goes to Paris.*

After you have decided on the kind of style you want to

achieve, and the market slant, try to professionalize it by following these tips:

I) BALANCE SIMPLICITY WITH ORIGINALITY

All writing must be clear since its purpose is to communicate ideas in a way that they are easily understood. The great best-sellers of all time, from the Bible to the works of Hemingway and Pearl Buck, are epitomes of simplicity, directness and clarity.

If there is any doubt as to the advisability of simplicity try to guess the meaning of the following paragraph:

> Beware of platitudinous ponderosity. Let your communications possess coalescent consistency and concatenated cogency. Eschew all flatulent garrulity and asinine affectations. Use intelligibility and veracious vivacity without rodomontade or thrasonical bombasity. Sedulously avoid all proxility and psittaceous vacuity.

It means, "Be intelligible and brief," but obviously it fails to practice what it preaches because of the overwriting, exhibitionistic words which are Latinized rather than Anglo-Saxon in origin. This should be a lesson in the choice of words!

Simplicity has been emphasized by so many writers, teachers and critics that some novices may get the impression that the secret of writing success is to say what's on your mind in second-grade language. Artless over-simplification can be as dull as pedantic ponderosity. Both omit the writer's individual contribution, the original *creativity* which John Ciardi defines as "the imaginatively gifted recombination of known elements into something new."

An ingenious writer never describes anything the way it has been described before. Try to add sparkle to your style by originating fresh

A. *Similes* and *metaphors*. Examples:

> "Mr. Langer, I'm like a canary—and my mother has one of those, too. She has it and me, and she wants us to sing her tune, because we're all she's got and no one else in the world will do it for her." She seemed to speak from a distance. "We're weak, Mr. Langer, that canary and I. But whenever the cage is open just a little, we fly out. We know it isn't safe, but we'll do it every time." She looked at the restaurant ceiling, away from the agitated and the dozing people. "We'd burn our wings on the sun, Mr. Langer, if we could fly away. I don't know whether it's canary courage or just desperation with wings on."
>
> ("The Storm," by Williams Forrest, *McCall's*)

> Tensions made the seconds crawl like ants over my skin, and it could be relieved by whisky, work or exercise.
>
> (*A Sense of Values*, by Sloan Wilson)

B. *Symbols*. Examples:

> My son, life is a party. The more you enjoy it, the more the other guests will and the more successful it will be. And I should say it was a mighty poor and ungrateful guest who departed gloomily.   (Irvin S. Cobb)

> Each day is like a furrow lying before us; our thoughts, desires, and actions are the seed that each minute we drop into it, without seeming to perceive it. The furrow finished, we commence upon another, then another, and again another; each day presents a fresh one, and so on to the end of life . . . sowing, ever sowing. And all we have sown springs up, grows, and bears fruit, almost unknown to us.
>
> (Charlotte M. Yonge)

C. *Sensory details.* Example:

> I stepped into the narrow front hall, and was assailed by the fragrance peculiar to Bettina's house, a mixture of sandalwood she had brought from the Orient long ago, the lavender she kept in her linen drawers, moth balls, Turkish tobacco, coffee, the perfumes of the many old women who visited her . . .   (*A Sense of Values,* by Sloan Wilson)

D. *Personification.* Example:

> The train creaked and puffed on its way into the wood, hardly able to drag itself along, as if it were an aged forest guard walking in front and leading the passengers, who turned their heads from side to side and observed whatever was to be seen.   (*Doctor Zhivago,* by Boris Pasternak)

E. *Sharp visualization* that creates pictures. Example.

> In the world of curtains of snow, people were moving up the road like ghosts, some with brave energy, some being helped, some stumbling. Car engines were working, but fewer than before. People held flashlights, but the light hit the falling snow and was dim.
>
> ("The Storm," by Williams Forrest)

H) KEEP STUDYING WORDS, THEIR MEANINGS, SOUNDS, CADENCES, USES AND DERIVATIONS

Read dictionaries, thesauruses, word-finding and etymology books and take vocabulary tests to enrich your own word prowess. Robert Frost wrote: "We need prowess in politics, in statesmanship, in production,—even in poetry." Whenever you meet an unfamiliar word in reading, look it up immediately, so you can use it in a logical context. Many words have several meanings and you must know how to use them correctly. Never be satisfied with the words you already know. Your vocabulary is like a bicycle—when it stops moving forward, it'll fall down. Decide right now to have a lifelong love affair with words!

(III) USE FORCEFUL, VIVID VERBS AND NOUNS: FEW ADVERBS AND ADJECTIVES

Remember: "Nouns are bullets; verbs are powder; adjectives are smoke." Try to avoid a preponderance of adverbs and adjectives which are really crutches to prop up weak nouns and verbs. If the latter are independently strong and hard-hitting, they do not need crutches.

(IV) BE BRIEF

Brevity is an important element in successful modern fiction style. Writers advised and practiced brevity long before our Age of Concentration that manifests itself in every phase of life from instant foods and brief bathing suits to book condensations. Chekhov ruled out any details that didn't have plot meaning, in fact a character could take a shower only if he were going to: 1. slip and break his neck, 2. get badly scalded, 3. catch pneumonia, or 4. discover that he had an operatic voice. And back in 1906 Mark Twain wrote:

> An average English word is four letters and a half. By hard, honest labor I've dug all the large words out of my vocabulary and shaved it down till the average is three and a half . . . I never write *metropolis* for seven cents, because I can get the same price for *city*. I never write *policeman,* because I can get the same money for *cop*.

Not only is the pay higher for skillfully compressed writing, but an editor won't read a story that's much longer than anything he publishes. He's like the newspaper boss who told the verbose cub reporter, "Young man, I hate to fire you, but you're lazy. You prefer to *waste words* in order to *save work*. You won't take time to write clearly and concisely."

Your stories will be fired, too, if they are replete with redundancies. Never be satisfied to mail a script until you have pruned, whittled and weeded it out to the best of your ability. Use concentration and focus to avoid dullness and ambiguity.

Don'ts

1) Don't use words that are Clear Only If Known. If you're writing for a technical magazine read by experts, you can use terminology they understand. If you write a Christmas holiday story for a Scottish publication, you can speak of "Hogmanay," "first-footing" and Santa coming down the "lum" (*chimney*). For a non-Scottish readership, you could still use these colorful terms but you'd have to define them. In your search for local color and a rich X-plus factor, strive for clarity and accuracy.

2) Don't use clichés. Many clichés are tempting because they come so easily and are vivid and appropriate. That's why they've been used so often that they're trite and taboo in good writing (unless you use them in dialogue to characterize a corny person). Weed out phrases like "cool as a cucumber," "eats like a horse—or bird," "eager as a beaver," "so quiet you could hear a pin drop," "sober as a judge," "pale as a ghost," "nuttier than a fruit cake," "turn over a new leaf," "slow as molasses," "quick like a rabbit" or "pretty as a picture."

3) Don't use a style that is out of style. Readers dislike timeworn, out-of-date devices like villains hiding in suits of armor, skeletons popping out of closets and phrases like "Excuse me while I seek habiliments suitable to the occasion." One student wrote a contemporary teen-age shipboard romance story with a style that reeked of the 20's. If she had put the whole story in a flashback frame or told it in that era, it would have been flavorful and effective instead of phony and unreal for today's teen-agers.

4) Don't use sloppy language, dangling participles or glaring language boners. Examples: "Running out into the storm, her eyes saw a strange sight." "Lying in bed, the red, neon signs winked their merry messages at her." "She dropped her eyes to the floor." "He seated himself upon his entering." Man to hotel clerk, "Do you have suitable accommodations where I could put up with my wife?"

5) Don't contradict or be inconsistent in physical description (character has green eyes on page 14, blue on page 20) or characterization. *The New Yorker* panned a book for saying "I knew I was being watched by so many people; I was an insect under a microscope. Oh, how I detest publicity" in one place, and soon afterward: "What a thrill to hear oneself mentioned. I love to have my name in the paper."

6. Don't indulge in any confusing statements. If a passage is not understood, it's not the reader's fault, but yours. Every paragraph should be clear to all readers and not be like the muddled theory which the college student said was "as clear as if it had been translated into Hindustani by Gertrude Stein and read aloud by a tobacco auctioneer."

XXIV | REACH FOR A SYMBOL

IN MOST PHASES OF LIVING, a symbol is used as a suggestion of the essence. In fiction, even more than in life, symbolism adds an extra fillip and is a clue to an inner, deeper meaning. You can turn a story from humdrum and superficial to professional quality by using dynamic pertinent symbolism: "the representation of any idea, thing, or person by means of a definite sign, which may or may not be part of or closely related to what is represented; an emblem or sign representing something else through association." For example, an insurance company uses the Rock of Gibraltar to suggest reliability; a motion picture company uses a roaring lion, and another moving picture company prefers to be represented by Liberty holding the torch of truth.

Editors are on the constant look-out for stories with symbolical dimension like that used in William Inge's *The Dark at the Top of the Stairs* which represents the universal fear of the unknown. In childhood, it is the youngster's reluctance to leave the warm, cozy, familiar downstairs for the cold, lonely dark upstairs; in adulthood, it stands for our wary suspicion of anything unknown or unexperienced. John Hersey's novel *A Bell for Adano* shows the human need for a symbol of peacetime and sanity, when the people of the Italian town prefer a replacement for the bell which the Fascists took from the tower of the Mayor's office, to food, clothing and other necessities.

One symbol can have different meanings to various people, and you must think through your symbolism before planning your story and know how and when to bring it in. A bridge may represent the transition between ages, between wealth and poverty, enslavement or freedom. In *Land Without Moses* by Charles Curtis Munz, the oppressed sharecroppers who have no leader think of Habishaw County as the Promised Land. But there is a toll bridge—which is a symbol of the fact that the world's downtrodden people must pay a high price to achieve liberty. *The Bridge over the River Kwai* suggests the superiority of British know-how which transforms defeat into victory, and it also represents Col. Nichol's personal achievements that satisfy his ambition. The three-dimensional meaning of Thornton Wilder's *Bridge of San Luis Rey* appears in the last line: "There is a land of the living and a land of the dead; the bridge is love, the only survival, the only meaning."

There are many other bridge symbols with different meanings, but you should try to select symbols that haven't been used too often or too similarly before. Try to select one that comes naturally from the environment of your story. Effective symbolism must also be:

1) emotional in quality
2) universal enough to apply to the reader's problems

3) subtle, yet unmistakably there

4) graphic, tangible, pictorial and vividly described

5) planted early in the story, then referred to later

6) important in affecting the plot action, usually changing the character's decision and solving a crucial problem.

The protagonist, wrestling with a situation, sees an obvious parallel in the symbol and acts differently because of it. In Robert Edmond Alter's *Storm Gamble*, David Barron's yawl, Wee Winkie, symbolized everything he loved about the Virgin Islands to which he had come to enjoy freedom and to write. When his first book doesn't sell, he considers himself a failure and plans to sell the boat and go back to New York. Before he can sell it to the Tortola fishermen who will rip her open and drop an old donkey engine into her, the boat and the man battle a tropical storm to save a little boy's life. The brave little yawl proudly fights even though, at the end of the storm, she sinks into the sea, almost happy to have been of service. Thus the boat-symbol of independence and adventure becomes the symbol of tenacity, and causes a change in her owner:

> The sea had won; yes, as of course it must sooner or later. But the *Wee Winkie* had also won and had gone to rest where she belonged.
>
> And suddenly in the yawl's victory Barron saw his own. He wasn't going to run for home. He'd stay here, somehow, and write another book—a better one. The *Wee Winkie* had taught him to hang on. It was the only thing to do, the only thing he wanted to do—keep trying until he either went under or made a strike . . .

Anything can be a symbol as long as you follow the above six rules. Take birds: Paul Gallico's "The Snow Goose" represents a staunch spirit in a crippled body. The snow goose, which has been restored to health by the crippled English artist, returns to help him rescue the stranded soldiers at Dunkirk. Poe's raven symbolizes death; Coleridge's albatross—conscience; Shelley's skylark—unrestrained freedom; Maeterlinck's bluebird—happiness which we search for all over and finally find in our own backyard.

Or take trees. Katherine Mansfield's "Pear Tree" is only one of many stories in which a tree represents life after death, as fresh buds burst forth from winter-dead limbs. The ugly aloe in her story, "Prelude" (which was originally titled "The Aloe") represents the refusal to give love. There is detailed description of ". . . its cruel leaves and fleshy stem." The curving leaves seemed to be hiding something; the blind stem cut into the air as if no wind could ever shake it. " 'Does it ever have any flowers?' " the (unloved) little girl asks her mother. And Linda (the mother) replies, " 'Once every hundred years!' "

How different from *Redbook's* "The Climbing Tree," which represents the old, traditional things we all need and which are lacking in a modern too-new tract of land—for instance, trees for children to climb.

A symbol name is often more effective than the character's real name especially for a title, as you can see from the following: Lloyd Douglas' *The Big Fisherman* suggests the physical hugeness of Simon Peter, but there is an additional symbolical meaning since he was called upon to become a fisher of men from the sea of life. Margery Allingham's novel, *Tiger in the Smoke,* refers to a ruthless man in London. The sadistic wife in *The Shrike* is truly like the vicious butcherbird which impales its prey on thorns.

Occasionally the subconscious mind works out symbolic ideas so cleverly that the author claims to be unaware of the deeper meaning until after the story is written. This is true of Nancy Hale's story, "The Empress's Ring," about a little girl who feels inferior to curly-haired Mimi until she is given a gold ring with five turquoises that has once belonged to the beautiful Empress Elisabeth of Austria who used to climb mountains. This precious possession cures her inferiority complex until (loving it so much she wears it everywhere) she loses it playing in the sandpile. She never finds it, even though she looks for it throughout her life, and her middle-aged dreams show her still looking, "scratching and clawing at the sandpile, trying to find my little blue ring." Only after writing the story, did Miss Hale recognize that the ring symbolized connection:

> the closed circuit, of both narcissism and wholeness . . . this ring of connectedness . . . that has been given to the little girl was lost in the sand. It was not destroyed, for it is there somewhere, if the little girl, who becomes a woman still with the same sense of inferiority could only find it again. Now there is no more alienating force than a sense of inferiority. It negates both self and society by placing them in a false relation to each other.

The subconscious cannot be relied upon to work out symbolism, and most authors begin either 1) with an abstract idea and then select a tangible symbol to represent it; or 2) with a specific object which they build up as a symbol.

1) The abstract idea of worry or fear can be expressed

by blackbirds, cranes, ravens, dark thunderclouds; or hope can be symbolized by a bright rainbow after a storm; a budding crocus in the snow; a candle burning bravely in the darkness; a new-born baby. In "The Lying Days," Nadine Gordimer discusses conformity and chooses appropriate symbols for the pseudo-sophisticated party-goers who always flock together:

> Their friends were all people whom I knew; a kind of distillation of the acquaintances I had been meeting over and over again for some time. Like a school of fish these people appeared at Isa Welsh's, at Laurie Humphrey's, disappearing into the confused stream of the city again, and then reappearing, quite unmistakably, known at once by the bond of the species which showed them unlike any other fish and like one another, although they were big fish and little, tame fish and savage, as if they had all worn a pale stripe around the tail or a special kind of dorsal fin. Now I was permitted to see what went on when they had whisked out of sight round the deep shelter of a dark rock; in this home water they swam more slowly and clustered, two or three, in a favorite shade.

2) It may be easier for you to start with specifics and work through to abstract meanings. Take that vase in your living room. To you it may symbolize the person who gave it to you, the country it came from. In one story and TV play the vase represented perfection to the perfectionist wife who abhorred weakness of any sort. When her husband's health broke he thought she'd stop loving him, but he was reassured when the vase suffered a simultaneous crack, and, instead of throwing it away, the wife mended it and moved it so that the imperfection would never show.

For a different treatment of the vase symbolism, see Adela Rogers St. Johns' "The Story Without an End."

Here a vase is the symbol of widowed Bitsy's devotion to her late husband, Peter. Desperate, even suicidal in her grief, Bitsy disbelieves in the Hereafter, because if Peter were anywhere he would let her know, and he hasn't. However, she keeps a fresh flower in Peter's vase as constant proof of her love until she has no cash to buy one, having loaned all her money to Noreen for a new dress (to lure a proposal).

When Bitsy apologizes to the empty vase she receives contact from Peter for the first time! His voice assures her that her constant mourning and tribute to the dead kept his memory from being alive . . . that, as soon as she put life first and helped the *living*, she enabled him to come through to her. By the time the story comes to the last word (no love story *ever* ends, says Miss St. Johns), Bitsy has smashed the vase—symbol of her tribute to her *dead* husband—and has decided to follow his advice and honor his memory by living, loving, and comforting.

A colorful bit of symbolism which you hear or read about can be the starting point of an entire plot. Let's take a trip from Symbol-to-Story as we guess how Bruce Marshall probably wrote his *Cosmopolitan* story, "The White Carnation":

Symbol: The Noranian funeral custom of throwing a white carnation into the grave of the deceased in order to give him or her your virtues to help him through the Judgment Day test.

Hero: An Englishman who is ignorant of this custom. To make him important enough to be an honorary pallbearer at an important Noranian funeral, the author makes him a member of the British Foreign Office, also a famous writer who is invited to be a pallbearer at the funeral of the great Noranian writer, Dysnia Postockyn.

Plot Complications Developing from Symbolism: Selected to represent England at the great writer's funeral, the hero and other pallbearers are given white carnations. He assumes they are to be worn. Later when the other pallbearers from other leading nations throw their carnations into the grave, he is taken offguard, hastily tries to follow suit, but his carnation misses the grave and falls at the feet of a beautiful widow—symbolically offering his virtues to her instead of to the dead national heroine and insulting the entire nation of Norania (precipitating, of course, an international incident).

In trouble back in England, he addresses a large group confessing his error and reinforcing his confession by saying the widow was *ugly*. But unfortunately she is in the audience and leaves weeping, which makes him realize he is in love with her. Later more symbolism enters when she sends him the faded carnation, meaning that she is wilting with love for him. Since he loves her and wants to marry her, he has to say that he aimed the white carnation at her in the first place. This statement loses him his job in the Foreign Office and all his English friends, but he wins the widow.

To keep us from scoffing at the foreign-seeming flower symbolism of Norania, Mr. Marshall ends with the hero sending his new wife red roses, *our* symbol of love: "What the world stands most in need of . . . and . . . what people might get if they weren't too frightened to give it."

That's the kind of symbolism working hand in hand with premise or story theme that seems to be the trend throughout the literary and dramatic scene.

Rumer Godden relies on symbolism in "Kingfishers Catch Fire," in which Sophie, the plain widow in India, is symbolized by the kingfisher of Kashmir, which is dull and unnoticeable until it dives underwater; then it is transformed into an exquisite flash of blue! Plain-Jane Sophie, too, is unremarkable until she dives into amazing ideas, then—flash! sparkle! Unforgettable vivid symbolism which pleases the reader who chooses to use it for self-identification.

See how simple symbolism can be. You can use a familiar object which may call up emotional associations in any of us. Maybe you're overlooking precious symbol stimulants for salable stories. For instance, gardening, raking the leaves, cleaning the patio—almost any everyday activity contains usable symbols. O. Henry may have been raking leaves when he got the idea for the "Last Leaf" in which the girl with no will to live likens her life to the last ivy leaves clinging to the wall outside her window. As wintry blizzards rip off the leaves, she decides that if the last one clings, she will live, otherwise . . . After the crucial night, she looks out to see the leaf still there and knows she will get well. (Twist: an artist-neighbor has painted the leaf on the wall during the freezing night. Although he died, it saved her life and proved the verisimilitude of his art.)

There is symbolism in the clothes you wear and the perfume or lotion you use. "The Necklace" by de Maupassant symbolized artificiality; "The Lost Earring" represented the wife's infidelity; "Red Shoes" stood for the artist's obsession for her art; and Robert Fontaine's "The Blue Homburg" was the symbol of a young bridegroom's happiness and anticipation, so that when he found it in the attic ten years after he had worn it at their wedding, honeymoon emotions were rekindled.

You may find inspiring symbols right in your pocket in any object you find there. Coins, for example. There's the situation of the good luck coin and man's dependence on it for his feeling of success. The superstitious Milquetoast goes to work without his good luck piece and is so irritable that he barks at everyone and shows a new virility that causes the boss to give him a raise. In a *Post* story, "I'm Hungry, Darling," a Hadrian good luck coin bearing the word *securitas* is the symbol of security. For an original twist, after the coin brings luck to the starving artist-hero, he generously gives it to his benefactor. In Dan Gallery's *Post* story, "The Great Golden Coin," a nuclear war between U.S. and Russia is averted when their representatives, Joe and Ivan, realize how easily tossing a coin settles their argument about who should pay for their drinks. This leads to the construction of a giant golden coin to be used to settle international disputes. This brings world peace because, Joe says, "On certain matters no nation can bow to any human agency. We say it would involve a loss of sovereignty if they did. But all that it really means is a loss of pride." And in Kathryn Forbes' *Mama's Bank Account* (which later became the basis of the "I Remember Mama" television series), the money which Mama always says she has in the bank for a "rainy day" is the symbol (even though only a figment of Mama's imagination) of security which keeps the family from worrying.

The keys in your pocket look uninspiring, but in Bud Lesser's "A Bunch of Keys," the young Wall Street wizard hero has a habit of twirling his bunch of keys so characteristically that they become a barometer of the stock market, unconsciously tipping off financiers and finally ruining his own prosperity. Each key symbolizes an epitome of achievement: keys to his town apartment, country house, custom-built convertible, country club locker, etc. As he loses each one, he sheds false, superficial values and gains real love and one single, meaningful key.

You can build a story from any symbol, even the paper

clip that came back on your last rejection. Here's one possibility: A paper clip, tightly clasping, tries to hold too much too tight. A jealous, domineering wife, husband or parent holds all facets of another character's life and personality, in other words, overloads the paper clip. In the bang-up crisis, the clip loses all power and the papers spill all over, symbolizing the fact that love, trust, and enjoyment go out of marriage or any other relationship when restraint is enforced. Doom is threatened and may actually occur. For a happy-ending story, you can reverse the paper clip, actually giving it a new spring or power when it is used in the other direction. The possessor can change his or her tactics and happy harmony results!

Try symbolism-developing with everything around you: Typewriter ribbon, eraser, ball-point pen, TV, Deepfreeze, transistor radio, etc. You'll find searching for symbolism a revitalizing, rejuvenating exercise that makes you a better fiction writer. You may even recapture the thrills you had as a tot when you stared up at a summer sky and saw ships, swans, ice cream cones, meringue pies, and herds of sheep in the clouds.

Open your eyes and your imagination. Look for invisible signs in the visibles all around. For, as John Greenleaf Whittier wrote: "Nature speaks in symbols and in signs."

XXV | THE CRUX OF PLOT: MOMENT OF DECISION

You've probably heard about the battle-toughened soldier who cracked up when he was given a K.P. detail to separate large potatoes from small ones. In a few hours he was blubbering: "Decisions! Decisions! I can't stand it another minute!"

Although this is a gross exaggeration, it contains sound psychology: Many of us can endure almost anything but the pressures of decisions. This is due to the tremendous responsibility and importance of some decisions, since the choice we make of a school, a career, a mate, a neighborhood, a political or ethical direction may spell the difference between success or failure, happiness or unhappiness.

In fiction, no matter how intriguing the character and incidents are, if the protagonist does not have to make any decisions whatsoever, the story will not sell. But give this same character specific *Moments of Decision* which place the fate of the yarn in his hands, have him decide in a way that does not ameliorate things but complicates them and leads to more Moments of Decision—and you're on the way to a salable story.

Why will the same Moments of Decision that make a true-life person crack up keep a story from cracking up? Is your decision-pressed reader sadistic enough to enjoy having his troubles transferred to others? Or does he learn how to cope with decisions from similar experiences of your hero which are more clearly presented and more satisfactorily solved? Or are the reasons less psychological and more technical? With each Moment of Decision ("Should I do this or should I do that?") we have a knotty problem which has two or more solutions. This means CONFLICT between the choices, SUSPENSE as the reader guesses which decision will be made, and PROTAGONIST-RESPONSIBILITY as the Moment of Decision makes the hero dynamically active in solving his dilemmas.

One of the main differences between an amateur round-tripper and a professional, salable script is that the former presents a protagonist marching through a series of incidents or experiences, perhaps from an interesting problem to a satisfying solution. The professional story adds the "something extra," the sharp decisions or dilemmas in which the hero is forced to choose between two or more courses of action. The choice he makes changes the course of the story and leads to other Moments of Decision. The amateur writes about a boy who goes to college, plays football or basketball, meets a girl, falls in love with her and marries her. No sustained decisions. The professional author's hero is a fine athlete who wants desperately to go to college, to be a doctor, lawyer, engineer or ? (he decides which); then financial crises at home pressure him to get a job instead of continuing his education. Papa's death gives

Mom a heart attack and there's no one but our Hero to foot the bills. When he decides to do the noble thing and sacrifice his own ambitions, Mom insists that his education is the most important thing in the world to her. She has spoken to the coach or some authority who has managed to get the boy an athletic scholarship. She can help by hand-painting neckties or china, or by typing envelopes at home. He decides to accept the scholarship, and then other Moments of Decision develop: to cheat or not to cheat in order to pass? to favor the son of a bigwig even though he is undeserving, rather than arouse the hostility of the bigwig? to date the rich coed who can help him or the poor waitress whom he really loves? to testify against a rival to get him out of the way? Finally, perhaps, when more money is needed for Mom's heart surgery, to accept a lucrative bribe to throw the game or turn down the much-needed money?

To make your story professional, plan a mounting progression of Moments of Decision, each of which:

1) Gives the hero a choice between moral Right and Wrong.

2) Throws light on characterization and intensifies motivation. The choice parallels the character's major traits.

3) Seems to solve pressing problems, but, instead, usually leads to subsequent Moments of Decision and stronger ACTION.

Let's consider these points in greater detail:

1) Right or Wrong.

Antipodal moral values must be pulling your hero in opposite directions, with the *wrong* way being more tempting and leading directly to the achievement of the hero's goal. For example, in Rod Serling's television play, "Patterns," in Robert Ruark's *Poor No More,* and also in the plethora of similar stories of success in the business world, the protagonist gets to the top by riding roughshod over others or by destroying an innocent person. The hero in the motion picture *Career* sacrifices his marriage, wife, and unborn child, as well as his pride and self-respect, in a series of dramatized Moments of Decision in which he makes the morally wrong, selfish choice which he feels will lead to the theatrical success he so passionately wants.

In most cases, the character and the reader are aware of which decision is morally *right,* which is *wrong.* (The best conflict and suspense result when the choice is a difficult one.) But sometimes in fiction as in life, the issues are not clearly White versus Black, and our basic beliefs are sorely challenged, even reversed. For instance, we are taught to tell the truth and that "honesty is the best policy." But is it always? Is it best to tell a truth that will hurt innocent people, shatter revered reputations, destroy worthwhile lives and do no good to anyone? In *Ben Hur,* Esther is an honest, loyal girl who sympathizes with Ben Hur's desire to find his mother and sister. When she learns that they are lepers and they beg her to tell him they are dead—to save him agony and themselves humiliation—is Esther justified in withholding truth and lying to the man she loves (for his sake and theirs)?

We are taught that it is honorable to keep our promise, but what of this moral value in the case of a kidnapping where the victim's father has given his word to pay and protect the kidnappers if they return his child safely? Is there a clear vision of right-versus-wrong in the father's concern over keeping his promise to the criminals and to cooperate with the police in apprehending the kidnappers?

These more complex Moments of Decision require more profound psychological treatment, a more intellectual market and a longer script. Until you are established, it's best to stick to the one-dimensional Moments of Decision where the hero and the reader can recognize good from evil, choose sides emotionally, and understand the nature of each character in accordance with the decision he makes. This leads us to:

2) Moments of Decision reveal and affect characterization. An honest person will not easily make a decision to cheat or lie and a gentle, kind person will not choose to inflict sadistic violence.

Ambition (social and financial) motivates many modern fictional protagonists. In the beginning of the novel (and movie) *Room at the Top*, by John Braine, Joe Lampton is determined to break the British social barrier and soar to the top, no matter who is hurt or what it costs. Later, he wavers toward his real desire to sacrifice this goal for his love of Alice, who is married, older, and definitely not the social and financial asset that rich, young Susan is. After he realizes that marriage to Alice is impossible and his duty is to marry Susan, who is carrying his child, his original ambition is eclipsed by independent pride as he defies rather than kowtows to her rich, industrialist father.

Another ruthlessly ambitious modern protagonist who eventually changes and regenerates is Tony Lawrence in Richard Powell's novel *The Philadelphians* ("the book that cracked upper-crust society wide open"). Throughout most of the Moments of Decision in the novel, Tony chooses the selfish, unethical, morally wrong course of action. In his desire to achieve prestige, fortune and fame in Philadelphia Main Line society, he chooses only rich socialite friends. He plans to elope with his wealthy sweetheart, Joan, but he relinquishes love and is "bought off" by Joan's dad. In law school when he learns of an opportunity that a classmate is excited about, Tony sacrifices friendship and honesty by deliberately sneaking ahead of the boy to steal the chance, not hesitating to connive and butter up the wife of the Big Wheel to clinch the deal. He makes another unethical decision to steal a client, wealthy Mrs. J. Arthur Allen, from a rival law firm, an act that could make or break him since it may lead to disbarment and disgrace.

Notice how this element of chance or gambling sharpens and adds spice to a Moment of Decision:

> Anthony came to a very big decision. He was going to try to steal Mrs. J. Arthur Allen and the Allen Oil Co. from the firm of Dickinson and Dawes. If he made any important mistake he might find himself facing disbarment proceedings. If he made the slightest mistake he might be asked to resign from Morris, Clayton, Biddle and Wharton. This was one of those jobs like General Brimmer deciding to go after the Royalty Islands and to hell with the Joint Chiefs of Staff. You couldn't attack in full force. You had to make it appear that you were just walking innocently along, and the Royalty Islands or Mrs. J. Arthur Allen happened to fall into your pocket. If he won without any taint of unprofessional conduct, his career would be made.

In a modern novel, TV play or drama, the lead character is more lifelike and interesting if he grows and changes, so that all his Moments of Decision are neither negative nor positive. Even ruthlessly ambitious Tony Lawrence has "good" moments, such as when he refuses to make love to his benefactor's wife even though she begs him to, and again when his down-and-out, socially disgraced, alcoholic friend is accused of murder and needs a lawyer. In this Moment of Decision, Tony acts unselfishly: To save his friend's life he accepts his first criminal case even though he is not a criminal lawyer (inviting defeat in court). Furthermore the opposition threatens Tony with exposure of his own illegitimacy, thus disgracing himself and his mother. Tony's negative, then positive decisions all add up to the premise or moral theme: that no one is really as good as he wants to be or as bad as he's afraid he is.

3) Although each Moment of Decision promises to solve a pressing problem, it leads to others and to drastic action which would not be the same if the decision had been different. The father who overindulges his son in the play *Edward, My Son* not only makes a dishonest, lying, cheating wastrel of the boy, but each of Papa's immoral decisions leads to tragedy and destroys another life. To get money for the boy's operation, he burns his business and blames his partner, who is sent to jail while he collects the insurance money. After the innocent man is released and asks him for a job, he turns him down, causing the latter's suicide. The father's immoral, self-centered decisions lead to his wife's alcoholism and death, his sweetheart-secretary's taking poison, and his own loneliness and imprisonment as his crimes catch up with him.

One of the main reasons Moments of Decision are necessary to add drama to your script is that they always create action that adds suspense and excitement to a scene.

There are such exciting Moments of Decision in every professional story or play. Many can be found in newspaper items and life all around you. See how many successful stories you can build from them. For instance, here are three local incidents that would make good stories:

1) A young internist was eating dinner in a restaurant when a woman coughed and choked violently, then fell to the floor unconscious. The doctor's first Moment of Decision: Should he interfere, since the woman was a stranger, not his patient, unconscious, and could sue him later; or should he disregard the risks to himself and try to help? Unselfishly, he chose the latter, leading to the diagnosis and prognosis Moment of Decision. Was it a stroke, heart attack or food stuck in her windpipe? He decided on the last and realized the only chance to save the unconscious woman was by surgery. But this doctor was an internist, not a trained surgeon. He had no instruments, not even proper lighting, but a woman's life was in danger. She would be dead in five minutes if he didn't take a chance. Of course, if it didn't work, his entire career would be finished, but he made the altruistic decision, and there was a happy ending.

2) Another local split-second Moment of Decision concerned a mother whose 16-year-old son was trapped beneath a station wagon. Her unselfish decision was to risk her life for him by superhumanly lifting the car to free his body.

3) A controversial Moment of Decision: Should a high-school student (or parent) testify for or against a physiology teacher accused by some of improper action?

You probably have better Moments of Decision in your own newspapers, life-experiences, or imagination. Start clipping and jotting them down to enliven your plots and articles: Should a woman dress her age or as young as she looks? Should parents put a blind or mentally retarded child in an institution or rear him at home with other children? Should a scientist or psychologist use his own

244 MODERN FICTION TECHNIQUES

children or friends in experiments he considers harmless? Should a wife try to slow down her overactive, partying, trying-to-be-young husband? Should a woman work after marriage and motherhood? Should you pick up a hitch-hiker or not?

Should a ruler desert his threatened capital and flee to safety, or stay with his people? Should the ex-doctor tell his sweetheart why he had to stop practicing medicine? Should a woman tell her fiancé she's older than he is? Should the warden capitulate to the rioting prisoners, to free the hostages they are holding? Should the C.O. give the order for bombing, knowing his own brother will be killed? Should a person ruin his own success to champion an unpopular cause? What should a lonely boy do when he finds a dog, gives it a home, comes to love it as his pal, and then the rightful owner shows up? Any strong Moment of Decision can be the crux of a plot for you to develop!

XXVI | LITERARY GIMMICKS

WHAT IS a gimmick?

A literary gimmick is much like any other gimmick, which the dictionary defines as: 1) "Any small device used secretly by a magician in performing a trick"; or 2) "A secret device by which a grifter controls the mechanism of a prize wheel; anything tricky."

As an author, you must be the grifter in control, the trickster who operates a wheel of chance, who makes the gimmick do what you want it to do. It cannot be just a "cute" tricky addition or an afterthought. It must be a legitimate part of the story, often solving the problem, aiding the premise or theme, or setting off crucial action.

It is not unusual for a non-professional writer to dream up a splendid gimmick, then make the mistake of falling so in love with the gimmick itself that he dashes off a "story" that will show it off, without working hard enough to build up strong story factors which will best blend with the gimmick. The best thing to do is to collect clever, timely, not-often-used gimmicks or bits of information from everywhere: science, medicine, psychology, law, philosophy, etc.

But don't hasten to write a story on the basis of gimmick alone. Be sure you first develop characters, situation, emotional conflicts, and theme in line with the gimmick before writing the actual story.

One of the most popular formulas of all time is a gimmick that gives extraordinary powers to an ordinary person. Let's see how the specific gimmick controls the story and leads to the premise. How does the protagonist use this superhuman power? For good or evil? How does the sequence of events add up to a universal meaning? Rod Serling has worked this formula out in many ways with a variety of specific gimmicks. In his "A Most Unusual Camera," Chester Dietrich, a petty thief, is checking his loot from his last robbery and finds a camera that looks beat-up and usual but is really unusual in that it takes pictures of events before they occur. He considers using it to help humanity by previewing and preventing tragedies, wars, crimes, etc. but decides instead to use it avariciously. He takes it to the races to photograph winners before each race and make a fortune—which attracts another thief and leads to death for all the characters involved. (Theme: Just as happiness comes from unselfishly helping others, unhappiness results from selfish greed.)

In another Serling story, he uses the ancient Aladdin's lamp gimmick to give a needy antique-shop-owner and his wife three wishes. Their first is for money; which they spend and give away until they don't have enough left to pay taxes on it. Their second is for power, and he becomes a Hitlerian tyrant who is about to be killed by the angry mob. The third wish is to escape and be as they were. (Theme: The grass is *not* greener. No matter what troubles we have, things could be worse.)

These are just a few of the possibilities of this "extraordinary-power" gimmick in relation to theme. From the ancient classics and folklore to Dickens' "The Magic Fishbone," and from "Superman" to "The Millionaire", the gimmick alone has not been enough. It has had to be synchronized with characterization, action, and theme.

Gimmicks are all around you—waiting to be developed. For instance, telephone automation: once a number is dialed, that phone will continue to ring unless someone breaks the connection at either end. It can ring for hours or days until either the dialer hangs up, or someone picks up the receiver at the other end. How can a plot be built around the item so that a specific character uses it for his own purposes? So that a true symbiotic relation between gimmick, character, and plot will exist? In Helen McCloy's story, "Thy Brother Death," an apparently devoted husband goes to the D.A.'s psychiatric assistant, Dr. Basil Willing, to show him a threatening quotation his wife received in the mail. He leads Willing back to his office where the phone is ringing when they arrive. Willing overhears the husband's end of a conversation with his wife who reports prowlers snooping around. The men hurry to the house and find her dead. Eventually you learn that the husband killed her, making it look like a theft-murder; then dialed his office from their house, knowing the phone would keep ringing and his supposed conversation with her would serve as his alibi. This phone-automation gimmick, plus a quotation gimmick (Shelley's "Thy brother Death came and cried, 'Wouldst thou me?'" in the handwriting of the girl he planned to frame); plus a psychological gimmick that the wife signed her maiden name after fourteen years of marriage (her unconscious mind's "counter-will" indicating she hated her husband and was unhappily married)—all these gimmicks are integrated with characterization, motivation, and whodunit plot.

There are many types of gimmicks that can give a story freshness, sparkle, and surprise. Study the ones used in stories and start a gimmick file of your own, collecting choice bits from reading, research, and living.

Here are just a few gimmick categories:

1. *Word gimmicks*

Word meanings, pronunciations, and misinterpretations have produced tricky results ever since Biblical Jephtha used the word "shibboleth" to distinguish his men (the Gileadites) from enemy Ephraimites, who pronounced it "sibboleth." Such differences in pronunciation have inspired passwords to catch spies in many wars ever since. Derivations or original meanings of words add gimmick-interest—such as our word "worry" which is derived from the Anglo-Saxon word for "strangle." A charming story was built on the word, "budget": A little Mexican boy tries to sell one of his mother's homemade dresses to a nice American couple, who can't buy it because the Budget won't let them. When Budget holds them back in other ways, and the boy realizes they are dominated by it, he tries to kill Budget with a magic silver bullet to free his friends. When he is hurt in a heroic crisis, the Americans realize how they have overemphasized materialistic wealth and how well off they really are.

Our slang word for psychiatrist, "headshrinker," might have inspired the Alfred Hitchcock story in which the white man in the jungle kept mentioning that he should take his disturbed wife to the headshrinker. When he asked his native boy to take her to the doctor, the lad returned with the wife's shrunken head.

Develop your word-consciousness. Millions of plot-ideas are lurking in your dictionary, thesaurus, almanac, or the fascinating Encyclopaedia Britannica Book of the Year, which defines brand-new words like "artsaker," "meter maid," "moonlighter," "moonwatcher," and "calypsomaniac." There's even an idea in words like "sidewinder"!

2. Character trait gimmicks

These are especially effective, since the best plot action stems from characterization. This tightens the integration of the story. The specific trait of the character (like Walter Mitty's daydreaming, Macbeth's ambition, Othello's jealousy, Pollyanna's optimism, Craig's wife's ultra-fastidiousness, or any special trait like boasting, gossiping, excessive punctuality) causes interesting situations or helps the protagonist's success or failure. In the best biter-bit stories, the villain's main trait trips him up. Titles like "The Shrike," "The Show-Off," "The Worrier," "The Meanest Man in Washington County" prepare you for character trait gimmick stories.

3. Fact or information gimmicks

This kind of gimmick may be gleaned from all fields: history, medicine, law, science, electronics, anthropology, sports and hobbies, etc. What could you do with such bits as the following:

> Nyctaphonia is a peculiar nervous state in which the afflicted person is unable to speak during the night, although his vocal powers return at daybreak.

or,

Pies were once considered an exotic delicacy reserved only for the rich and powerful. During the 15th century in Scotland, Parliament banned pie-eating by anybody below the rank of baron.

or,

The irritant poison of *Rhus toxicodendron* (poison ivy) is as catching from the smoke of its burning as if you actually touch it.

This last gimmick was used in Frances and Richard Lockridge's story "Allergic to Murder" in which it solves a murder. When Roger Handley is murdered, his hearth is smoking with a fire made from poison oak brush. His niece's husband, who admits gathering the brush, has the rash on his wrists, therefore seems guilty until Roger's brother-in-law, Clement Parkins, develops a bad case of poison oak proving he *was* in the smoke-filled room when Handley was killed. This jibes with a strong motive.

The facts do not have to be scientific or academic, but may be extremely simple gimmicks that provide the trick to turn the story. In C. B. Gilford's story, "Terrified," a delinquent teen-age couple cause a fatal accident, then kill the injured man with a huge rock so there won't be any witnesses. They tell the highway patrolman that the man was thrown from his car and hit his head against the rock, but an elementary gimmick trips them up. But, the trooper says, "There are two sides to a rock . . . The top side stays clean washed by the rain. The bottom side is dirty from contact with the ground. Now you tell me, sonny, how (he) was thrown from his car so that he hit his head on the bottom side of that rock?"

Prentiss Combs' *Post* story, "The Substitute Son" uses

the red flag on rural mailboxes as a gimmick to symbolize the loneliness of the isolated farmers who put up the red flag, not just when they have mail to be collected, but when they want Tribus Afton, the genial mail-carrier, to stop for a visit.

4. Mystery gimmicks

Many magazines of the crossword puzzle variety, as well as some syndicates, buy vignettes built on mystery gimmicks or simple facts. For example, a naturalized U.S. citizen loses his American citizenship if he stays out of the U.S. for more than five years; or a native-born American citizen cannot be deported. Fascinating lawsuits often hinge on surprise gimmicks, and it often pays for writers to wade through legal tomes, serve on a jury, or attend trials. Mystery or detective gimmicks can be sold as miniature "puzzle" stories or can be built up to whodunits. In either case, be sure that the clues are valid—honestly planted but cleverly concealed.

5. Object, thing, or symbol gimmicks

Almost anything or any object can be used as a story gimmick if it is cunningly sprung, integrated into the story naturally, and has an important part in solving the problem. Once when Robert C. Dennis was sharpening a pencil, he observed that the plastic catch-all that holds the shavings would be a good place to hide something small and valuable. In a future story, that's where the diamond ring was hidden! An object that has a symbolical meaning and strong emotional significance is best: a trophy that has been dearly won; a gift from a dear one; etc. In my *This Week* story, "Return to Life," a captured enemy flag was an emotional gimmick used to cure the hero's psychosis.

6. *Psychological gimmicks*

Studying psychology and abnormal psychology pays rich dividends in gimmick-ideas for stories, whether in phenomena like hypnosis, dream interpretations, subliminal perception, *déjà vu*, extra-sensory perception, or retroactive inhibition.

Start collecting psychological gimmicks, which can be found in strange places. For instance, the overheard remark at a cocktail party: "I'm glad I'm neurotic. That's the only thing normal about me." The title of Elaine Dundy's novel *The Dud Avocado* comes from a European's opinion of American girls: "These American girls are just like avocados. A hard center with the tender meat all wrapped up in a shiny casing. How I love them. So green—so eternally green!"

Editors will love your stories, too, if the gimmick is kept the hard center surrounded by tender, fleshy plot and characterization—wrapped up in a shiny casing of philosophical theme. Then you'll no longer be a greenhorn, for your scripts will bring in a goodly share of greenbacks!

XXVII | DON'T REPEAT IT, REVERSE IT

THERE IS a magic secret device to help those writers (1) who tire of manufacturing conflicts to make a plot; (2) those who run out of story ideas; and (3) those who are discouraged by the fact that professionals often repeat the same plot formulas but an unestablished author must come up with something startlingly fresh and original to break into print. This situation may seem like a stalemate because if you *should* come up with a plot that's never been used before, it would be so bizarre, weird, taboo, or lacking in credibility and reader identification that no one would publish it anyway!

The solution is *Reversal*. Don't try for a brand-new plot. Don't repeat the often used ones. Just *reverse* familiar trends, ideas and situations and you will produce something fresh and salable.

Even pros use this trick of Reversal effectively, reversing widespread ideas. For example, in *Visit to a Small Planet*, Gore Vidal reverses the general feeling that people from other planets are inferior, showing the "visitor" far more intellectually advanced than we. *Paths of Glory* reverses the popular admiration for military efficiency, and *The Bad Seed* reverses our romantic concept of children as innocent darlings.

Even our age-old, time-tried philosophies like "Do unto others" and "Cast thy bread upon the waters" are up-ended in such books as Francis King's *The Man on the Rock* in which the Greek orphan, Spiro, hates those who help him and destroys everyone who loves him. You can add hundreds of other literary reversals to widely accepted ideas, and you can learn to work your own fresh angles as you observe general tendencies and popular concepts—then reverse them. Juvenile literature frequently idolizes the "reverse" character like Ferdinand, the non-belligerent bull; Horton, the elephant who hatches an egg; *The Horse Who Lived Upstairs; The Ugly Duckling; The Duck Who Flew Backward;* etc.

If there is another name for our era, it could be "The Positive Thinking, Sweetness-and-Light-Mean-Charm-and-Success" era. Reversals of these overdone concepts appear in stories like Hannah Smith's *Woman's Day* yarn, "Scowling Success." Here Katie Allison, optimistic, positive-thinking, Carnegie-charming, and generous, has a toothache and phones for an immediate dental appointment. Through a mistake in the dentist's intercom, she overhears him tell his assistant, "That sweet, smily blonde won't fuss if we put her off until Friday." Enraged, Katie tells the assistant to go to - - - - and gets the appointment immediately. She realizes that being sweet merely makes you a sucker and a fall guy; that the tough, demanding people reap all the harvests while the nice folks get pushed around. Up till now she's worked overtime for the other girl in the office—and the other girl got the promotion *she* deserved; she's been letting her roommate wear her clothes, and the ingrate smooched with Katie's boy friend, etc. So she *reverses* her behavior pattern, becomes selfish and tough, with resulting success that sweetness never achieved. "Scowling Success" gives us a double reversal:

1) reversal of the overdone philosophy of today

2) reversal of the old "worm turns" plot which formerly concerned a male Milquetoast, not a young blonde. Lest lady readers are urged to lose their femininity (perish the thought!), the end presents a bonus reversal: After landing the repentant young boss (who liked her "sweet, smily" old self and gave the other girl the promotion just to keep Katie in his office), she reverts to her former feminine charm with him.

You can cash in on the reader's wanting to know the other side of anything (whether you choose to call this trait curiosity or fickleness). Cater to this by training your mind to be a weathervane to see how the winds are blowing. Learn to develop story ideas by reversing current news items or even gleaning ready-made reversals from headlines like, "Younger Generation Sheds Cloak of Conformity."

We've always been told that stories must abound in drama—the basic conflicts: internal, character versus character, character versus nature, fate, situation, automation, or society. Yet, *Teahouse of the August Moon,* which John Patrick dramatized from a novel by Vern Sneider, is a fast-paced, absorbing play without genuine dramatic conflict. The civilized, sophisticated American military occupy primitive Okinawa in order to *teach* the natives democracy, but the Americans *learn* more from the natives than they teach them.

There are many reversals in customs: the impoverished

natives give gifts to the American military to "save face"; and many reverse contradictions occur within the characterizations. Col. Purdy bellows: "I will democratize these people if I have to shoot them all!" Throughout, he roars whenever his orders are not carried out. But later, after he has ordered the destruction of the Teahouse and the brandy stills (Congress unexpectedly approves of them), he complains because his orders *were* obeyed. "Why can't someone disobey an order?" he rants. "What's happened to the American spirit of rebellion?"

A final reversal solves the problem satisfactorily: We are led to think that the subservient Tobikians have destroyed the Teahouse and the stills. But have they? No. Reversal: They've only dismantled and hidden sections of their beloved Teahouse. After getting the supervising sergeant drunk on brandy, they substituted water barrels for the brandy kegs to be shattered.

For long scripts you need more and varied reversals, for short ones, less complicated ones. But be sure to plan them thoroughly before writing. Study, too, how reversals are maneuvered by professional authors. There are standard reversal plots that never wear thin: the non-athletic Dad who's looked down on by his son becomes the hero (*To Kill A Mockingbird*) or vice versa (the child who shames or embarrasses his parents becomes their pride); the blacksheep is whitewashed or the opposite; enemies become friends or battling neighbors become bosom pals (you can't watch an evening's TV entertainment without seeing this one); the coward is really courageous. All ugly duckling, Cinderella, and Jack-and-the-Beanstalk formulas are really reversals. Still a favorite is the unwanted, unloved-dog-becomes-the-treasured-pet yarn and the dear old amnesia story in which the protagonist has opposite reactions under different situations.

Most TV shows are loaded with reversals even though the conflict may be nil. In a popular "Private Secretary" script, Ann Sothern and her rival went to a dead author's haunted house to land the contract for his works. The rival (a man) is so terrified and Ann so calm about the ghostly shenanigans, that she wins the contract. (She has read the author's works and recognizes all the spooky gimmicks.) After she wins out, the rival reverses her success by saying *Ann* was the scaredy-cat, that he knew the author's books, wised her up, and pretended his fright so poor Ann wouldn't lose her job. She reverses his reversal, however, by dressing in a sheet, pouncing at him, and scaring him out of the picture.

A reversed attitude is the nucleus of the "come-to-realize" stories. It is a positive reversal from failure to success, from weakness to strength, from frustration to fulfillment, such as you'll find in Horatio Alger and Pygmalion plots. There is an opposite reversal in *Not as a Stranger*. From medical-student days to doctorhood, Luke Marsh is a perfectionist—strong, excessively demanding of others and of himself—never tolerating mistakes or weakness. It isn't until he weakens, errs, and fails that he becomes a successful human being, who in the process of needing others realizes his first promise of happiness.

All novels, movies, and longer scripts utilize many reversals to keep interest from fading. There are specific clear-cut types of reversals. One may be enough for a brief vignette or short-short, but in longer scripts several should be integrated.

How many types of reversal will you be able to concoct

to add surprise, suspense and change of pace to your own stories? Plan to integrate several of the following in every story you write:

Character Reversals may present a 1) regenerated or degenerate person who travels from one pole to another in the course of the story (the skid-row bum who becomes a missionary, the society doctor who becomes an alcoholic, the selfish snob who becomes an altruistic humanitarian, the self-righteous moralist who becomes an incorrigible gambler, etc.); or 2) a character with simultaneous opposite traits that alternate (like Doctor Jekyll and Mr. Hyde, Eve in *The Three Faces of Eve,* or the Damon Runyon fellow who could calculate a friend's death as coldly as a horse-race but who was kind-hearted.)

Psychological Reversals range from a definite change in psychology to the currently popular "reverse psychology" of the hard-to-get man-hater being alluring to men, or Shelley Winters' reverse psychology for dieting—she buys a favorite dress too small so she'll *have* to reduce to get into it!

Philosophical Reversal abounds in the come-to-realize story where there is an about-face in attitude: from "revenge is sweet" to "it is cancerous and corrosive to seek revenge for a wrong . . . better forgive and forget" or any other change in basic philosophy.

Situation or Fortune Reversals create an ironic effect, reminding us of the flexibility of Fate. The mighty fall, the poor grow rich, the lowly and despised become honored or vice versa, as in *The Egyptian, Gone With the Wind, View From Pompey's Head, Giant, The Leopard, Executive Suite.*

Place Reversals offer dramatic scene changes either

within our shrinking world or from our earth to other planets. In one story the unemployed American husband travels to the moon to earn a steady salary for his wife. When she tries to keep him there because she's paid for each day he's on the moon, he reverses the experiment, returns, not to the U.S.A. but to a remote paradisical island far from her mercenary demands . . . and to a reverse type of naïve, native girl.

Humor Reversals create more laughs than any other comedy device. As in all reverse planning, you merely build up anticipation, then radically reverse the expected outcome.

Attitude Reversal spikes Isabel Langis' *McCall's* story "Almost Any Man Will Do." In the beginning Peggy needs to be married to get a radio job. She proposes to Sam who is anti-marriage; then later when he agrees to marry her, she runs away. When he goes after her and proves it's love, both reverse their anti-marriage sentiments.

Whenever you are tempted to repeat a usual situation, try reversing it, (naturally multiplying the number of reversals for a novel over a short story). Many professionals begin this way, as Mona Williams did when she switched the familiar set-up of the poor babysitter in a wealthy home, to the rich producer's wife who baby-sits in an underprivileged home and winds up revamping her own moral values and solving her psychological problems.

In a *Redbook* short-short, "Sister Act" by John Savage, harried housewife Marge is suffering one of those "all wrong" days when her young actress sister, Sally, comes over to discuss her own possible marriage. During the conversation, Sally decides against matrimony since married Marge complains so much. In defending marriage,

Marge realizes her blessings and her own deep happiness with her husband and children. In the end, it dawns on her that Sally invented this scene for that very purpose: for her own benefit. *Psychological Reversal:* Marge's disgust with marriage reverses to grateful appreciation of her blessings. *Character Reversal:* Marge's emotionality vs. Sally's clear-headed logic. Marge's character matures from selfish shortsightedness to long-range emotional maturity. *Emotion Reversal:* Complaining self-pity changes to satisfaction and realization: "What a lucky gal am I!"

You can concoct exciting stories by working out reversals on your own. Instead of the dominating parent who controls the children's lives and love affairs, why not dominating children who object to the widowed parent's plan to remarry? Instead of the girl "going home to mother," why not the bride who has a better rapport with hubby's mom than with her own? Instead of a gossipy old woman being the antagonist, how about a handsome young man being the real trouble-maker by disseminating scandal? Or how about the traveling saleslady and the farmer's brother? the lady plumber? Robin Hood? pilot? crop-duster? used car salesclerk? forest ranger? cowgirl? detective? minister? baseball player? wrestler? Or the male nurse? babysitter?

In Sloan Wilson's novel, *A Summer Place,* the adults are the delinquents, whereas the teen-agers are stable, moral and mature. There are many other possibilities with this reversal. If your wife-seeking hero has to choose between the naïve-seeming poor girl and the sophisticated rich girl, he finally learns that the poor girl is really a gold digger whereas the rich girl sincerely loves him for himself.

Here are just a few of the many reversals in Herman Wouk's *Marjorie Morningstar,* which, in its wholesome recommendations of chastity, American homelife, and religious adherence, reverses our strong Fitzgerald-begun emphasis on cynicism and abhorrence of patriotic, religious, or moral enthusiasm: *Situation Reversal:* At first, Marjorie is a throbbing young girl with theatrical ambitions, later she is a mature woman happily settled. *Philosophy Reversal:* The book opens with Marjorie's feeling that her religion is outmoded, but later she realizes it fulfills her inner needs. *Character Reversal* travels from superficiality to maturity. In her youth she is physically attracted to ne'er-do-well Noel, but as her own character develops she becomes aware of his shallowness and unworthiness. A *Fortune Reversal* is illustrated by Marsha, the daughter of poor immigrants who marries a rich man. *Attitude Reversal:* the family laughs at and looks down on the old Uncle as a financial failure during his life. After he dies, however, they respect him, realizing that he actually held the family together with his humor and his habit of harmonizing family quarrels.

If you don't have *conflict* be sure you have *reversal* in your story—in anything you write. Look around you, think up situations, characters, and ideas to reverse for your own scripts: the sophisticated child and the naïve adult; the mother-in-law siding with her daughter-in-law against her own son; the step-parent who loves the child more than the natural parent does; the sloppy wife who's a better spouse than the meticulous one; the sweet thing who turns sour, etc.

After you have decided on your *Major Reversal* for the

all-important plot problem or situation, work out several subsequent reversals in character, philosophy, psychology, fortune, place. Whenever the story is bogging down, seeming monotonous or static, spring a logical reversal. Then you'll experience the most thrilling reversal of all: from rejections to steady sales!

XXVIII | TIME LIMIT

CAN YOU RECOGNIZE the common denominator in the following situations taken from fiction, drama, and life? A young couple has one year in which to produce an heir and inherit grandfather's millions; a sheriff has until ten minutes after five to get himself and his prisoner on a train before the gang comes to kill him and free the prisoner (*Five-Ten to Yuma*); to another sheriff the arrival time of a train means threatened death instead of salvation (*High Noon*); a parolee has six hours to prove himself innocent of a fresh crime or he will be returned to the penitentiary; a man, locked in an auto trunk, breathes air from the spare tire and stays alive till rescuers come; bank robbers have a limited time to break into one of two vaults to get a fortune—they toss a coin and are lucky enough to be led to the right one, but in their haste they leave the coin behind—with fingerprints!

The common factor is Time Limit, without which the above have no drama or excitement. This time element can usually be depended upon to heighten a rather dull, ho-hum plot. Try it.

If you're having a tough time giving your story that professional zing, perhaps you can tenderize that toughness the same way you tenderize tough meat—with pressure. For tough meat you use the pressure-cooker, and for tough plot-knots, you use the pressure of a Time Limit. This invisible character can be a help to your hero or an added villain to foil him, increasing the obstacles which he must overcome, thereby building more drama and increasing suspense.

Everyone would like to have $3,000. But it's more vital and dramatic if your hero must have $3,000 by tomorrow night to pay the balloon mortgage on his business or the home he's put his life savings into; or to bring the surgeon-specialist to this country to save his child's life; or to meet the kidnappers' ransom demands; or as in Rod Serling's *Requiem for a Heavyweight*, Maish Loomis must have $3,000 to pay Hensen in one week.

If it's impossible to get, yet *must* be obtained by a certain time, the pressure is on. Suspense and excitement are kindled, and we are assured of action, one way or another, by a definite time. Life offers us no such certainty, and yet every admirable, successful life is the record of making impossibles possible.

You can hardly turn on TV, go to a movie, or read a story without bumping into some sort of a Time Limit: "You have one week to solve the murder!" "I'll give you until midnight to clear out of town!" "If you wish to see your child alive, you must fly us and our cargo to the coast by nightfall!" "You can have three hours to water your cows at my trough, then you must get them off my property!" "Entries must be postmarked before December 31." "Your income tax must be paid by April 15." "If the boy who brought the whiskey doesn't confess by three o'clock, no one will graduate." "Don't go near the typewriter for six months; if after that time, you still want to write, go ahead!" "If you don't have $1,000 by six o'clock, we'll beat you to death!" "If I don't lose five pounds by Saturday, I'll never be able to squeeze into my new formal!" (There's a story in each of these—help yourself!)

Whether the time limit is humorous, spine-tingling, or magic, it must be *urgent* to the protagonist. It has always been so:

The children of Israel had to rush through the Red Sea before it closed up again. Cinderella had until midnight to be glamorous, then . . . *Rumpelstiltskin* contains many time pressures: Lord Karsh gives the king *one week* to sign the marriage contract with the rich queen he doesn't love. Several times, wicked Lord Karsh gives Elsa *one hour* to weave straw into gold. The dwarf helps her but later comes to collect payment: the baby she has after she marries the king. The only way they can keep their son is to guess the dwarf's real name *within three days*. Just as the time limit is ending and tragedy looms, the problem is solved . . . Rumpelstiltskin's name is revealed—happy ending!

Time limit adds excitement and suspense to all types of stories and dramas all through the ages and in various languages, from *Faust* to *Rip Van Winkle* to *Maverick*. In the play, *Dark of the Moon*, the Witch Boy falls in love with mortal Barbara Allen and wants to marry her. He gets his wish with the stipulation that if she kisses another man within the first year, she'll die and he will be reclaimed by the Conjure-Woman and the witch girls. In another story, a fortune will go to the man who tells the truth and nothing but the truth for *twenty-four* hours. The time limit is always a Damocles' sword hanging over the head of the hero and making the reader hold his breath. It also must exert a real influence on plot and characterization.

The time limit and its importance are established, and the outcome of the story depends on whether or not the hero meets the deadline. 1) If he does, there is a happy ending; 2) if not, it's a tragedy; or 3) rarely an ideological ending lets the reader guess what happened. Examples:

1) HAPPY ENDING. Time limit forms the motive, constant throughout, and even appears in the title of *Around the World in Eighty Days*. At the crisis, Phileas Fogg thinks he had failed and lost the bet, but the international dateline-time-change gimmick reverses it to a happy ending. In *Bells Are Ringing,* time limit proves a friend to the answering-service-switchboard heroine, enabling her to meet playwright Jeffrey Moss who has to meet a noon deadline with his play. Since she must wake him and can't reach him by phone, she goes to his apartment and this meeting develops into a romance.

2) UNHAPPY ENDING. The writer, architect, contractor who doesn't meet the tight deadline loses his great opportunity to a rival; the contestant, racer or duelist can be sadly defeated by minutes or hours. A lifetime of happiness can be lost if one is late for a definite appointment, as happens in *Back Street,* when the heroine's kindness makes her late to meet her sweetheart's family and costs her marriage. Limitless tragedies result from the time limits in wartime. Other time limit failures cause tragic endings like those of *Romeo and Juliet,* where Juliet takes poison

before learning the real plan; *La Tosca,* in which Tosca doesn't kill Scarpia *before* he has given the order for her lover's death.

3) IDEOLOGICAL ENDING. Only in rare controversial cases is the time limit problem left unsolved. The play, *Time Limit,* asks if there should be a time limit on courage in wartime, a time limit before men who have been heroes in two wars break down. Should they be condemned and discarded if they do? Because the Major accused of collaborating with the enemy in Korea had unselfish, therefore sympathetic, motivation in trying to save the lives of his eleven fellow-officers and the reputation and feelings of his general, we do not want to see him court-martialed. *But,* because we cannot condone treachery and collaboration with the enemy in wartime, we don't want him to go scot-free. The author doesn't force his opinion on us, but lets us choose our own solution.

Likewise, time limit is sometimes offered as a solution to a controversial love affair involving divorce or marriage between members of different religions or races: a separation of a given time—three months, six months or one year to think it over. If, after this "cooling off" period they still love each other, they can marry. Readers who are for their getting together smell orange blossoms and hear wedding bells on the horizon; those who oppose such a union are convinced that the time limit test will make the characters change their minds. I suggested this type of ending to a TV love story between a Hindu boy and an American girl, but the author insisted that they get married. The teleplay was rejected as taboo, then later the same plot appeared on the same program with the identical ideological time limit ending I had recommended.

The ideological can seem frustrating to the reader who expects the author to solve the problem completely.

It's wise to become time-limit-conscious. See if your story can be spiked and made more exciting by adding this pressure-factor. Study examples of time limit in professional stories and in life all around you, all the way from simple acts like catching the 8 a.m. commuter train to time limits in the international missiles race. Ask yourself how meeting or missing deadlines can change individual lives and even history. Start collecting and categorizing different types of time limits and see how they suggest specific conflicts, therefore drama, and eventually whole plots! Here is a possible classification with a few examples. You can add many more, I'm sure:

1) COMPETITION TIME LIMIT. Any kind of race: swimming, car, boat, skiing, horse, dog and others. Two rival companies have a stagecoach race to determine which will win the U.S. Government Mail contract; or steamboats race up the Mississippi River for the same purpose; or homesteaders race to stake their claims. Perry Mason and other detective-heroes try to solve the murder before the police do.

2) NATURE-IMPOSED TIME LIMIT. When natural disaster threatens your hero, the odds rise against him and there is more challenge, suspense, and a stronger David-and-Goliath plot: the raging forest fire or rising floods rushing to destroy hero, home, or town and a desperate time limit to strengthen the levees with sandbags or to water down the property within vital minutes! Escape or invasion (like D-Day) depending on high or low tide, or a full moon or no moon at all! The Big Freeze or Blizzard on the way to

kill all the cattle on the cattle drive or the wagon train or a group like the Donner party or the lady school bus driver and her load of kiddies.

3) Man-Imposed Time Limits include all chase stories and threats (like the convict who promised to kill the judge within twenty-four hours); the thugs who'll beat up the protagonist if he doesn't give up information or money by a certain time; a prison sentence, pardon, or time of execution; so many hours before a race or battle or some crisis to fix a crippled plane, car, boat, tank, etc. A definite time on the court docket, before which the attorney must have all his evidence prepared.

4) Scientific Time Limit. The time-bomb or rocket will go off within an hour (perhaps it must be defused, stopped, or launched properly). Medical time limits include discovering the cure or obtaining medicine before character dies; many especially dramatic operations involving transplanting bone, skin, glands. A newspaper report of a corneal transplant that had to be performed within forty-eight hours grew into a TV play.

5) Emotional Decision Time Limit. The girl has hours, minutes, or weeks to make up her mind to marry the boy before his plane leaves, etc. Or the man has to make a vital decision on his job, trip, marriage, divorce, whether to charter his plane or boat to smugglers, or some other course of action, by a given time.

Whether your time limit is short or long, little or large, plant it where it will do the most good, and keep it ticking as suspensefully as a time-bomb!

Please let us know what happens when you recruit this invisible character—time limit—into your stories and into your life. Perhaps he'll help you as he did George Axelrod who read Robert Sherwood's statement that anyone who wanted to write a play should do so before he was thirty. He looked at a calendar, saw he had just six weeks to go, sat down at his typewriter and wrote *The Seven Year Itch!*

XXIX | THE MARKET FOR FICTION

THERE ARE THREE major categories of fiction markets: 1) slicks, 2) quality magazines, 3) secondary magazines. The slicks and secondary magazines publish commercial stories that attract readers by the crescendoing array of actions and scenes that travel from a problem to a solution, without straining the reader's intellect or challenging his belief in the eventual triumph of good over evil. The slicks often stress psychological problems and the style is polished, the characterization three-dimensional, the premise more philosophical and the atmospheric X-plus factor more pronounced. In quality stories, there is even more emphasis on mental and spiritual appeals than physical; sometimes the negative is highlighted instead of the usual affirmation of life through the triumph of virtue over villainy. The quality story is a realistic, slice-of-life yarn that delves into an unusual phase of living and provides fresh insight into human understanding. This insight must grow as a result of a deep emotional experience. Many quality stories break taboos and smash ikons in their attempt to mirror reality (which is not always pretty).

They pose questions that are not always answered satisfactorily, or perhaps are not answered at all. The quality story is to writing what Stravinsky is to music and what abstract painting is to art. It underscores a thinking author's individual interpretation of an experience.

THE SLICKS

The Slick Magazines are so-called because they are published on slick or "coated" paper that is receptive to photo engraving and 4-colors. They carry richly-illustrated advertising that enables them to pay highest rates, yet controls the material so that it cannot offend or belittle the advertisers. You should study the ads as well as the stories and articles and slant accordingly.

There are general slicks (*Saturday Evening Post*), women's slicks (*McCall's, Good Housekeeping, Ladies' Home Journal*), and men's slicks (*Esquire, Playboy*). Each buys stories that appeal to the specific readers, but all seek yarns that provide the essence of *Excitement, Entertainment, Enlightenment, Escape, Education*.

The slicks require an intriguing story-line with suspense-filled scenes that travel from the presentation of the *problem* to a satisfying *solution*. Whereas the secondary stresses *physical* problems, description, and action, the slick emphasizes the psychological and philosophical in addition to the physical; and the reader is given greater opportunity to exercise his imagination and intelligence. A polished style and sharp originality are necessary in the slicks. The specific X-plus factor with a thorough knowledge of a definite place, profession, or subject matter is vital to buck the terrific slick competition and to get those checks.

Slick Do's

1. Vivid, lifelike *dimensional* characters with more than one facet to their personalities.
2. Strong motivation for all action and characterization even though they may be out of the ordinary. Study cause and effect constantly for ideas and understanding of how they work.
3. Clever, pithy dialogue and deep-drawn emotion, preferably telling the whole story from the viewpoint of the one character most emotionally involved in the situation—the one who solves it.
4. An impressive, underlying *premise* or *theme* that adds fresh insight into the usual problems of everyday life. Not conventional, shocking, or taboo. Never one that upsets ingrained beliefs.
5. Reader Identification, so that the reader sees himself in a story.
6. A professional, pruned style that sparkles with suspense, sophistication, and a quick-moving tempo.
7. A special X-plus factor that adds gimmick and richness.

Slick Don'ts

1. Don't be too obviously trite, or contrived. The reader should not be able to anticipate the outcome, nor must the solution be incredible, illogical, or synthetic.
2. Don't have author intrusion. Keep your own opinions and axes-to-grind out of the story unless you create an Alter Ego who expresses your thoughts in his own way and as a natural part of his own fictional problem.
3. Don't have stereotyped characters, unchanging actors, or people who do not inspire an emotional reaction.

4. Don't have two similar characters with identical dramatic functions.
5. Don't have long uninterrupted narrative passages or solid dialogue sections. Narrative and dialogue must be integrated, with the story unfolding in carefully-planned, dramatized scenes like those of a TV play or motion picture.
6. Although the slick story may follow a general plot formula, it cannot be too much like an already-published story. It must offer a fresh angle, an unusual reversal or twist something different.

THE QUALITY STORY

There used to be a saying that this offtrail, "arty," literary story was written for posterity rather than prosperity, but now it hits the double jackpot. More and more slicks like *Cosmopolitan* and the *Post* are seeking realistic, slice-of-life quality stories which formerly were the exclusive fare of magazines of the intelligentsia like *Harper's, The Atlantic Monthly, The New Yorker, Vogue, Harper's Bazaar,* the "reviews" and "best stories" collections. Because the quality yarn does not follow the contrived, predictable, commercial formula, some readers consider it plotless and therefore easier to write. Plotless? Uncontrived with pat solutions to obvious problems, yes. But unplanned and unstructured? Definitely *not*. It requires more thoughtful perfection, experience and "criticism of life" than the other two forms. Also far-above-average style, challenging and profound ideas and sometimes a downbeat interpretation of life, since it mirrors life "as it is" rather than "as we'd like it to be."

The quality story must have:

1) *Emotion*—vividly enacted and leading to release. Granville Hicks says of the quality story: "More and more commonly the end is an emotional experience for the reader. Both events and characters are used to create a specific emotion, and, at the climax, to provide a release for it." Emotion building to *release,* and then to *insight.* It can be any emotion:—frustration, despair, grief, revenge, hate, hope, loneliness, etc. But the quality writer dramatizes and intensifies one emotion thoroughly until "something happens to give the reader the release he must have," says Mr. Hicks, adding: "What happens must, of course, be consistent with the facts we have been given and must be appropriate to the prevailing emotional tone."

The explored emotion that is the core of the quality story does not have to be morbid or unchanging. In George Garrett's "The Rivals" (*Harper's Bazaar*), the teen-age boy resents and scorns his father, until they share a thrilling experience getting their boat through a wildly dangerous surf, then his negative mood reverses:

> There weren't words for what the boy felt. He lay there beside his father with the sun and the breeze floating on his back in calm water, and nothing, not even the percussion of the surf, could interrupt his spent tranquility. The air seemed full of tunes his blood could dance to . . .

2) *Distinctive style* transfers the emotional experience and raises the quality story above the run-of-the-mill slick. Elmer Wheeler calls style "the sizzle that's more important than the steak." This applies to quality style which features sentences that are often more magically arresting than the

plot. In Ray Bradbury's "Too Late" (*Playboy*), a woman is wishing for the death of Roger's old, wicked mother who prevents her marriage to the mother-trapped son:

> . . . That night in bed I thought, what ways are there for murder that no one could know? Is Roger, a hundred yards away, this moment, thinking the same? Will he search the woods tomorrow for toadstools resembling mushrooms, or drive the car too fast and fling her door wide on a curve? I saw the wax-dummy-witch fly through the air in a lovely soaring arc to break like ridiculous peanut-brittle on an oak, an elm, a maple. I sat up in bed. I laughed until I wept. I wept again until I laughed again. No, no, I thought, he'll find a better way. A night burglar will shock her heart into her throat. Once in her throat, he will not let it go down again, she'll choke on her own panic . . .

Or Esther Wagner's "The Slip" (*The Atlantic Monthly*), which describes the alcoholic's first drink in many months:

> The cool, dark-tasting first minute passed, and the lovely little explosion, so gentle, so far-reaching, along all her tingling nerves up into her ringing ears, down into her curling toes, occurred faithfully, as if the long months of nothingness, and before that the long months of drearily diminishing returns, had never been. Each separate, delicate, dark needle, chartreuse-tipped, stood out on the bough of spruce which swung close to the deck . . . She drank and drank, her senses sharpening. . . .
>
> More swallows, another glass, and a new explosion of lucidity sent its brilliant rays up through her head to match the explosion of sense impressions earlier.

No matter what is described in a quality story—a sensation, character, experience or emotion—it must be delineated as to heighten the reader's insight into life. It makes him more *aware* of the world, which Ray Bradbury describes as "both noon and midnight, evil and good, a *terrible delight."* He claims that the writer's function is to "make us sad we are alive. He must make us glad we are alive. But above all, he must not make us sit still . . . He should make us want to go out and look, hear, smell, taste and touch the world. That is what we are here for."

Sean O'Faolain, whom *The Atlantic Monthly* calls "one of the best short story writers of our time," deserves this honor because he follows his own definition:

> A story is like a picture, caught in the flick of a camera's trigger, that comes nearer and nearer to clarity in the bath of hypo which is the writer's blend of skill and imagination; he trembles over it as the bleach trembles and wavers over the sensitive halides of the film, waiting for the final perfection of his certainty, of his desire . . .

3) *Distinctive subject matter.* Choose a problem or life-experience that is emotionally stimulating and challenging, although it may be negative and off-beat. Taboos can be broken here and the story can deal with any true-to-life phase of human weaknesses such as selfishness, greed, profiting from another's loss, ingratitude, sadism, masochism, intolerance, or the domination of a bad habit or state of mind. Be sure that the subject—no matter what it is—is dealt with in good taste and with dramatic consistency.

4) *Originality* is the keynote. This must be a story that has not been told too often before, or if the idea is familiar, there must be some hallmark of absolute differentness, either in the philosophy, characterization, style, time or place. "The Mask" by Mira Michal (*Harper's*) satirizes the eccentricity of a man who always wears a mask over his handsome face in line with his belief that one's countenance is the most personal, private, expressive part of one's

body and should not be exposed to strangers. The story ends with the girl who has broken off with him for being so zany, and she is applying heavy make-up, thus also covering her naked, soul-revealing face with a mask.

5) *A specific atmosphere* adds exciting color and authenticity. The most successful quality writers bring to life the places they are familiar with. Brian Moore, Liam O'Flaherty, James Stephens and Sean O'Casey write about the Irish; John Hearne writes about his native Jamaica; Lydia Davis about her New Zealand; Hugh Nissenson, a New Yorker who has lived in Israel, about this brave, new-old nation; Nadine Gordimer, about South Africa; and Olga Bergolts, Sholokov, Leonov, and Pasternak about Russia. Hugh Nissenson describes the barren Israeli desert graphically in "The Well" (*Harper's*):

> . . . Broken up by a network of wadis running east to west —dry water courses eroded by flash floods—the landscape always gives me the impression that it has been raked by the talons of some gigantic beast. Here and there, glaring in the sun, are white outcroppings of rock; ribs and spines and shoulder blades, only partly buried by the cracked earth. Yes. It is exactly as though some unimaginable animal has dug at the earth to bury the bones of its prey.

6) *Full-dimensional characters who are never stereotypes,* people the reader comes to know more intimately than his own friends; people he is usually the wiser for having known. From Nadine Gordimer's *Atlantic* story, "A Chip of Glass Ruby," here is Mrs. Bamjee, Indian mother of nine living in South Africa, who altruistically fights for Negro rights and goes to jail for her liberalism:

> She still wore the traditional clothing of a Muslim woman, and her body, which was scraggy and unimportant as a dress

on a peg when it was not host to a child, was wrapped in the trailing rags of a cheap sari, and her thin black plait was greased. When she was a girl, in the Transvaal town where they lived still, her mother fixed a chip of glass ruby in her nostril; but she had abandoned that adornment as too old-style, even for her, long ago.

Unselfish and as womanly as Mother Earth, Mrs. Bamjee is summed up by her daughter:

". . . she doesn't want anybody to be left out or forgotten . . . she always remembers where other people forget; remembers everything—people without somewhere to live, hungry kids, boys who can't get educated—remembers all the time. That's how Ma is."

7) *Realism*. Life in its naked naturalness, without glossing or glamour, sometimes disillusioning, occasionally shocking, often without sensible motivation or satisfying results. Perhaps as wanton as the boys destroying the Christopher Wren house in Graham Greene's "The Destructors" (*Harper's*); as grotesque as Isak Dinesen's "The Cardinal's Third Tale," in which Scottish Lady Flora Gordon is finally persuaded to kiss the toe of the sacred statue of St. Peter in the Vatican, and gets—not faith, but syphilis; as depressing as the blind souls in Hemingway's "Two Tales of Darkness"; or as wacky as S. J. Perelman's "Long Time No Sheepskin" (*New Yorker*), which explores the fact that college graduates have fewer children than high school graduates, then investigates the relationship between education and lower birth rates. Of course, not all quality stories are as starkly realistic as these, but neither are they pallid, vaporous airy-fairy tales. The readers want realism and can take it.

8) *Dynamic movement.* Though quality story characters may not dash about in physical movement and external conflict like those of the pulps and slicks, there must be vital, vibrant changes within them and/or their conditions and attitudes. Peter Ustinov's *Atlantic* story, "The Loneliness of Billiwoonga" concerns the many vicissitudes of Jiri Polovicka, a victim of Hungarian-Czechoslovakian-Polish boundary changes. Inducted into the Polish army, captured by the Germans, tossed into concentration camps, eventually liberated by the Russians, he finally emigrates to Australia where he starts a promising new life as George Pollens, with a wife named Ida, and a genial, efficient business partner, Bill Shoemaker. It all comes to a shattering standstill, however, when he recognizes Bill as one of the sadistic Nazi murderers from one of the extermination camps. Should he kill the German? report him? break up their partnership? At first he is impelled to avenge the millions so cruelly slaughtered, but he changes his mind for two reasons: 1) destroying Bill Shoemaker (Herr Willi Schumacher) will end his own prosperity and he cannot give up what he has never had before: position, security, a wife and son; and 2) having been the underdog all his life, he cannot resist the temptation to use his knowledge of Bill's Nazi past to see him squirm. When the slave ceases to be oppressed, he makes another person a slave. Here is realism—dynamic changes in both characters and a thought-provoking premise, which leads to the next.

9) *Significance and maturity.* The message or basic truth is always meaningful, even though it may be controversial or sophisticated enough to be a reversal of an accepted

maxim. Whereas a commercial premise insists that good-
ness is repaid and bread cast upon the waters comes back
cake, a quality story might state that generosity en-
genders not gratitude, but hate and resentment. In Frank
O'Conner's *New Yorker* yarn, "Francis," the tough gang-
leader in a private boys' school likes goody-goody, priest-
to-be Francis as long as he can look down on him as a
square and a sissy. But when he learns that Francis and his
parents have been sending him the generous packages he
hoped his own mother had sent, he hates being beholden
to them and despises Francis forevermore.

Another popular concept which quality yarns frequently
reverse is the idea of automatic love and respect that exists
between parents and children. Here, this relationship is
viewed from the standpoint of individual characterization,
not through rose-colored glasses designed to fit everyone.
In one case the girl has more rapport with her stepmother
than her mother. In Jane Bowles' *Vogue* story, "A Stick
of Green Candy," the child is not only misunderstood but
ignored by her parents and consequently lives in an imaginary world from which all human beings—children as
well as adults—are ultimately barred.

10) *Abstract values in conflict.* The premise or basic
truth is the philosophical conclusion of a fictionized debate between opposite values, such as revenge versus for-
giveness; conformity versus individuality; abstinence versus indulgence; courage versus cowardice; conscientious
hard work versus goofing-off; doubt versus faith; truth
versus deception; etc.

Sometimes the opposition of abstract values is merely implied and worked out subtly; sometimes it is stated obviously.

THE SECONDARY MAGAZINES

The secondary magazines replace the pulps (of which only a few in the science-fiction, sports, western, and detective field survive) as a training ground and market for new writers. Here they have a better chance of success.

There is such a variety of secondary magazines that you are sure to find a market suited to your interests and experiences, one you can sell to and earn while you learn. This experience will sharpen your plot sense and teach you to dramatize a clear-cut problem with its credible solution while perfecting the techniques of characterization, action, suspense and emotion. The secondary market can play an important role in your writing career. Novelist and slick-writer Cecilia Bartholomew enjoyed writing for the romance-westerns on her way up. She says, "I needed a place to learn plotting and incidentally to get small checks to bolster my ego." So will you if you observe the following:

DO'S FOR SECONDARY MARKETS

1. Study stories published in recent issues of the magazine for which you will slant your story.
2. Develop a definite premise which your story will prove (original but not controversial or taboo).
3. Sketch main characters so that they come to life. They may be one-dimensional with a strong major trait instead of several traits, but hero and villain must be clearly-drawn.
4. Begin with an attention-snatching opening.

5. Introduce action *immediately*—physical and/or psychological action. Keep it crackling throughout.
6. Be sure that suspense is maintained and the reader cannot guess the exact ending. Save a surprise for the last scene.
7. The style should be clear and direct, clarifying as many conflicts as possible.
8. Stay in one viewpoint throughout.
9. The protagonist must solve his own problem through characterization that is clear to the reader from the outset.

DON'TS

1. Don't be condescending or write down to the reader.
2. Don't forget to slant specifically, with right number of words, scenes, and characters for that magazine.
3. Don't be too intellectual or philosophical in theme, style or content.
4. Don't narrate when you can dramatize in action-scenes with dialogue and emotion.
5. Don't write about erudite, thinking-much-but-doing-little characters. Each person must inspire a definite emotional response in the reader, and each must represent virtue or villainy.
6. Don't let the action lag or the story sag at any point.
7. Don't write inconclusive or frustrating endings. Be sure the final scene leaves the reader with a good taste in his mouth and with a healthy respect for justice and courage, since these have conquered villainy so cleverly.

XXX | THE PROFESSIONAL APPROACH

OVERCOMING WRITER'S BLOCK

ONE OF THE SIGNS of a professional—and this is a goal which every writer must work towards—is learning to understand, accept, overcome, and make use of "writer's block." This is also called "black moment," "slump," "dry spell," and many other names, and is a stoppage of inspirational flow which every writer experiences at some time or other.

What should you do when it occurs? Decide that you're not cut out to be a writer and turn your typewriter in? Accept it as part of the game and twiddle your thumbs until it passes? These are both dangerously wrong alternatives for a writer, and the second not only wastes time, but can become habit-forming.

Fortunately there's no guaranteed, magic formula for overcoming writer's block. I say "fortunately" because writer's block can be your best friend if you learn to understand how and why it happens; that it can be a symptom that your story is careening off in the wrong direction. You are not so likely to be stymied if you have a sure knowledge of the specific techniques, and if you work out your formula, market slant, basic principles and abstract values before you start to write your story or novel.

A truly honest writer will confess to having had many slumps . . . and may even offer remedies, for there have been as many suggested cures for writer's block as there have for hiccoughs. Writer's block does not mean that you are not a writer. In fact, it is one of the occupational hazards and signs that you are. What may help one writer conquer writer's block, however, may make yours worse. Each writer is an individual and must discover his own mainsprings of inspiration. You must develop a deep knowledge of yourself, your subject, the basic techniques and mechanics of writing, and become familiar with some of the aids which have been used successfully in defeating writer's block:

1) *Increase your range of interests, hobbies, friends.* Go to night school, learn skin-diving, bowling, golf, tennis, bridge, square-dancing. Seize every opportunity to broaden your awareness, always being on the lookout for devices, characters, and methods of enriching your writing. As Storm Jameson has said, "A writer can never afford a holiday from idea-seeking. He must learn neither to evade nor waste any personal experience. He must get it down on paper and then utilize it."

Learn to understand and get along with people, but also learn to get away from them. Almost every great poet, philosopher and thinking writer has derived his greatest inspiration in solitude, often from walking in the woods or relaxing in a meadow. Even as a boy, Robert Louis Stevenson was dubbed "idler" because of his frequent

spells of apparently doing nothing. But he was thinking—
the necessary preamble to good writing—and he always
carried two books with him: one to read and one to write
in. Robert Frost was teased about his solitary hikes and
when asked, "What do you do walking by yourself in the
woods?" he replied, "I gnaw bark!" We, too, need to escape
technological civilization to "gnaw bark," to meditate, and
to ponder.

2) *Write about people, places, and subjects you know
well and have empathy for.* Concentrate on writing the
kind of thing you sincerely enjoy reading, and choose a
premise that coincides with your own philosophy. If you
try to force yourself to write something that antagonizes
you, your unconscious mind will stage a strike which, of
course, is one of the commonest causes of writer's block.

3) *Don't fall into the habit of starting stories that you
do not finish.* On the other hand, do not spend so much
time on one story that it becomes stale. Many writers have
the best results when they have two or three projects in the
works at one time, enabling them to break the tedium and
monotony of, say, a novel, with the writing of a quicker-
paced short story.

4) *Establish deadlines, word limits and a regular writing
schedule* of a certain number of hours and a set number of
words every day. Three writing hours at the same time
every day, seven days a week, are better than twenty con-
centrated hours in one day and then none for another
week.

5) *If you must interrupt or end your daily writing stint,
never stop at the end of a sentence or a scene,* but in the
middle, while the next words and actions are fresh in your

mind. You'll find it much easier to get back into the swing next day or whenever you return to continue it.

6) *If you come to a block or a blackout, instead of sweating and stewing over what should come next, retype the last page* once or twice until the story action moves forward of its own accord.

7) If any section of your script seems to be confused or muddled, *write it out in the simplest terms* or in a letter to yourself or a friend, then build it up to match the rest of the story.

8) If you are temperamental or moody with highly inspired and productive days alternating with low, depressing, dry-spells, *learn to anticipate the moods beforehand and exploit them.*

Most writers experience a seemingly unaccountable alternation of "gushers" and dry spells. John Keats insisted that when he ran out of inspiration he felt he was changing "not from a chrysalis into a butterfly, but on the contrary; having two little loopholes whence I may look out into the stage of the world." Acquaint yourself with Dr. Rexford Hersey's *Emotional Cycle* and learn to chart your ups and downs so you can use the "ups" for creativity, and the "downs" for reading, research and revision. Take advantage of the "dry spells" to look out of the loopholes into the world around you to study its people, places, things and ideas and soon your inspiration will be perking vigorously.

9) *Start keeping an idea file* with separate compartments for personal experiences, characters, interesting clippings, gimmicks, new discoveries and inventions, your own original thoughts, emotions, single words that intrigue you, objects that could be used as symbols, proverbs or apho-

risms, cartoons and jokes, action scenes, atmosphere descriptions, any notations concerning the arts, music, sculpture, architecture, etc. Whenever you come up with something worthwhile, no matter how small it seems at the time, jot it down when it's fresh (if it's not original, note the exact source) and drop it into the proper compartment. You'll find that many of these items grow and attract other ideas and serve as fuel to feed the flame of inspiration. Soon you'll have more things to write and more stimulus to create than there are hours in the year. That is, you will if you apply the tenth must:

10) *Work.* There's no substitute for making yourself write whether you feel like it or not. If you have trouble beginning a story, start writing the end first, or work on the middle section, or write about anything at all to rev up your mental motor!

Turning Trials into Triumphs

It is possible for you to follow every rule in these pages and still not sell every manuscript the first time out. We hope the technique tips will reduce the number of rejections, perhaps eventually eliminating them altogether, but you should be psychologically prepared to cope with disappointments and rejections as occupational hazards of the writing profession. Accept each rejection slip for what it is: a symptom that something's wrong, and that the amateur weaknesses are overbalancing your professional skills.

Editors are usually too busy to tell you why they didn't buy your story, and even well-meaning friends and relatives who aren't professional critics are as incapable of diagnosing your story troubles as they'd be of performing delicate brain surgery without experience. Develop your own objectivity and check a returned script against Mary Roberts Rinehart's seven reasons for rejections:

1) No writing ability
2) Wrong subject matter (your material's dull, taboo, or trite.)
3) Bad craftsmanship and hasty work (not enough conflict, plot, with rising action and suspenseful peaks of interest, no viewpoint, emotion; hero doesn't solve his own problem.)
4) Lack of sincerity of style and significance of meaning
5) Amateurish appearance of manuscript
6) Wrong market slant or length
7) The magazine is over-stocked, low-budgeted, or already has similar material. (Usually the rejection will say this and perhaps ask you to return it at a named later date. Do *not* smugly assume this is why the editor was forced to turn your opus down.)

There are additional reasons, such as wrong timing. Monthly magazines are made up six months in advance, weeklies, three, so a Christmas story shouldn't be submitted in November. An idea can be too late or too early in other ways, as well.

Except for the first rejection reason—lack of writing ability—all can be corrected. If the editor or reader has been nice enough to offer any criticism at all, be sure to treasure this help and act on it, rather than stubbornly sending the story elsewhere to prove him wrong.

Analyze and rewrite every story until it is your best work and in line with the type and length of the magazines to which you send it and be sure to enclose a stamped, self-addressed envelope with each manuscript. Develop a thick skin, expect an occasional rejection, and don't let it get you down. Learn a lesson from the thousands of authors who were panned, squelched and rejected, but who wouldn't take "no" for an answer. Failure is often the squeaky overture to success, and most geniuses have known rejection, many even sooner and more often than you.

The writers who succeed are those who are blessed with a confidence that overrides rejection. But this is a blessing only when the work is worthy of the faith the author has in it—when it is the very best he is capable of and is what the reader wants to read. Herman Wouk put his best efforts into *Caine Mutiny*, which several publishers turned down as ill-timed, since it was offered when the public was trying to forget World War II. But Wouk kept submitting it until it sold. Even after the reading public acclaimed it a success, it was turned down by eight motion picture producers, but the author kept storming gates until Columbia finally bought it.

Today's most popular authors will joke about their rejections as an inevitable part of their success. One of Ray Bradbury's favorite stories was rejected eighty times before it sold, and even his "The Swan" was turned down three times by *Cosmopolitan* before they finally bought it. Lloyd Douglas was never discouraged by the many times *Magnificent Obsession* was refused, because it was his very best writing. He followed his "inner fire" and kept submitting and resubmitting the manuscript which the religious publishers turned down because it had "too much story and not enough religion" and which several commercial publishers rejected as having "too much preachin' and not enough story." Douglas had faith in it, refused to change it and finally triumphed.

Rejection slips are like pills: bitter to swallow but good for what ails you. Some are even palatably sugar-coated, such as cordial letters offering criticism. Whether rejection slips are sour or sweet, you should accept them in a sporting spirit. Don't be like the doubting tyro who wrote to the editor accusing him of buying stories by robot—apparently submitted scripts passed by on a moving belt, and Mr. Robot seized every 500th for publication. Longing for some proof that his story was touched by human hands, the writer received a rejection slip marked with the red-pencilled outline of the editor's hand!

Rejection can be a stimulus to success, a storm-warning or symptom that something's wrong with your writing, or a spanking that will make you a better writer. Make rejection slips your friends. Let them help you turn obstacles into opportunities. Self-confidence and optimism, reinforced with technical know-how, can help you convert your pipe dreams into pay checks, your trials into triumphs.